SHE WHO IMAGINES

She Who Imagines

Feminist Theological Aesthetics

Edited by
Laurie Cassidy
Maureen H. O'Connell

Foreword by
Elizabeth A. Johnson

A Michael Glazier Book

LITURGICAL PRESS
Collegeville, Minnesota

www.litpress.org

A Michael Glazier Book published by Liturgical Press

1   2   3   4   5   6   7   8

Library of Congress Cataloging-in-Publication Data

    She who imagines : feminist theological aesthetics / edited by Laurie Cassidy, Maureen H. O'Connell.
        p.   cm.
    "A Michael Glazier book."
    ISBN 978-0-8146-8027-8 — ISBN 978-0-8146-8028-5 (e-book)
    1. Aesthetics—Religious aspects.   2. Feminist theology.   3. Feminine beauty (Aesthetics)   I. Cassidy, Laurie M.   II. O'Connell, Maureen H.

BL65.A4S535   2012
230.082—dc23   2012029421

Contents

Part 3: She Who *Imagines*

Elizabeth A. Johnson

Foreword

In her essay "On Beauty and Being Just," Elaine Scarry describes discovering the mistake she had made in ruling out palm trees as objects of beauty. One day under the canopy of a high palm, she realized that a pair of eyes was looking back down at her. A large owl, plumage interwoven with the fronds, was resting face-down over the sixty-foot column of air. Typical of its kind, the bird had sought out this inverted nest at dawn: "It was as though she had stopped to sleep in midair, letting the giant arcing palm leaves take over the work of her wings, so that she could soar there in the shaded sunshine until night came and she was ready to fly on her own again."[1] New appreciation replaced the earlier dismissive stance Scarry attributes to "failed generosity." Now she sees the featherlike tree capturing and scattering sunlight in cresting waves of aqua, green, and yellow, running its fingers up and down its own piano keys in the wind while its leaves stay perfectly parallel. Beautiful!

In my imagination, this incident provides an evocative symbol for reading *She Who Imagines*. Calling into question the overlooked reality of women as creators and interpreters of beauty, it opens new dimensions in the developing area of theological aesthetics as well as the traditional field of theological anthropology. And surprises await.

Introducing the issue of gender makes several lacunae apparent. To date, much recent discussion in theological aesthetics either neglects women and their work or describes them in ideal terms to which few, if any, actual women correspond. While theological anthropology has made efforts to rehabilitate the sacredness of the body, long identified with women and the earth and opposed to the supposed rational masculine spirit, the body remains a contested site of meaning in the overall

---

1. Elaine Scarry, *On Beauty and Being Just* (Princeton, NJ: Princeton University Press, 1999), 20.

structure of theology. All the while, pop culture promotes the ideal of a certain type of female body preferred for its youth, shapeliness, race, and sex appeal.

In the face of this mix of problems, this collection of essays represents the wisdom of practicing scholars who challenge the exclusion and false definitions while constructing capacious ideas that discover beauty in unexpected places. Drawing mainly on the visual arts, both religious and secular—painting, photography, portraiture, craftwork—their proposals join beauty to truth and, in a richly defining way, to the practice of justice.

Toward that end, the book's tripartite subdivision is inspired. "SHE Who Imagines" presents women as active creators of and theorizers about rather than passive recipients of definitions of beauty. "She Who IS IMAGINED" challenges racist and sexist conventions and their attendant violence toward women in religious and pop art. "She Who IMAGINES" returns to women's active roles in picturing and enacting possibilities of beauty that empower women's flourishing in and beyond debilitating situations. In a variety of ways, all the essays link women's definitions of beauty with experiences of suffering and hence with the yearning for justice. All clearly prize resistance to degradation as an essential element of thought. While focused on individual instances of women as agents making and interpreting beauty, contributors to this section see this action connected to wider communities: the family, local community, the whole world. Since this discussion is concerned overall with relationship to divine revelation about humanity, it moves in a dimension that honors religious experience and investigates with theological interest.

Amid the suffering of life, at times beyond endurance, beauty is lifesaving, "a plank amid the waves of the sea," as Augustine wrote. With its diverse instances of women creating beauty, imagining its meaning, analyzing how it functions, and resisting its distortions, this book floats as such a life-affirming plank. Its contribution to theology lies in the way it knocks on the door of theological aesthetics, showing the enrichment that could ensue if it opened to include women, their imaginative work of critique and their constructive work of interpretation. More broadly, it takes its place in the growing body of work that contributes to the struggle for human dignity and spiritual self-determination for women that is a hallmark of our time. Read it with anticipation of bracing critique and constructive ideas, especially regarding the linkage of beauty with justice. And keep your eye out for the owl.

**Laurie Cassidy and
Maureen H. O'Connell**

Introduction

"The world will be saved by beauty."
Dostoyevsky, The Idiot

Dostoyevsky's quote bespeaks the paradox for feminist theology in understanding beauty. How does beauty save women and young girls from violence, domination, and oppression? In contemporary American culture "beauty" is often associated with female physical appearance and judged in relationship to heterosexual standards of sexual attractiveness. Contemplating the global status of women, in which women and girls make up 70 percent of the world's poor, and looking into our own lives, we find the bitter consequences of these idealized notions of beauty.[1] The omnipresence of pornography in popular culture and the

---

1. "Globally, 1 in 3 women will experience some type of domestic violence. There is little difference between poor and rich countries on this measure." For these statistics and more on the status of women worldwide, see http://worldsavvy. org/monitor/index.php?option=com_content&view=article&id=548&Itemid=977 (accessed December 28, 2011). The Millennium Project describes violence against women as one of the global challenges facing humanity: "Violence against women is the largest war today, as measured by death and casualties per year. While the proportion of women exposed to physical violence in their lifetime ranges from 12% to 59%, a function of region and culture, sexual assaults remain one of the most underreported crimes worldwide, continuing to be perpetrated with impunity." See http://www.millennium-project.org/millennium/Global_Challenges/chall-11. html (accessed December 28, 2011). Another impact for women of these oppressive notions of beauty is in the rise in women and girls electing to surgically augment bodily appearance. The number of breast implant surgeries for women and girls has tripled since 1997, from one hundred thousand to three hundred thousand in

proliferation of global sex trafficking of women and girls reveal a perverse connection between sexist visions of women's beauty and women's subjugation.[2] Naomi Wolfe's now-classic *The Beauty Myth* draws the undeniable connection between cultural construction of beauty and women's continued political, economic, and social disenfranchisement, noting that "the beauty myth is not about women at all. It is about men's institutions and institutional power."[3]

Women do not fare much better in religious contexts when it comes to beauty. In the Catholic tradition, out of which contributors to this volume write, women's beauty is too often construed in narrow ways, either as something to be feared and denounced as evidenced by centuries of denigrating the female body as an invitation to grave sin, or as something to be understood vis-à-vis its relationship to masculinity as is the case in contemporary theologies of divinely intended gender complementarity. Too frequently in the Catholic tradition women's beauty is also measured against an equally narrow and idealized image

---

2008. See The National Resource Center for Women and Families information at www.breastimplantinfo.org/augment/implantfacts.html (accessed December 28, 2011). Body augmentation includes plastic surgery for younger facial features, buttock enlargement, calf sculpting, and "vaginal rejuvenation." For an excellent study on the race, class, and gender dynamics at work in our society's obsession with women's bodily appearance, see the YWCA's document "Beauty at Any Cost: The Consequences of America's Beauty Obsession on Women and Girls" (August 2008), available at www.ywca.org.

2. Pornography is a $20 billion industry and its economic success and access through the internet have made it more widely accepted in American culture. See Frederick Lane, *Obscene Profits: The Entrepreneurs of Pornography in the Cyber Age* (New York: Taylor and Francis, 2001). In his book, *Empire of Illusion: The End of Literacy and the Triumph of Spectacle* (New York: Nation Books, 2009), Chris Hedges gives a gruesome picture of the impact of pornography on women and men (55–88). There is an enormous amount of feminist scholarship on the relationship between pornography and women's social status and well-being. This literature is too vast to enumerate here. Nevertheless, the work of Andrea Dworkin, *Intercourse* (New York: Basic Books, 2006), and Catherine A. MacKinnon, *Are Women Human?* (Boston: Belknap Press, 2007), must be mentioned because of their groundbreaking feminist legal scholarship in this area. For a historical look at this question within American feminism, see Carolyn Bronstein, *Battling Pornography: The American Feminist Anti-Pornography Movement, 1976–1986* (New York: Cambridge University Press, 2011). For an excellent look at the shift to contemporary cultural acceptance of pornography in America, see Carmine Sarracino and Kevin Scott, *The Porning of America: The Rise of Porn Culture, What It Means and Where We Go from Here* (Boston: Beacon Press, 2008).

3. Naomi Wolf, *The Beauty Myth: How Images of Beauty Are Used against Women* (New York: HarperCollins, 2002), 13.

of Mary as acquiescent virgin and mother. The traditional attributes of Mary's beauty too often undercut women's agency when it comes to discerning what will happen to and in their bodies and domesticates women in private spaces, such as families, and in more public places, including the institutional church. Images of Mary's docility and purity iconoclastically trump other visual interpretations of her life that might empower women to become, like her, agents of God's loving justice in the world.

In contrast to these misappropriations of the power of beauty, women's dreams of a beautiful world fuel its creation. Creation of beauty by women in the arts and in communities of justice contest popular patriarchal defining. By creating art, women become subjects, not objects, of beauty. The novels of Toni Morrison, the activism of Delores Huerta, the poetry of Linda Hogan, and the radical hospitality of Dorothy Day reveal an inherent connection between beauty and justice. In the lives of these women we see human flourishing as the measure of what is beautiful. These women interrupt the popular notion of the beautiful solely as sexually attractive youthful physical appearance. Instead, these woman reveal beauty to be truth-telling, justice-making, welcoming, and essential for sustaining a world of flourishing for all creation. Beauty is not an ideal used to judge the appearance of bodies but the performance of justice and the flourishing of people and communities.

To define beauty, to understand beauty, to create beauty is for feminist theology, in the words of Elisabeth Schüssler Fiorenza, "a site of struggle."[4] As Schüssler Fiorenza argues in relationship to biblical texts, we contend that the concept of beauty cannot be abandoned to sexist imaginings or idealistically and uncritically embraced. Feminist theology must struggle to construct oppositional understandings of beauty rooted in the concrete material conditions of the well-being of women and girls all over the world.

It is not only the creation of beauty but also the theoretical discussion of aesthetics that has been conditioned by sexist, racist, and class dynamics of power and oppression. For example, regarding the gendered character of this literature, a database search for texts addressing theological aesthetics will generate a list of authors who are male with few exceptions. In addition, the intersection between aesthetics and ethics itself has been historically formed and informed by masculine perspectives on beauty, the good life, and justice. This Euro-American

---

4. Elisabeth Schüssler Fiorenza, *Sharing Her Word: Feminist Biblical Interpretations* (Boston: Beacon Press, 1998), 76.

patriarchal discourse has been separate from the concrete material conditions of women's flourishing and the history of their oppression. Moreover, women have reflected on, imagined, discussed, practiced, and created beauty for themselves and others for centuries. Yet their perspectives on aesthetics, as well as the ways in which they use the arts to create more just relationships among human beings and with the earth, remain largely peripheral in both theological aesthetics and ethics. As a result, women's ways of envisioning and creating a more just world through the arts have yet to be theologically examined. This collection of essays attempts to address that egregious lacuna by drawing on several aspects of the rich tradition of Christian feminist theology in order to illuminate theoretical, practical, and as yet largely unexplored connections between the disciplines of theological aesthetics and social ethics.

Method

Readers may wonder what makes our volume on aesthetics *feminist*. Are we able to claim our work as feminist simply because the editors and contributors are women? As editors who are American born, straight, white, able-bodied, and middle-class, we have often benefited from the very notions of beauty we seek to contest. Women of color have challenged us to see the privileges we have from dominant ideas of what is beautiful and to understand the history of violence it has inflicted upon them.[5] As editors, we take the question that orients our methodology from Elizabeth Johnson's groundbreaking work in *She Who Is: The Mystery of God in Feminist Discourse*, which inspires the title of this volume: how does theological discourse about and engagement of beauty impact *all women*, especially women of color who are poor and living in violent situations?[6] Our work must be accountable to the lived material conditions of women, particularly those who are suffering.

---

5. Katie Cannon documents the dynamic interaction of ideals of beauty for black and white women. These socially construed ideas of beauty were used by white women to oppress black women and were also the source of white women's oppression. See Katie Cannon, *Black Womanist Ethics* (Atlanta: Scholars Press, 1988), 31–76.

6. Johnson writes, "For me the goal of feminist religious discourse pivots in its fullness around the flourishing of poor women of color in violent situations. Not incidentally, securing the well-being of these socially least of women would entail a new configuration of theory and praxis and the genuine transformation of all societies . . . to open up more humane ways of living for all people, with each other and the earth" (Elizabeth A. Johnson, *She Who Is: The Mystery of God in Feminist Theological Discourse* [New York: Crossroad, 1992], 11).

Our feminist methodology examines and draws theological insight from specific social and cultural contexts in the creation or distortion of beauty. These loci may imply for some readers that our work is really a Christian social ethics or this emphasis on the concrete may be judged to be "not theological enough." Our method is rooted in our faith in God's taking flesh in Jesus. We demonstrate this faith by using interdisciplinary tools to explore the theological significance of human experience—human experience that was made a medium of God's self-communication in Jesus. The incarnation demands that we explore God's presence and activity within our human experience—a presence both revealed and concealed in everyday life. Recognizing and responding to God at this time in history is a particularly urgent task for all Christians, and for theologians in particular. And this task is an inherently feminist one.

In her multivolume project, *Death and the Displacement of Beauty*, Grace Jantzen observes, "Violence is ugly."[7] Violence holds us hostage in fear, torturing bodies, distorting relationships, snuffing out hope, and posing extinction for many of God's creatures—all of this threatens the existence of God's creation. Our interdisciplinary methodology takes seriously the good and beautiful as pointing to God's gracious presence and activity at this precarious moment in history. The opening quotation of our introduction reveals the theological depth of beauty's import. Dostoyevsky claims that the world will be saved by beauty. This equation of beauty with salvation indicates that Christians interpret beauty as revealing God's activity. Jantzen questions the metaphor of salvation as the primary means of understanding the work of Jesus, exposing, along with other feminist scholars, the theological and historical implications of Jesus' violent death as that which saves humanity. Our "cultural preoccupation with death," she notes, "shows itself in destruction and violence, in a focus on other worlds and in the degradation and refusal of beauty in this one, in fear and hatred of bodiliness, sensory experience, and sexuality."[8] By way of an alternative, she argues for human flourishing as a metaphor for understanding God's saving action. Beauty saves since, according to Janzten, beauty can "reconfigure consciousness toward creativity and new life."[9] Jantzen's scholarship

---

7. Grace Jantzen, *Foundations of Violence* (New York: Routledge, 2004), vii.
8. Ibid.
9. Ibid., viii.

demonstrates that "beauty, creativity, seeks to bring newness into the world, newness that is at odds with violence."[10]

The image on the cover of our volume illustrates our feminist theological method. This image is of a *cuadro* titled *The Spiral of Life* by Nora Vasquez Liñares from the Pamplona Alta region of Peru. Rebecca Berru Davis explains the significance of this masterpiece in her chapter of this volume. We see in Liñares's piece of art the three methodological turns at work in this volume of feminist aesthetics. *The Spiral of Life* reflects women as subjects of interpreting beauty, women contesting oppressive representation, and women creating beauty. This stitched textile represents the life story of the woman who created it. To stitch her life journey from the countryside to the city, Liñares is the subject of her own story. In this artwork, she takes her life seriously and presents us the image of a spiral that is an interpretation of her sojourn. The size of this work is seventy-six inches by seventy-eight inches, which further amplifies Liñares as a subject because her work takes up a significant amount of space in exhibition and cannot be ignored in any gallery where it hangs. Also, as a medium this textile can be deceiving in its simple and direct means of communicating. The colors, fabrics, and images can appear happy and childlike. Upon closer examination, however, the work reveals the struggle to survive, the reality of domestic violence, and the effort to gain basic human rights. The work not only tells a woman's story but also holds up a mirror challenging the ways we imagine women in Peru. Finally, as Rebecca Davis documents, these *cuadros* are a way Peruvian women "picture paradise" for their families and community, not only through creating this art, but also in organizing an art cooperative that brings much-needed income to their neighborhoods.[11]

Spiral Turns in This Book

These three methodological moves—women as subjects of beauty, women as objects of beauty, and women as agents of beauty—are reflected in the three sections of this volume.

10. Ibid. For a historical look at the issues of beauty and violence within Christianity, see Rita Nakashima Brock and Rebecca Ann Parker, *Saving Paradise: How Christianity Traded Love of This World for Crucifixion and Empire* (Boston: Beacon Press, 2008).

11. See www.convida.org for more information on the Peruvian women's art cooperative Compacto Humano Group. We are grateful to Nora Vasquez Liñares and Convida for permission to use this image.

Contributors to the first section, *"She* Who Imagines," explore what happens when women become subjects of beauty and not merely objects of it. In other words, the contributors examine the contribution of women to the field of theological aesthetics; they also explore how the personal experiences and notions of beauty carried forward by women artists illuminate connections between the beautiful and the good. In her essay "For the Beauty of the Earth: Women, Sacramentality, and Justice," **Susan A. Ross** fills in the gaps in dominant theological aesthetics where women's voices have been absent, noting the links between our sacramental and ethical lives that emerge when we take women's experiences of beauty seriously. "For too long," Ross notes, "God's hidden-yet-revealed presence in the world, which the Christian tradition has named sacramental, has found itself more often in men's ways of seeing and doing than in women's." Given the centrality of Marian devotion in the lived experience of believers throughout Christian history, several of our contributors engage images of Mary. The first to do so is **Jeanette Rodriguez**. In "Theological Aesthetics and the Encounter with Tonantzin Guadalupe," she considers theological aesthetics through the history, cultural impact, and image of Our Lady of Guadalupe. Devotion to Tonantzin Guadalupe witnesses to a new way of understanding aesthetics, as Rodriguez describes: "Devotees have a unique opportunity to proclaim to the world the Guadalupan message of hope, love, and justice, a message of care and 'connectedness' to the wider community that is fed through the theological aesthetics of narrative, image, and popular religion, including song, dance, altars, and fiesta." **Jayme M. Hennessy's** essay, "Kollwitz: The Beauty and Brutality of the *Pietà*," considers twentieth-century German artist Kaethe Kollwitz's reflections on and renderings of the Pietà, linking beauty not only with women's experiences of suffering but also with resistance to war. **Colleen Mary Carpenter** draws on the work of Minnesota photographer Kristi Link Fernholz in her essay "Contemplating the Landscapes of Motherhood: The Discovery of Beauty in a Place We Thought We Knew." Through Fernholz's photographs of seemingly everyday images, Carpenter brings into clear focus the inherent beauty in caring for children and the earth, noting, "There is beauty here, wild and breathtaking beauty: we just need to learn to see it."

The second section, "She Who *Is Imagined*," is a phrase coined by its first contributor, **M. Shawn Copeland**, to describe how the politics of representation reinscribes the dynamics of race, class, and gender oppression. Contributors critically interpret representations of beauty in "the canon" of both religious art and pop culture, highlighting women's bodies as the locus of a narrow social and culturally oppressive imaginary. These essays serve as a form of resistance by making women the subjects of beauty, which can challenge convention. Copeland's essay, "The Critical Aesthetic of Race," explores implications of racialized conceptions of dark bodies on understanding the beautiful and the good. Who in a racist society can tell us what beauty is? Copeland answers, "Beauty is consonant with performance—that is, with ethical and moral behavior, with habit or virtue. In other words, beauty is the living up to and living out the love and summons of creation in all our particularity and specificity as God's human creatures." In "The Jennifer Effect: Race, Religion, and the Body," **Michelle A. Gonzalez** considers the social construction of the persona and aesthetic of Latina pop artist Jennifer Lopez to illuminate racial attitudes about Latinas in American society, claiming that "J.Lo. challenges and affirms the work [Latinos/as] have done and pushes us into a serious consideration of popular culture in our future theological collaborations." **Laurie Cassidy**, in "Picturing Suffering: The Moral Dilemmas in Gazing at Photographs of Human Anguish," focuses on the photograph of a small Sudanese girl child to explore how photographs of suffering serve women's flourishing. Cassidy argues that rather than shedding much-needed light on the material conditions of women and girls, these photographs often reinscribe or lend a "common sense" to the status quo of violence against women's bodies. In her essay "AIDS, Accountability, and Activism: The Beauty of Sue Williamson's Resistance Art," **Kimberly Vrudny** examines Williamson's public art that resists abuses of power that result in sexual violence against women in South Africa. Vrudny's essay demonstrates that "by living creatively and in solidarity with those mistreated by systems as they stand, Williamson embodies how to live beautifully, actively attentive and resistant to powers that seek to damage and destroy human community and human thriving."

Contributors to the third and final section, She Who *Imagines*, celebrate the moral agency that women experience as creators of "the beautiful" in their lives, families, and communities. Here we see women using their encounters with beauty as touchstones for imagining alternatives to the way things are, or to living justice. Here beauty offers the opportunity for increased capacity for relationship, for abundance, for alternative ways of thinking and knowing. **Rebecca Berru Davis**, in "Picturing Paradise: Imagination, Beauty, and Women's Lives in a Peruvian Shantytown," examines theological anthropology and notions of flourishing in the craftwork of Peruvian women. **Maureen H. O'Connell** examines the relationship between Dorothy Day's notion of beauty and love in the context of her radical Catholic witness in "A Harsh and Dreadful Beauty: The Aesthetic Dimension of Dorothy Day's Ethics." Attention to what Day understood to be beautiful as well as ugly "implicitly underscores the moral agency of women as creators, as well as the power of beauty to pull us into the ugliness of social injustice and to sustain us to love the neighbor in radical ways." **Mary Ann Zimmer**, in "Being Immaculate: Images of Oppression and Emancipation," considers alternative renderings of the Immaculate Conception for feminist understandings of sin and salvation, noting that often "merely critiquing oppressive representations is not an adequate response; the creation of new images—a counterfiguration of Mary—is essential." In "The Feminine Face of God Is My Face: On the Empowerment of Female Self-Portraiture," **Susie Paulik Babka** explores the role of portraiture in the lives of migrant women detained at US borders, noting that the "cultural symbol of the Virgin of Guadalupe adds a new dimension of meaning and contextuality that enables young women to see beyond their circumstances, as bearers of the divine, as worthy of respect, opportunity, and the leisure necessary to enrich the self."

The title of our volume reveals the central theological issues at stake in theological aesthetics: how do we imagine the Creator, and are all human beings made in God's image and likeness? The creativity, insight, and challenge in the scholarship of these essays reveal the importance of feminist aesthetics to American Catholic theology in addressing who God is and who we are as God's image and likeness. Future work in Catholic feminist aesthetics must engage the artistic expressions of dance, theatre, poetry, and music. In addition, feminist aesthetics must analyze other forms of contemporary culture, such as hip-hop, social media, film, and fashion. Our hope is that the conversation in this volume is merely a beginning, and we will work to widen our circle to include the voices of First Nation women; women with ancestry in Asia, the Subcontinent, and the Pacific Islands; and Africans in Diaspora. In addition, women who are not straight can open our eyes to see the ways that sexuality determines our understanding of beauty. Women with different physical abilities will challenge the dominant ways we create, experience, and embody the beautiful. We believe there is so much beauty in God's creation yet to be discovered and celebrated; our intent is that as a community of feminist theologians our work will contest the violence in our suffering world and join women around the world in creating a future filled with hope.

Acknowledgments

This volume has come to completion through the assistance of many people. Beauty was created in the kindness, vision, and generosity of many colleagues and friends. First, we are indebted to Hans Christoffersen from Liturgical Press. Hans believed in this project, encouraged its development, and saw the book come to birth. Lauren L. Murphy and Julie Surma were its midwives. Robin Jensen, Luce Chancellor's Professor of the History of Christian Art and Worship at Vanderbilt University and president of the Society for the Arts and Religious and Theological Studies (SARTS), not only gave us encouragement but also practical and sound counsel in how to bring together written material and images in our text. We are very grateful to Elizabeth A. Johnson for her generosity in writing the foreword to our text. Thanks goes also to M. Shawn Copeland who offered a more expansive vision of feminist aesthetics by suggesting her idea of "she who is imagined" as an integral deconstructive step for our method.

Maureen O'Connell would like to thank the Theology Department at Fordham University for the financial support of this project and SARTS for opening up space within the academy for theologians to take up questions of the theological and practical significance of beauty in our lives. I am also grateful to Laurie for her tireless enthusiasm for this project and her even more unwaivering friendship.

Laurie Cassidy would like to thank Maria Montoro Edwards, assistant vice president for research, and Mike Foley, dean of the College of Liberal Arts at Marywood University, for their enthusiasm and support of this project. This book was made possible through two Research Initiation Grants from Marywood and the award of a SARTS Luce Faculty Fellowship. I am also grateful to Kim Vrudny and John Stomberg for engaging conversations on this project as well as on ethics and photojournalism. Amanda Lass and Katherine Demo were research assistants extraordinaire! Amanda's expertise as a photographer and Katherine's talent as a writer were invaluable gifts to this book. This book and my chapter benefited from the generous reading and comments from my colleague and friend Alex Mikulich. I am blessed to have Maureen O'Connell not only as a coeditor but also as a friend.

ⓔ ⓔ ⓖ ⓖ

Excerpts from Susan A. Ross, *For the Beauty of the Earth: Women, Sacramentality and Justice* (Mahwah, NJ: Paulist Press, 2006). Used by permission.

Excerpt from pp. 11–12 (140 words) from *Truth and Beauty* by Ann Patchett. Copyright © 2004 by Ann Patchett. Reprinted by permission of Harper-Collins, Publishers.

"The Broken Spears" and "The Fall of Tenochtitlan" by Miguel Leon-Portilla. Copyright © 1962, 1990 by Miguel Leon-Portilla. Expanded and updated edition © 1992 by Miguel Leon-Portilla. Reprinted by permission of Beacon Press, Boston.

Käthe Kollwitz, "The *Pietà*/Mother and Son," 1938. © 2011 Artists Rights Society (ARS), New York / VG Bild-Kunst, Bonn. Used by permission.

Kristi Link Fernholz, "Sister," "Tutu Bike," and "Laundry," photographs. Used by permission.

M. Shawn Copeland, "Disturbing Aesthetics of Race," *Journal of Catholic Social Thought* 3, no. 1 (Winter 2006): 17–27. Used by permission of *Journal of Catholic Social Thought*.

Laurie Cassidy, "Picturing Suffering: The Moral Dilemmas in Gazing at Photographs of Human Anguish," *Horizons* 37, no. 2 (Fall 2010): 195–223. Used by permission of *Horizons, The Jounal of the College Theology Society*.

Sue Williamson, "From the Inside: Busi Muqongo," digital print. Used by permission.

Upper Rhenisch Master, ca. 1415, "Little Garden of Paradise" (Das Paradiesgärtlein), Städel Museum, Frankfurt am Main, © Städel Museum – ARTOTHEK. Used by permission.

At time of publication, the following permission was pending:

Excerpt from Adrienne Rich, "Rape," in *Diving into the Wreck: Poems 1971–1972* (New York: W. W. Norton & Company, 1994).

Part 1

She Who Imagines

Susan A. Ross

For the Beauty of the Earth
Women, Sacramentality, and Justice[1]

In the world of academic theology, the last two decades have seen a surge of interest in theological aesthetics as the work of Hans Urs von Balthasar and his disciples has become more widely known and as other theologians find themselves drawn to ideas of the good, the true, and the beautiful. Catholic and Protestant authors have joined their Orthodox colleagues with a renewed interest in icons. Even scientists describe the cosmos in the language of beauty. Yet, with very few exceptions, mainstream theology takes little notice of women's perspectives on beauty. Although feminist scholars have contributed to nearly every discipline imaginable, their ways of rethinking scholarly discourse have not had a noticeable effect in the field of theological aesthetics. This volume, then, is a welcome addition to a serious lacuna.

My reflections attempt to fill some gaps in this literature. It is significant that in recent years attention has shifted away from theological method and the limits of rational explorations of theology to beauty. It is important to (re)value theologically what touches our senses and hearts as well as what challenges our thinking. For too long God's hidden-yet-revealed presence in the world, which the Christian tradition has named sacramental, has found itself more often in men's ways of seeing and doing than in women's.

1. I am grateful to St. Mary's College, Notre Dame, Indiana, for permission to reprint excerpts from my 2006 Madeleva Lecture, *For the Beauty of the Earth: Women, Sacramentality and Justice* (Mahwah, NJ: Paulist Press, 2006).

3

I first began to think seriously about the connection between beauty and justice during the five years I lived in a condominium on the far north side of Chicago. My neighborhood seemed always to be fighting a losing battle against the forces of ugliness and violence. Our small six-flat condo building was one of the few bright spots on a block that was marginal, at best. One of the owners spent hours landscaping our tiny front yard with flowers and a small white picket fence. But the flowers got trampled, and the fence was torn. Some of the neighbors threw their garbage onto the sidewalk. My car's hood was dented by the young men who used it for a bench. I came to dread warm weather, since the noise and litter seemed to increase with every degree. Late one summer night, I came home alone after a party and was mugged in the vestibule of our building. Four months later I sold my condo and moved to a much smaller and more expensive rental apartment in a nearby suburb. I felt both guilt and relief after the move: guilt because I felt I had abandoned my solidarity with the poor, and relief because I felt safe. I was now surrounded by beauty: well-maintained homes, carefully tended lawns, trees, flowers, quiet. I felt better able to work, calmer, and more optimistic, better able to tackle the challenges of life. I felt whole. I kept thinking, though, of the people in the neighborhood I had left behind.

Was there a connection between my new feeling of well-being and my surroundings? And was there a connection as well between the ugliness of my old neighborhood and the ugliness of some people's actions? I think there is. It seemed to me then, as it still does, that what it takes to be a good person is not simply *doing* the right thing because it *is* the right thing. Stories of the courage and selflessness of people in terrible situations of poverty or cruelty tell us that our external conditions do not wholly determine our actions. But often these are the exceptions.

From my mother and others along the way I have learned that beauty is to be shared, that creating beauty is a statement that one cares about others and about oneself—not so much that others will think the wrong thing, but rather that they are worth the time and effort to be cared for, with attention to the details. Ultimately, beauty's power to draw us in and beyond ourselves is a significant element—indeed, a necessary element—in our moral development. And, I would also venture, the beauty of the world gives us a sense of the care with which God holds us, a care that is attuned to our senses and to our delight and God's. In this essay, I will develop an idea of beauty and justice related to one's own self, to the church, and to the world.

Beauty and Ourselves

Most of us are familiar, I think, with the feminist criticism of fashion magazine standards of beauty. Yet these criticisms, while important and necessary, may unwittingly overlook the fact that we are embodied creatures and thus we depend on our physicality. In fact, our senses seem to have some kind of innate sense of beauty, which we share with other living species: we are drawn to the plumage and song of birds, the softness of animal fur, the aroma of flowers, the tastes of ripe fruit.[2] So while there is a very real ambiguity in beauty, in that we may only initially see or experience one of its dimensions, genuine beauty signifies a depth beyond its appearance.

In one of her books, Annie Dillard writes poignantly about two young children, a girl and a boy, who both suffer from the condition of femoral hypoplasia (very short legs). About the younger of the two, a little girl, Dillard writes, "She has dark hair, bangs, and two wavy ponytails tied with yarn bows. Sure of her charm, she smiles directly at the camera; her young face shines with confidence and pleasure. Am I not cute? She is indeed cute. She is three."[3] Dillard then writes of a five-year-old boy with the same condition: "He has a handsome young face, this boy; he stands naked against the black-and-white grid wall. He looks grim. He tilts his head down and looks up at the camera. His eyes accuse, his brows defy, his mouth mourns." At some point between the ages of three and five, Dillard says, "these kids catch on."[4] They come to see that they *will* be judged by their looks, that they *will* face stares and taunting, that their appearance *does* play a role in how they are perceived by others.

A second example: in her memoir about her friend Lucy Grealy, Ann Patchett recounts how Lucy was convinced that no one would ever love her, that she would ultimately die alone, that she would never be happy. Lucy had had cancer of the jaw as a child, had endured chemo and radiation therapy, and had had multiple reconstructive surgeries, most of them unsuccessful. Patchett describes Lucy's face when they roomed together in graduate school:

> Her lower jaw had been a ledge falling off just below her cheekbone when we started college, making her face a sharp triangle, but now the

2. National Public Radio Report, "In Evolution, A Taste for Beauty Has Purpose," October 4, 2004; http://www.npr.org/templates/story/story.php?storyID=4057069.

3. Annie Dillard, *For the Time Being* (New York: Vintage Books, 1999), 65–66.

4. Ibid.

lines were softer. She couldn't close her mouth all the way and her front teeth showed. Her jaw was irregular, as if one side had been collapsed by a brutal punch, and her neck was scarred and slightly twisted. She had a patch of paler skin running from ear to ear that had been grafted from her back and there were other bits of irregular patching and scars. But she also had lovely light eyes with damp dark lashes and a nose whose straightness implied aristocracy. Lucy had white Irish skin and dark blond hair and in the end that's what you saw, the things that didn't change: her eyes, the sweetness of her little ears.[5]

Lucy was also a talented writer but struggled all her short life—she died of a drug overdose in her thirties—with the complications of her looks. Would she have had the same struggles, insecurities, addictions if she had not gone through what she did? We do not know. But we cannot really say that "looks don't matter," especially when it comes to severe disfigurement. We read of doctors and nurses who go to poor countries and perform surgeries to correct cleft palates, of plastic surgeons who donate their time to repair disfiguring injuries on those who cannot afford the care, and, on a much more mundane level, of women who donate good used clothing so that poor women who cannot afford to buy them can have attractive clothes to wear to work, or prom dresses so that high school girls without the means to buy their own can have a pretty dress to wear.

Appearances *do* matter: we would consider it tragic if someone were unable to correct a disfigurement from birth or an accident, if a child with a correctable problem went without surgery because of a lack of funds. Yet we—or at least I—find it problematic when a sixteen-year-old girl has breast augmentation surgery, when Hollywood stars have so much cosmetic surgery that their faces can no longer express any emotion, or when a slight young man has pectoral implants so that he can appear to be muscular. There is a line somewhere between the examples of the two children and Lucy Grealy and our culture's obsession with young, thin beauty, when the importance of appearance for a decent life develops into an obsession with appearance that verges on, if not actually becomes, immoral.

As I have reflected on these examples, it seems that *caring* for others' beauty and for our own is central. We wish for the other's good and happiness, a happiness that is *in some way* tied to our physicality, and we do what we can to promote this happiness. Yet I do not think

5. Ann Patchett, *Truth and Beauty: A Friendship* (New York: HarperCollins, 2004), 11–12.

that the mother who spends $5,000 on her teenager's breast implants is necessarily really caring for her child. What makes the difference? I want to suggest here that a central dimension of genuine beauty is the quality of generosity. Real beauty both has and elicits generosity, and such generosity plays a central role in the Christian moral life.

Beauty in Church

In her fascinating book *A History of Women in Christian Worship*, Susan J. White describes her experience of visiting an ancient cathedral in Macedonia. Knowing that women and men were separated from each other in worship, she went into the narthex, where the women would have stood while the liturgy was going on, so that she could have a feel for what worship was like for them. She expected to feel angry and excluded, but as she looked around the narthex, she became aware of large frescoes of female figures covering the walls and ceiling. She writes:

> Suddenly, I knew something about women's experience of worship that I had not known before: I understood that when women gathered to pray in this place, surrounded by the presence and prayers of the great cloud of women witnesses to the faith from the past, it was an experience of solidarity and empowerment rather than an experience of segregation and repression.[6]

Although women were, and in many cases still are, excluded from sacred spaces in worship, we ought not to jump to negative conclusions too quickly. White's book itself shows why the history of women and worship is not "the shortest book ever written," as one of her friends commented, but rather a rich and complex story. And as Sandra Schneiders wrote a number of years ago, there is a "flip side" to women's experiences of exclusion and marginalization.[7] Nevertheless, it is instructive to note how carefully women's physical presence or absence in the presence of the holy has been regulated by canon law.

Let me give you a few examples. The 1917 Code of Canon Law held that "consistent with ancient discipline, women be separated from men

---

6. Susan J. White, *A History of Women in Christian Worship* (Cleveland, OH: Pilgrim Press, 2003), 1.

7. Sandra J. Schneiders, "The Effects of Women's Experience on Their Spirituality," *Spirituality Today* 35, no. 2 (Summer 1983): 100–116.

in church."[8] Women also were not to distribute Holy Communion, not to be altar servers, to have their heads veiled, and the last choice to be an extraordinary minster of baptism.[9] Now these canons make no reference at all to beauty; at their core remains what I would describe as a strong though unarticulated sense of concern for ritual purity. But I would argue that this regulation against women's presence and voice or even their handling altar linens is also a fear of men being distracted, or, at worst, seduced, by the physical presence of women, which would then prevent men from being in the presence of God. Women's physical presence and their beauty detracts from or even obscures the beauty of God.

Since the revision of the Code in 1983, these regulations may seem somewhat quaint to modern ears. Surely women's presence is no longer a problem in churches, and even I, for one, would suggest that women *and* men consider a little more carefully how they dress for church! Yet there remain a number of practices and regulations that concern women's physical presence. For example, in the new Code of Canon Law (1983) only men can be formally installed as acolytes (altar servers) and lectors (readers). Women can be "temporarily deputized" to fulfill the functions of these roles but cannot formally assume them, as can men. Women can also and indeed do serve as eucharistic ministers, but they, like laymen, do so in an "extraordinary" capacity—that is, when the "ordinary" minister cannot.[10] Basically, women serve in these capacities as a "last resort."

Liturgical worship is meant to draw the mind and heart to God, so let us just digest this point: in ideal circumstances, as Canon Law would require, when one's eye is on the altar, there are *no women* in the picture. We are so accustomed to this that the presence of women in liturgical roles is, for some, problematic. But let us consider how women have indeed graced the presence of churches in ways that often are ignored or trivialized.

8. *The 1917 Pio-Benedictine Code of Canon Law*, in English Translation, Edward N. Peters, Curator (San Francisco: Ignatius Press, 2001), par. 1262 (p. 427).

9. Pars. 845, 813, 1262, 742. It is interesting to note that a woman can baptize if "a woman knows the form and manner of baptism better than does a man."

10. The 1980 document *Inestimabile Donum* reiterated the instruction that "the faithful, whether religious or lay, who are authorized as extraordinary ministers of the Eucharist can distribute Communion only when there is no priest, deacon, or acolyte; when the priest is impeded by illness or advanced age; or when the number of the faithful going to Communion is so large as to make the celebration of Mass excessively long."

My mother, like many church-going women, was a needleworker, and our house is graced with many of her pieces. She hated to have her hands idle. One of the most humorous projects she ever undertook was to knit uteruses so that my sister, a nurse who taught childbirth classes to expectant parents, could demonstrate how the uterus stretched during pregnancy and opened up for the baby's head. She loved to recount how she would answer when someone politely asked her what she was knitting. "It's a uterus," she would respond, with a straight face. She taught my sisters and me how to knit and do needlepoint, and I think of my mother whenever I pick up knitting needles or a needlepoint canvas.

In the process of writing this essay, I came across a number of references to women's altar societies and other women's organizations. From one perspective, one could dismiss the work of altar societies—cleaning pews, washing and ironing altar linens—as demeaning women's work, a way to keep the elderly ladies of the parish busy. Yet consider the work itself and consider the fact that all of this is necessary work. Like maintaining a home, these tasks need to be done yet are considered to be the liturgical equivalent of "housework," something that most of us would rather not do ourselves and hire out if we can. But without this work, churches, like houses, would not be clean or inviting and would utterly lack beauty. Beauty, as we are so often told by the "beauty industry," requires a great deal of work, and some of this work is far from glamorous. I want to raise up the work of these countless anonymous women who have helped to maintain the beauty of our churches. Without them, we would not be able to behold this beauty as well as we have.

Let me also mention briefly another way that women have beautified churches. Generations of African American women have worn beautiful and sometimes elaborate hats to church.[11] The one who wore a hat well had "hattitude." She had pride in herself, a love for beauty, and a desire to wear her best in the presence of the Lord. One woman portrayed in the book *Crowns* comments, "I think that [putting on your best] grows out of the African American tradition that says that when you present yourself before God, who is excellent and holy and most high, there should be excellence in all things, including your appearance." Another says, "As a little girl, I'd admire women at church with beautiful hats. They looked like beautiful dolls, like they just stepped

11. See Michael Cunningham and Craig Marberry, *Crowns: Portraits of Black Women in Church Hats* (New York: Doubleday, 2000).

out of a magazine. But I also knew how hard they worked all week. Sometimes, under those hats, there's a lot of joy and a lot of sorrow."[12]

Wearing hats, like belonging to an altar society, is no longer widely practiced, even in the African American community. Most women have welcomed the relaxing of the requirement that our heads be covered, and I do not know a single woman who is involved in an altar society or who has special hats for church. I suspect that these traditions will soon be quaint reminders of the past. Yet I think it is worth considering what these practices tell us. In both cases, women were either barred by men from sacred spaces and given menial work to do or they had a rule imposed on them by men—both so that women would not intrude on the sacred beauty of the church. But in both cases, women from all ends of the social and economic spectrum turned these situations into opportunities for beautifying their worship spaces.

So when we walk into a beautiful church, with clean stained-glass windows that allow the light to filter in, with pews that are free from dust and clutter, with tapestries or artwork that draw our hearts heavenward, with women crowned with elaborate millinery, we should be grateful for the work that women have done to maintain this beauty and for the love of self and of neighbor that moves them to share their love of beauty with the whole church. And while I deplore the demeaning attitudes that have prompted exclusion and sexist requirements for women's exclusion, at the same time I celebrate the creativity with which centuries of women have turned these prohibitions into occasions of beauty and grace.

Beauty in the World

In the summer of 2002, I went to Africa with a small group of Loyola faculty and staff members. We were part of an "immersion trip" to Kenya and Tanzania, where we visited a university, orphanages, schools, women's cooperatives, and training centers and also encountered the magnificent natural beauty of Africa. Yet even with all this spectacular beauty, one of the most memorable places we visited was the tiny village of Lwak, near Kisumu in western Africa, on the shores of Lake Victoria. Lwak is a desperately poor place, and the people there struggle to survive amid the crisis of HIV/AIDS, the effects of governmental corruption, and the vagaries of the weather. Shortly before we arrived in June, most of their tomato crop had been washed away by torrential rains.

12. Ibid., 75.

While we were there, we were also gifted with the hospitality of the women of Lwak. After we had spent the better part of a day touring the fields, visiting the village where the cooperative store sold soaps and preserves, and driving along muddy, rutted "roads" to see some of the cooperative projects, the women of the village threw us a party. They brought their couches and chairs outside and covered them with lace doilies, and they served us food that they must have spent days cooking. There was a small band of male musicians, and although we were all exhausted, we ate and danced and sang with our generous hosts into the evening. I was struck then as now by these women who beautified themselves, their homes, and their village in honor of their guests. The women who belonged to the cooperative wore matching dresses that they had sewn by hand, and their homes had pictures on the walls and flowers in their tiny gardens. The woman who hosted the party had buried her husband a few months before, after he had died of AIDS, and she herself was HIV positive. Somehow, though, her love for beauty had survived, as had her generous sense of hospitality and her commitment to her village.

As the magazine *National Geographic* described in its September 2005 issue, Africa is much more than it may seem to the West. What I have learned from the women of Africa are lessons in beauty and justice that extend from their families to their communities and, ultimately, to the world. In this last section, I would like to describe the work and contributions of a handful of African women. I will then reflect on what they have to teach me—a white, privileged, highly educated, middle-class American woman—and perhaps some of the rest of us. For many of the women of Africa, beauty and justice go hand in hand.

One of the most well-known African women was the late 2004 Nobel Peace Prize winner Wangari Maathai. In the summer of 2005, Wangari Maathai visited my church in Evanston, Illinois, and I heard her speak about her life and work. The church was filled to overflowing as we heard her talk about her efforts in reforestation and with women's groups. The words of the Nobel committee described her contributions this way:

> Peace on earth depends on our ability to secure our living environ-
> ment. Maathai stands at the front of the fight to promote ecologically
> and viable social, economic and cultural development in Kenya and in
> Africa. She has taken a holistic approach to sustainable development
> that embraces democracy, human rights, and women's rights in par-
> ticular. She thinks globally and acts locally.[13]

---

13. Presentation of the Nobel Peace Prize, December 10, 2004, as found at http://
www.nobelprize.org.

It is not immediately evident that either Wangari Maathai or the Nobel Prize committee thought of her work in the language of beauty and justice. But her work shows evidence that beauty is at least an implicit, if not an explicit, dimension of it. My own thesis is that historically, and for the vast majority in the present, women have seldom taken the time, or have had the time, to theorize about beauty. Beauty for women is, rather, tied closely to the way one lives and acts. It is interwoven into women's lives and is much less an ornament than a central thread: a practice and not an idea.

After I returned from my trip to Africa, I was on the lookout for things that related particularly to African women. In the fall of 2002, I was on a plane to New York for a conference and happened to flip through the in-flight magazine. There was a very small sidebar that described an exhibit in New York City. Although I couldn't go to the exhibit, eventually I tracked down some books by the photographer whose work was the exhibit's focus. Margaret Courtney-Clarke has spent decades photographing the work of African women, from the Berber women of Morocco to the Ndebele women of South Africa, whose artistic work is not only stunningly beautiful but also practical and of service to the community.

Courtney-Clarke's first book describes the house painting and bead-work of the Ndebele women of South Africa.[14] For generations, these women have painted murals on their homes in bright colors and designs and have also worked beads into intricate patterns to be worn. These practices have survived years of civil war and apartheid, and, sadly, they are no longer as widely practiced as they once were. Globalization, modernization, and urbanization mean that fewer younger women are learning these skills. The house paintings involve complex geometric patterns in distinct designs. Some of them have in recent years begun to incorporate features of modern life, such as cars, planes, and electric lights in their murals, but they are transformed and adapted into Ndebele culture. Beads are also a significant part of Ndebele life. Children wear beads before they wear clothing, and initiation ceremonies for both boys and girls involve wearing beadwork especially designed for these rituals of passage.

It would be both inappropriate and presumptuous of me to say what the meaning of these practices is. But for this particular Western observer, the incorporation of the house painting practices into the lives

---

14. Margaret Courtney-Clarke, *Ndebele: The Art of an African Tribe* (New York: Thames and Hudson, 1986, 2002).

of the Ndebele people raised for me the issue of beauty and its role in everyday life. The Ndebele people have endured apartheid, forced relocation, civil war, and worse, and yet, these women continue to paint their houses as expressions of the craft they learned from their mothers and, I think, as a way of keeping their daily lives not only functioning but also beautiful. House painting is not something these women do to "while away the time." It is, rather, a part of their culture, a means of both self- and communal expression.

In another one of her books about African women—Berber women from Algeria, Morocco, and Tunisia—Courtney-Clarke again documents the craft of women, this time in weaving and pottery.[15] In her introduction, she describes her search for these women's work and the reactions of the Berber men when she asked about it: "The Berber men had no concept of what I was in search of and thus could not comprehend my passionate interest in their wives' seasonal domestic activities."[16] It has been the men's work in pottery and jewelry that has achieved renown, not the women's. Moreover, the work of the women, as is true of much of the work of non-Western cultures, is under attack from the same processes I described above. As much as, if not more than, their creativity and practicality, these are works that make sense only within their community. They are not individual works of art, with no precedent, unique unto themselves. Each house is very much like the next, although it is also different. Baskets and pots resemble each other, although each has the stamp of its maker. They are interwoven into the community's life. The skills are passed down from mother to daughter. And as we have seen, even the term "beauty" does not quite capture these objects. They are good: pleasing to the eye yet also functional. Might we say they also embody the truth of the lives of these women? Might we say that they are examples of the unity of goodness, truth, and beauty?

Women, Sacramentality, and Justice

As I have written elsewhere, "feminist theology shares with the Christian tradition a reverence for the earth and for the body. . . . All of creation is potentially revelatory of God and has intrinsic worth, not just that worth bestowed by humans."[17] In the previous sections of these

15. Margaret Courtney-Clarke, *Imazighen: The Vanishing Traditions of Berber Women* (New York: Clarkson Potter, 1996).

16. Ibid., ix.

17. Susan A. Ross, *Extravagant Affections: A Feminist Sacramental Theology* (New York: Continuum, 1998), 46.

reflections, I have emphasized the ways that women's works of art and craft are indeed sacramental: they are ways of encountering the beauty of God in both expected and unexpected places. Like the sacraments, they are not purely individual creations but rather connected to wider communities: the family, the local community, the world. Yet there is a sense in which the sensual dimension of human experiencing and knowing still carries a hint of the old dualisms. For example, in the *Summa Theologiae*, Thomas Aquinas writes:

> It follows, therefore, that through the institution of the sacraments, man, consistently with his nature, is instructed through sensible things; he is humbled, through confessing that he is subject to corporal things, seeing that he receives assistance through them; and he is even preserved from bodily hurt, by the healthy exercise of the sacraments.[18]

Although having to be "instructed through sensible things" may be for Aquinas a humbling experience, one can also consider the benefits of our corporeality, as does the music theorist Victor Zuckerkandl, who writes:

> A God enthroned beyond time in timeless eternity would have to renounce music. . . . Are we to suppose that we mortals, in possessing such a wonder as music, are more privileged than God? Rather, to save music for God, we shall hold, with the Greeks, that God cannot go beyond time. Otherwise, what would God do with all the choiring angels?[19]

Indeed, what would God do with them? But we know that, in fact, God so loved the world that God became one of us and, in the process, made the earth and all who live upon it to be the place where we encounter God.

I have suggested in these pages that having to choose between goodness and beauty is a false dichotomy, much like the false dichotomies that have plagued our tradition for millennia: spirit and body, male and female, reason and emotion, light and dark. And although women have found themselves so often on the lesser side of the dualism, they have also refused to accept this situation.

It seems appropriate to close these pages with the words of a song written on behalf of women workers, words that suggest the bread that

---

18. *Summa Theologiae* III, q. 61, a. 1.
19. Victor Zuckerkandl, quoted in Jeremy Begbie, *Theology, Music, and Time* (Cambridge: Cambridge University Press, 2000), 128.

fills us not only materially but also spiritually.[20] The song also brings to mind the work that women have done for so long on behalf of themselves, as well as on behalf of men and children:

As we go marching, marching, in the beauty of the day,
A million darkened kitchens, a thousand mill lofts gray,
Are touched with all the radiance that a sudden sun discloses,
For the people hear us singing, Bread and Roses! Bread and Roses!

As we go marching, marching, we battle too for men,
For they are women's children, and we mother them again.
Our lives shall not be sweated from birth until life closes;
Hearts starve as well as bodies; give us bread, but give us roses.

As we go marching, marching, unnumbered women dead
Go crying through our singing their ancient call for bread.
Small art and love and beauty their drudging spirits knew.
Yes, it is bread we fight for, but we fight for roses too.

As we go marching, marching, we bring the greater days,
the rising of the women means the rising of the race.
No more the drudge and idler, ten that toil where one reposes,
But a sharing of life's glories: Bread and Roses, bread and roses.

Our lives shall not be sweated from birth until life closes;
hearts starve as well as bodies; bread and roses, bread and roses.

20. The most popular version of this song was written in Lawrence, Massachusetts, during the mill strikes of 1912. The original lyrics were by James Oppenheim; music is attributed to Martha Coleman and/or Caroline Kohlsaat. See Edith Fowke and Joe Glazer, eds., *Songs of Work and Protest* (New York: Dover, 1973).

Indigenous children dressed in traditional clothing for the celebration of Our Lady of Guadalupe. Photo courtesy of Dr. Jeanette Rodriguez.

Jeanette Rodriguez

Theological Aesthetics and the Encounter with Tonantzin Guadalupe

The significance of Tonantzin Guadalupe in the history and contemporary experience of Latino/as is more fully appreciated when we bring certain dimensions of theological aesthetics to bear on our encounter with this event and we situate her in the religious-aesthetic sensibilities of the Náhuatl culture in which she originally appeared and into which she was appropriated. Doing so enables Tonantzin Guadalupe to become a subject of beauty, that which moves the heart, as one who imbues beauty with a sense of identity and resistance and as a source of hope reflected in the prevalence of her image in indigenous religious piety and popular culture.

The term "theological aesthetics" was first coined by Alexander G. Baumgarten in 1735 as the "science of sensory cognition."[1] Latino/a popular religion is an example of this understanding of theological aesthetics with its altars, incense burning, candles, and flowers. I intend to include and highlight, however, a way of understanding theological aesthetics proposed by the late theologian Alejandro García-Rivera. He asks a profound question: "What moves the human heart?"[2] He contends that aesthetics "has existed since the first human heart was

---

1. Alexander G. Baumgarten, *Meditationes Philosophicae de Nonnullis Ad Poema Pertinentibus* (1735); quoted in Alejandro García-Rivera, *The Community of the Beautiful: A Theological Aesthetics* (Collegeville, MN: Liturgical Press, 1999), 9.

2. García-Rivera, *The Community of the Beautiful*, 9.

moved by the influence of the beautiful."[3] In addition, I draw on the work of Georgina Zubiria, RSCJ, a theologian from the province of Mexico-Nicaragua, and Gesa Elsbeth Thiessen, both of whom highlight the importance of the senses and affect to understand that which moves the human heart. In Scripture we find that the heart is the center of the human person. So in the sense that I am calling for our hearts to be moved, I am retrieving a language of Christian spirituality that regards "the human heart as the special organ of the love of God."[4]

A New Framework

In her article "Mi Corazon Me Dice Que te Busque" ("My Heart Tells Me to Look for You"), Zubiria contributes three important points for developing my framework for understanding theological aesthetics.[5] First, she states that to speak about God is difficult, and it is even more difficult to try to articulate a communal experience of the divine. We always run the risk of reducing the experience of the divine into finite words and ideas that ultimately place God in a box.[6] Yet, she argues that our very senses and feelings mediate this experience of God. Zubiria contends that "our experience of God is born, grows, and is nourished through our humanity, through words and gestures, symbols, human experience and conviction."[7] Moreover, she contends that, through the senses, we further "discover and manifest God. It is our senses and even our sense of smell and skin that permit us to recognize the presence or the absence of God."[8]

Second, she draws on the insight of the famous Spanish philosopher, Xavier Zubiri, who recognizes that "our intuitive and perceptive capacity, our intelligence and feeling is what permits us to recognize the transcendent in the imminent."[9] Third, Zubiria reminds us that our feelings return us toward God; our feelings are "wired and manifest and make transparent God's love and presence and commitment to humanity."[10]

---

3. Ibid.

4. *Oxford Dictionary of the Christian Church*, ed. F. L. Cross and E. A. Livingstone, 3rd ed. (New York: Oxford University Press, 1997), 740.

5. Georgina Zubiria, "Mi Corazon Me Dice Que te Busque (Sal 26, 8)," in *Diabonia Servicio De La Fe Y Promocion De La Justicia*, trans. Jeanette Rodriguez (Managua: Centro Ignaciano de Centroamerica, 2001), 61–65.

6. Ibid., 60.

7. Ibid., 61.

8. Ibid.

9. Leonardo Boff, "La experiencia de Dios," Confederación Latinoamericana y Caribena de Religiosos y Religiosas (CLAR) (n.d.), quoted in ibid., 61.

10. Ibid., 62.

In *Theological Aesthetics: A Reader*, Gesa Elsbeth Thiessen paraphrases Richard Viadesau when she writes that "theological aesthetics is concerned with questions about God and issues in theology in the light of and perceived through sense knowledge (sensation, feeling, imagination), through beauty, and the arts."[11] Together, then, these insights create the framework of theological aesthetics in this article. The framework includes three movements: attending to all the senses, reflecting on how the experience moves the heart, and pondering how God is revealed. I explore the Guadalupe experience to flesh out this approach.

The Tonantzin Guadalupe

Much has been written about the narrative, image, and iconography of and devotion to Our Lady of Guadalupe. Tonantzin Guadalupe is the most important religious symbol of Mexico and one of the most powerful female icons of religious culture. Indigenous people of Mexico refer to her as Tonantzin, the Náhuatl word for "Our Mother." The debates on, speculations about, and articulations of this experience are well-documented, extremely interesting, and complex.[12] The narratives bring together the world and spirituality of sixteenth-century Spain with the cosmic vision of the Náhuatl indigenous communities.

In order to fully understand the power and impact of the Guadalupe image and narrative, we must understand culture. At the heart of culture is religious understanding. Many cultural anthropologists and theologians have utilized a variety of sources to understand this notion

11. Gesa Elsbeth Thiessen, *Theological Aesthetics: A Reader* (Grand Rapids, MI: Eerdmans, 2004), 1 and 361.

12. A sampling of studies on the Virgin of Guadalupe include anthropologist Eric R. Wolf, "The Virgin of Guadalupe: A National Symbol," in *Ritual and Belief: Readings in the Anthropology of Religion*, ed. David Hicks (Boston: McGraw Hill, 2001); historians D. A. Brading, *Mexican Phoenix: Our Lady of Guadalupe; Image and Tradition across Five Centuries* (New York and Cambridge: Cambridge University Press, 2001); Stanford Poole, *Our Lady of Guadalupe: The Origins and Sources of Mexican National Symbol, 1531–1787* (Tucson and London: The University of Arizona Press, 1995); William B. Taylor, "The Virgin of Guadalupe in New Spain: An Inquiry into the Social History of Marian Devotion," *American Ethnologist* 14, no. 1 (February 1987): 9–33; art historian Jeanette Favrot Peterson, "The Virgin of Guadalupe: Symbol of Conquest or Liberation," *Art Journal* 51, no. 4 (Winter 1992): 39–47; and theologians Virgilio Elizondo, *Guadalupe: Mother of the New Creation* (Maryknoll, NY: Orbis Books, 1997); and Jeanette Rodriguez, *Our Lady of Guadalupe: Faith and Empowerment among Mexican-American Women* (Austin: University of Texas Press, 1994).

of culture.[13] In this essay, I define culture as that which flows from an understanding that people develop regarding unique sets of categories, including languages, political organizations, rituals, and ceremonies. Historically, marginalized groups have additional categories that reveal the cultural forces that have resisted annihilation from dominant groups by accessing forms of spiritual resistance. Foundationally, culture provides frameworks of meanings that include attitudes, values, and beliefs.

As we unpack the story of Guadalupe by utilizing the work of Clodomiro L. Siller Acuña, the Mexican cultural anthropologist, we will see that Our Lady of Guadalupe's message calls those in positions of political and ecclesiastical power to leave their palaces and move to the periphery and stand with the poor and the marginalized.

Siller Acuña presents the narration and tradition of Guadalupe as that which incarnates the traditional values of the indigenous peoples. It is these values that become the "meat and the body and blood of the message."[14] In order to understand and appreciate this message, it is necessary to know something about the Náhuatl culture because the Guadalupe experience is a Náhuatl event. All theology and experience is contextual. It is grounded and mediated through specific cultures. While mediated in the Náhuatl culture, I believe the narrative of Guadalupe transcends time, place, and culture because what lives within the story is that which is deeply human. Everyone is ultimately in search of satisfaction for "an unquenchable fire, restlessness, a longing, a hunger."[15] Located in concrete time and culture, the original Tonantzin Guadalupe experience transcends that particular time (1531) through the Mexican aesthetic *flor y canto*. That is, the original event is transmitted to and received by subsequent generations through narrative, visual images, and popular religious practice, including drama, symbol, fiesta, and other contemporary expressions. These practices impact people's hearts and draw people to experience their own relationships with Tonantzin

13. See the following for the interplay between culture and theology: Aylward Shorter, *Towards a Theology of Inculturation* (New York: Maryknoll, 1988); Pedro Arrupe, "Letter to the Whole Society on Inculturation," *Aixala* 3 (1978): 172–81; Aylward Shorter, *African Culture and the Christian Church: An Introduction to Social and Pastoral Anthropology* (London: G. Chapman, 1973). Insights are also drawn from informal conversations with and unpublished class notes of Dr. Ted Fortier, cultural anthropologist at Seattle University.

14. Clodomiro L. Siller Acuña, "Guadalupe: Luz Y Cambio De Nuestra Realidad" (n.p: n.p., 2000).

15. Ronald Rolheiser, *The Holy Longing: The Search for a Christian Spirituality* (New York: Random House Inc., 1999), 4.

...ge of Our Lady of Guadalupe is displayed in a many
...n home altars, around one's neck in jewelry, hanging
...r mirrors, and even tattooed on the body. Photo courtesy
...d Fortier.

The image of Our Lady of Guadalupe as it is displayed in the
Basilica of Mexico. Photo courtesy of Dr. Jeanette Rodriguez.

Guadalupe. Thus, she becomes a vehicle for communicating God and
drawing people to faith.

The narrative speaks of an intimate encounter between human and
the divine. The elements—of belonging, restoration, healing—within
the narrative transcend time, place, and culture.

The original language of the *Nican Mopohua* is Náhuatl. Náhuatl is
a symbolic language communicating meaning far beyond words. It is
a simple language, direct, smooth, precise, elegant, resounding, beautiful, significant, and even sublime. An important aspect of the Náhuatl
language is its use of *disfrasismos*, a way of communicating the most
profound thought or feeling using a complementary union of two words
or symbols that express one meaning.[16] The phrase "flower and song" is
an example of *difrasismo*. The Náhuas believe that only through flower
and song, only through *flor y canto*, can truth be grasped. Truth intuited
through poetry, therefore, derives from a particular kind of knowledge
that is a consequence of being in touch with one's inner experience as

16. Clodomiro L. Siller Acuña, "El metodo de la evangelizacion en el Nican
Mopohua," *Servir* 17 (1993–94): 255–93.

lived out communally. Truth is mediated through the cultural constructs of the community as understood through the individual seeker.[17]

The sixteenth-century Spanish conquistadors and the indigenous communities they encountered led to the devastation of the Náhuas and their culture. Those secular and religious individuals who objected were powerless to stop the systemic violence. In their enthusiasm to convert the natives, the clergy lost their humanity even as they pursued divinity.[18]

The social structure of the indigenous people underwent tremendous upheaval. Aztec society had been made up of a social structure with rigidly defined roles. With the coming of the Spaniards, the Aztec priests and princesses once revered by their people found themselves on the same level as the Aztec peasants.[19] Land, formerly held in common for the welfare of the people, became a place of slavery where the Indians worked to provide wealth for the Spanish landlords.

The indigenous people were forced into a state of helplessness, powerlessness, fear, anger, and eventually self-hatred. In the midst of this deep cultural and personal upheaval, the intellect falls silent, unable to make sense of it. Only poetry can begin to express the depth of struggle and loss. Thus, just as the Israelite peoples used poetry to lament their plight, so too the following poems express the depths of devastation experienced by the Náhuatl and other indigenous cultures at the time of the Spanish Conquest.

> *Broken Spears*[20]
> Broken spears lie in the roads;
> We have torn our hair in our grief
> The houses are roofless now, and their walls
> Are red with blood . . .
>
> We have pounded our hands in despair
> Against the adobe walls,
> For our inheritance, our city, is lost and dead
> The shields of our warriors were its defense.
> But they could not save it.

17. Jeanette Rodriguez, "Latina Activists toward an Inclusive Spirituality of Being in the World," *A Reader in Latina Feminist Theology: Religion and Justice* (Austin: University of Texas Press, 2002), 127.

18. Siller Acuña, "Guadalupe: Luz Y Cambio De Nuestra Realidad," 9.

19. Alfred Mirande and Evangelina Enriquez, *La Chicana: The Mexican-Misioneros del Espiritu Santo* (Chicago: University of Chicago Press, 1979), 2–12.

20. Miguel Leon Portilla, *The Broken Spears: The Aztec Account of the Conquest of Mexico* (Boston: Beacon Press, 1962), 137–38.

The Fall of Tenochtitlan[21]
Our cries of grief rise up
And our tears rain down
for Tlatelolco is lost. . . .
Weep my people:
Know that with these disasters
We have lost the Mexican nation
The water has turned bitter,
Our food is bitter![22]

Tonantzin Guadalupe appears in the setting of the "post-guerra," ten years after the conquest. She enters the devastation as Tonantzin, her original title meaning "our mother" to honor the Náhuatl religious understanding. In addition, although she is now known as Our Lady of Guadalupe, "in the experience of the people then and now, references to the Mary of the Gospels are notably absent in connection with devotion to Guadalupe. What is mediated instead is profoundly engaging sacred love and compassion that gives heart, wisdom, and fortitude to adherents."[23]

The Narrative

Thus, the experience drew people to her heart and the community kept the experience alive through the theological aesthetics of narrative, image, and popular religion. Students and scholars of the origin of the devotions to/of Guadalupe assert that the narration of the apparitions was transmitted, at the beginning and for some time thereafter, in the manner common to the Indians of that time, orally and through "charts" on which they were able to draw the events of history. From Indian to Indian, from community to community, the word of what had happened to Juan Diego at Mount Tepeyacac began to be told along with the other marvels that took place in the presence of the Virgin of Guadalupe. The deeds rapidly entered into the traditions of the people.[24] Only afterward, according to the demands of the circumstances, was the narration written down, first in Náhuatl and later in Spanish. This written

---

21. Ibid., 146.
22. These poems can also be found in my book, *Our Lady of Guadalupe: Faith and Empowerment*, 11–12.
23. Elizabeth A. Johnson, *Quest for the Living God: Mapping Frontiers into the Theology of God* (New York: Continuum Press, 2007), 142.
24. Clodomiro L. Siller Acuña, "Flor y canto del Tepeyacac: Historia de las apariciones de Sta. Ma. De Guadalupe; Texto y comentario" (Xalapa, Vercruz, Mexico: Servir, 1981).

Indigenous women preparing for the celebration of Our Lady of Guadalupe with incense burner and lute. Photo courtesy of Dr. Ted Fortier.

form is referred to as the *Nican Mopohua*. Siller Acuña contends that the original author of the *Nican Mopohua* was Don Antonio Valeriano, an indigenous student and later teacher at the Colegio de la Santa Cruz de Tlatelolco.[25] The tradition tells us that he was what ethnography would call an informant of the First Bishop of Mexico and that the document was written under the direction of Bernardino de Sahagun.[26] While Siller Acuña recognizes the significant contributions that Don Antonio Valeriano made in the transcriptions of the *Nican Mopohua*, however, he also finds it hard to believe that he is the only author of the *Nican Mopohua* and makes a compelling argument that the writing of the *Nican Mopohua* was a result of a collegial and collective contribution.[27]

The text states the day, the date, and the time of the apparition: Saturday, December 9, 1531, early in the morning. For the indigenous, *muy de madrugada* (very early in the morning) referred not only to daybreak but to the beginning of all time. Tonantzin Guadalupe appears early in the morning, just as the day is coming out of darkness and night. This meaningful time defined the Guadalupe event as fundamental, equal in significance to the origin of the world and the cosmos.[28]

She associates herself with *El verdadero Dios, por quien se vive* (the true God for whom one lives). This expression is one of the names that the Náhuatl gave to their gods. When Tonantzin Guadalupe states that she is from the one true God, the God who gives life, the Náhuatl recognized this God to be their God.[29]

Religious principles penetrated the very existence of the pre-Columbian people. Every stage of each person's progress from birth to death; the rhythm of time; the arts; their public and private life; and even games were informed by their religious understanding and commitments.[30] This all-pervasive religiosity of the indigenous peoples

25. The authorship of the *Nican Mopohua* has been intensely researched. Please see Siller-Acuña's *Para comprender el mensaje de Maria de Guadalupe,* and Rojas-Sanchez's *Nican mopohua. Dn. Antonio Valeriano, traducción del náhuatl al catellano.*

26. Siller Acuña, "Guadalupe: Luz Y Cambio De Nuestra Realidad," 8.

27. Ibid., 9. While Siller Acuña recognizes the contribution that Don Antonio Valeriano made in the transcription of the narrative, he also indicates that it is difficult to believe that Valeriano was the only author of the *Nican Mopohua* and makes an argument that the *Nican Mopohua* was a result of a more collegial and collective contribution. Please see Siller Acuña's book, pages 9–11.

28. Ibid.

29. Siller Acuña, "Flor y canto del Tepeyacac."

30. Jacques Soustelle, *Daily Life of the Aztecs on the Eve of the Spanish Conquest* (Stanford, CA: Stanford University Press, 1970), 119.

continues to be a large part of the assumptive world of many Mexicans and Mexican Americans.

At the time of Tonantzin's apparition, the Christian faith had begun to flourish, albeit slowly, given the conquest. The narrative centers on a Christian Indian man by the name of Juan Diego, who was on his way to continue his Christian formation in Tlatelolco. Juan Diego was born in 1474 in a small village of Cuautitlán. "His pre-conquest Indigenous name was Cuautitlatoatzin, which means 'venerable eagle that speaks.'"[31] The *Nican Mopohua*[32] states, "It was Saturday, very early in the morning when Juan Diego was on his way to learn more about God and the commandments" (NM 6). And as he approached this little hill named Tepeyacac, it was nearing dawn. He heard singing coming from the top of the hill. It was the song of many fine birds. As he listened, he asked himself if he was, in fact, dreaming. He looked up toward the top of the hill, toward the "place where the sun rises" (NM 11), from where the precious celestial song was coming. He came before a maiden. She called out to him and asked him where he was going. He admired her grandeur: "her clothing was shining and giving out rays like the sun, the rocks . . . were casting out rays of light. Her radiance was like that of precious stones. . . . [T]he ground was shining with the splendors of the rainbow in the mist. And the mesquitas, prickly pear, cacti and the rest of the little plants that usually grew there looked like emeralds" (NM 17–21). He prostrated himself; apparently he recognized her. It is here that she reveals herself to him by saying,

> Know for sure, my youngest and dearest son, that I am the Perfect, Ever-Virgin Mary, the Mother of the Most True God, the Giver of Life, the Creator of Persons, the Owner of What is Near and Immediate, the Owner of the Sky, the Owner of the Land. I greatly wish and desire that they build my scared little house here, in which I will show Him, I will exalt him on making Him manifest. I will give Him to all the people and all my personal love, in my compassionate gaze, in my help, in my salvation. For I am truly the compassionate mother, of you and of all the people who live together as one in this land, and of the other diverse races of people, who love me, cry out to me, who seek me, who trust me. There I will listen to their weeping and their

31. Carlos de Siguenza y Góngora, *Piedad Heroyca de Don Fernándo Córtes* (Madrid: José Porrúa Turanzas, 1960).

32. Translation of narrative drawn from Náhuatl-Spanish text of the *Nican Mopohua*: Mario Rojas-Sanchez, ed., *Nican Mopohua*, Don Antonio Valeriano, traducción del náhuatl al castellano por el presbitero Mario Rojas Sanchez (Mexico: Imprenta Ideal, 1978).

sadness in order to remedy, to cure all their different afflictions, their miseries, their suffering. (NM 26–32)

This is her message. In order for her message to be carried forth, she asked Juan Diego to go to the bishop and to tell him what it was she asked for: that there be built here on Tepeyacac a home, a house. But when Juan Diego arrived home to the house of his uncle, Juan Bernadino, he was confronted with an illness that had come upon his uncle. The uncle begged him to summon a priest for his final breath. Juan Diego agreed to his uncle's request. When he reached the hill of Tepeyacac, he avoided the road that might lead him to an encounter with the Lady. He decided to take a different road. To no avail; the Lady encountered him and asked, "What is happening, my youngest son? Where are you going?" (NM 107). He proceeded in an embarrassed tone to tell her, "It grieves me to cause anguish to your face and heart. Know, little girl, that my uncle and a dear servant of yours is seriously ill. A grave illness has taken over him for which he will surely die"(NM 111). It was at this point that Tonantzin articulated her most intimate, caring words:

> Listen, be convinced in your heart, my youngest son, what frightened and afflicted you is nothing. Do not let it disturb your face and heart. Do not fear this sickness or any other sickness that afflicts or over-whelms. Am I not here, I, who am your mother? Are you not under my shadow and protection? Am I not the reason for your happiness? Are you not in my lap, in the crossing of my arms? Are you in need of anything else? Let nothing else afflict and disturb you. Do not let your dear uncle's illness cause you anguish because he will not die of it now. Rest assured in your heart that he is already well. (NM 118–20)

With his heart at peace, Juan Diego followed Tonantzin's instructions to climb up the hill, gather the roses, and take the roses to the bishop as a sign of her proof so that he would believe Juan Diego. "When he arrived at the top, he greatly marveled at how many diverse kinds of precious flowers like those of Castile were in full bloom with their corollas wide open when it was not quite their season" (NM 128). He cut the flowers; he gathered them and brought them back down to the Lady. She took them in her hands, once again put them all together in the hollow of his tilma, and told him, "My youngest son, these differ-ent flowers are proof, the sign that you are to take to the bishop. You are to tell him on my behalf that he is to carry out my will which is my desire. And you, you are my messenger; in you I absolutely place my confidence" (NM 137–39). Juan Diego took the flowers to the bishop. Before presenting the flowers, Juan Diego told the bishop everything he had seen and experienced and encountered. As soon as the bishop heard all that Juan Diego had to share he sensed in his heart that this was the proof.

The Image of Tonantzin Guadalupe[33]

When the Náhuatl saw Tonantzin Guadalupe, they did not see a mere image or photograph of something, as we might suspect. For the people who inhabited Central and Southern Mexico, the image of Tonantzin Guadalupe contained codices—ancient symbols and words. It was a codice that they could read perfectly and that consisted of everything that was important to them.[34] The image of Guadalupe, then, is a *Conjunto symbolos*—a collection of symbols creating a codice. The codice functions in the same way, I believe, that images function in spiritual direction. Mary Rose Bumpus writes, "Images have both a mediating and a holistic function. Images occupy an in between space, the place between thought and feeling. . . . Images can mediate between dimensions of the self and can assist us in moving from one dimension to another. At the same time, images have the capacity to bring together disparate aspects of our experience. They may summarize or gather up the whole of the experience in a way that discursive language cannot do."[35]

If we look at the image of Tonantzin Guadalupe through the eyes of the Náhuatl, there are a number of key factors that stand out that deepen the understanding of this dynamic language of symbols that speak to the heart.

The Face[36]

A person's face held great importance for the indigenous people because they felt that through the face one could come to understand the inner person. The person was considered by the Náhuas to be born faceless and with a nameless heart. It was through education that the

---

33. Detailed description and interpretation of the indigenous and European overlays of the iconography of the Virgin of Guadalupe can be found in Louise M. Burkhart, "The Cult of the Virgin of Guadalupe in Mexico," in *South and Meso-American Native Spirituality*, ed. Gary Gassen (New York: Crossroad, 1997), 198–227; and Rodriguez, *Our Lady of Guadalupe: Faith and Empowerment*, 22–30.

34. Siller Acuña, "Guadalupe: Luz Y Cambio De Nuestra Realidad," 92.

35. Mary Rose Bumpus, "The Hopeful Imagination: A Place God Comes to Meet Us" (unpublished paper, 2009).

36. Rodriguez, *Our Lady of Guadalupe: Faith and Empowerment*, 23.

child was introduced into the tradition of the group, and thus one's face was gradually formed, and a person received individuality by the unique way in which he or she assimilated unto him- or herself the tradition of the group. Thus, the face could be defined as the embodiment of the self as it had been assumed and developed through education. Face and heart (*rosto y corazon*), then, for the Náhuatl, is approximated by our contemporary notion of personality. The face reflected the internal physiognomy of the person.[37] Thus, the purpose of education for the Náhuatl at this time was

> to find one's face, find one's heart and search for a "foundation," a truth, a support, a way of life and work through which one could express one's life. To this end, the Aztec developed schools they called the "Calmecac," in which the "tlamatinimine," the philosopher poets of Aztec society, taught by using poetic chants that they called "flower and song." Through a variety of formal and informal methods including the use of mythic complexes, the tlamatinimine encouraged their students to "find their face" (develop and express their innate character and potential); and to "find their heart" (to search out and express their inner passion); and to explore "foundations" of life and work (to find that vocation that allowed the student the fullest expression of self and truth).[38]

By looking upon the young face of Guadalupe, her skin bronzed by the sun, with mature eyes and a smile of compassion, the Náhuatl saw her as compassionate.[39] Her face also told the indigenous people that she was not a Spaniard; she was one of their own.

The Hands[40]

Another aspect of the image of Tonantzin Guadalupe that draws attention is her hands. Her hands are poised not in the traditional Western style of prayer but in an Indian manner of offering, indicating that something is to come from her.[41]

---

37. Virgilio P. Elizondo, "Our Lady of Guadalupe as a Cultural Symbol: The Power of the Powerless," in *Liturgy and Cultural Religious Traditions*, ed. Herman Schmidt and David Power, 25–33, *Concilium* 102 (New York: Seabury, 1977), 18.

38. Maria Williams, "Indigenous Mysticism," in *Religion as Art: Guadalupe, Orishas, and Sufi* (Albuquerque: University of New Mexico Press, 2009), 147.

39. Ibid., 83.

40. Rodriguez, *Our Lady of Guadalupe: Faith and Empowerment*, 27.

41. Elizondo, "Our Lady of Guadalupe as a Cultural Symbol," 1.

Further, scholars conclude that Tonantzin Guadalupe's arms were not simply in a position of offering but resting on her stomach in the same way a woman would place them if she were pregnant.[42]

The examination of her hands on the tilma, using infrared photography, indicates that the hands have been modified to shorten the fingers and convert the original hands from elongated fingers to shortened Indian fingers. The gold bracelet and fur cuffs around the wrists have been added to fit a Gothic pattern, and the original hands are of unknown pigment.[43] One could speculate, however, that such alterations were made in an attempt to clarify the Náhuatl symbology contained in the image for the Spanish. Adding the gold and fur trappings of royalty makes it clearer that Guadalupe is an important figure, almost divine. Shortening the fingers, while more difficult to explain, would make more obvious the Náhuatl understanding that Guadalupe was an Indian, one of them, and not a foreigner.

The Eyes[44]

As with most human images, the eyes of Our Lady of Guadalupe are both intriguing and revealing. The eyes of the image are looking down, indicating that she is not a proud creature, "neither did she show the impersonalism of the Mayan gods nor the masked presence of the Aztec gods."[45]

The Pregnancy[46]

Guadalupe's pregnancy is indicated by another important element of the image: the tassel or maternity band that she wears around her waist. *Estoy en cinta* means "I am pregnant." The skeptics say that the waist tassel was added to the painting some time after the original image was formed,[47] presenting a dilemma: was the original image of Our Lady of Guadalupe one of a pregnant woman or not? Yet further investigation of the symbolism of the image reveals that below the tassel there is a "four-petaled flower, the symbolic solar flower familiar to Náhuatl hieroglyphics whose petals are joined in the center to form

---

42. Interview with Margarita Z. Parente-Martinez, Mexico City (March 1986).

43. Philip S. Callahan, *The Tilma: Under Infra-Red Radiation*, CARA Studies on Popular Devotion, vol. 2; Guadalupan Studies, no. 3 (Washington, DC: Center for Applied Research in the Apostolate, 1981).

44. Rodriguez, *Our Lady of Guadalupe: Faith and Empowerment*, 25.

45. Elizondo, "Our Lady of Guadalupe as a Cultural Symbol," 85.

46. Rodriguez, *Our Lady of Guadalupe: Faith and Empowerment*, 29.

47. Callahan, *The Tilma*, 9.

the Quincunce—meeting place between heaven and earth, the human and divine. The Quincunce was a symbol of transcendence and fullness designating the place of encounter with ALL that exists."[48] The flower's position on Our Lady of Guadalupe's womb verified for the Náhuatl that she was pregnant.[49] Perhaps the *cinta* was added to make the Náhuatl symbol of the flower clearer to Spanish missionaries. Siller Acuña offers an interesting insight, stating that "the black belt Guadalupe wears during her pregnancy also has significance, in the color itself, the color black, or *intlilli*, is the symbol for death, or the sacrifice of the Sun God."[50] The significance is that it reminds the people of their ancient religious beliefs in a generous and compassionate God that sacrifices himself so that humanity might survive.

Other Aspects[51]

The virgin wears on her dress, a broach with a figure that is a cross within a circle, and this is a symbol of Ollin Tonatiuh, the sun in movement, which symbolizes the presence of God in our natural history. The time that we live in is called the fifth sun and since there is no evil in this epic, we are living in the best of all times.[52]

According to Clodomiro L. Siller Acuña, "the image of the Virgin completes our experience of God ever present to us on Earth." In the eyes of the indigenous people who experienced her, she appears as *la tierra*, the earth. Her title, Tonantzin, which means "our mother," and her appearance link her to the earth.[53] The combination of the stars, moon, and the rays of the sun together forge an image of God as Father and Mother, *como Cielo y Tierra*.

The most notable aspect of Tonantzin Guadalupe's image is the robe. Virgilio Elizondo contends that the color of the robe was the color of the spilled blood of sacrifices, the color of Huitzilopochtli, the sun god who gave and preserved life and was himself nourished with the precious liquid of lifeblood.[54]

And finally, at the feet of the virgin, holding her up is not an angel but a "*macehual*, a poor indigenous changed into an eagle knight trans-

---

48. Benedictine Sisters, *Inninantzin in Ipalnemohuani: Mother of the One Who Gives Us Life* (Mexico), 13.

49. Interview with Margarita Z. Parente-Martinez, Mexico City (March 1986).

50. Siller Acuña, "Guadalupe: Luz Y Cambio De Nuestra Realidad," 94.

51. Rodriguez, *Our Lady of Guadalupe: Faith and Empowerment*, 29–30.

52. Siller Acuña, "Guadalupe: Luz Y Cambio De Nuestra Realidad," 94.

53. Ibid., 92.

54. Elizondo, "Our Lady of Guadalupe as a Cultural Symbol," 3.

mitted by the people of faith. He represents a person with dignity chosen for service of the community; that is to say, the message of Guadalupe is based upon and sustained by persons who are willing and available to be of service to their people."[55] The Náhuatl culture did not include angels but the face or *el rostro* (*in ixtli*), a symbol representing one's personality or one's humanity. The precious feathers on the back of the *macehual* represent mediation or service. Thus, according to Náhuatl aesthetics, the feathers on the figure remind us of the service one ought to give by being a Guadalupana.[56]

From an artistic viewpoint, the robe of Our Lady of Guadalupe is especially notable because of its unusual luminosity: "It is highly reflective of visible radiation, yet transparent to the infrared rays. . . . It is the most transparent . . . as in the case of the blue mantle the shadowing of the pink robe is blended into the paint layer and no drawing or sketch is evident under the pink pigment.[57]

The artistic and technical explanations are a testimony to the extraordinary nature of the image. The description makes clear that the image is not simply a picture but a story made up of a number of symbols, which spoke to the Náhuatl people in the sixteenth century and still speak to twenty-first-century people.

Popular Religion

Contemporary believers continue to celebrate Tonantzin Guadalupe. In her fiestas the children carry roses to her image, indicating that a proper celebration of a divine event must contain beautiful elements of nature. In the celebration of Guadalupe, sacred space and time are particularly important. There is a specific day, December 12, designated to celebrate the feast and a specific time, dawn. The people rise at daybreak, the time of new beginnings and the rebirth of the sun, to sing *Las Mananitas* to her.[58]

Tonantzin Guadalupe clearly represents a familial and relational component in Mexican American life. She identifies herself as the mother of Mexican Americans and they are all brothers and sisters to each other. Tonantzin Guadalupe takes a central role regarding the vital necessities of life—food, shelter, safety, and concern for family. She

55. Benedictine Sisters, *Inninantzin in Ipalnemohuani: Mother of the One Who Gives Us Life* (Mexico), 14.

56. Elizondo, "Our Lady of Guadalupe as a Cultural Symbol," 95.

57. Callahan, *The Tilma*, 10.

58. Ibid., 147.

is petitioned for everything from health to the protection of a family owned business. Her image is found in homes and businesses in the form of pictures, statues, and altars and is worn on people's bodies in the form of necklaces and even tattoos.[59]

All of these examples are significant to the people and their religious life, but they are not institutionalized, that is, they are not formally structured with rigid rules and procedures. Rather, the touching, the processions, the intimate whispers, and the worn relics are manifestations of a deep intimacy, hearts touched and transformed.

As seen in the practices of popular devotion, presence and immediate contact are vital in the world of symbols. The image of Tonantzin Guadalupe in the churches must be accessible and within reach so that devotees may touch it or rub their hands across the frame or touch the candle before the picture. It is not enough to recognize a symbol; it must be held, experienced, and received. The symbols that emerge from the Guadalupe event are concrete: flowers, music, the sun. She not only comes in her full presence adorned with cultural symbols that the people recognize but also enters into their history. Through her affirmation and acceptance of her people, she gives them a reason to hope and to live.[60]

The symbol of Tonantzin Guadalupe manifests the creating energy and creative power of God. She is nothing less than God's self-giving, or grace. I understand grace in relational terms: not so much God as a person I love or God as a person who loves us, but God as love itself. God is love and the way of experiencing that love is within the dynamic of a relationship. Divine nature is relational and self-sacrificial: to share in the life of God, for God to give God's whole self to us, means that we live in some kind of relationship. How do we know we are living in that kind of relationship? We need to look at the relationships in our lives to answer this question: Are they life-giving? Are they hopeful, affirming?[61]

Conclusion

Tonantzin Guadalupe manifests, symbolizes, and activates the power of the people, in this case the power of the poor. In the *Nican Mopohua*, it is the poor Indian Juan Diego who evangelizes the bishop, whose conversion enables him to work with the poor, the marginalized, and the indigenous. Siller Acuña emphasizes the Náhuatl image of *yollo* (the

59. Ibid., 148.
60. Ibid., 149.
61. Ibid., 150.

heart), which moves us to action; if a devotion to Tonantzin Guadalupe does not bring us closer to action and to solidarity with the cause of the poor, then the devotion is not authentically Guadalupana. Her tender words to Juan Diego ask him to tell the bishop to construct a temple where she can manifest her love, compassion, help, and defense to *all* who call her, trust her, and love her. She will hear their lamentations and relieve their suffering. As the story is told and heard, people experience her promise of love and inclusion as directed to themselves. Her invitation and promise inspire and prepare those who respond to her to live their lives, relationships, and consciousness as action for justice on behalf of and with the poor. In accepting this invitation to be loved, believers accept their own neediness and poverty of love, strengthened by the love she offers, and, in response, become those who love unconditionally.

Tonantzin Guadalupe's request for a temple (or *casita* in some translations) is not to be understood as a building or even a church. Rather, she is speaking of the rebirth of a people and a new world order based on dignity, justice, and solidarity. Other images of Mary include the tabernacle of God and the tent of God's abiding. The Apostle Paul also preached that each person is a temple of God inhabited by the Spirit through Christ. These powerful images provide a means to accept ourselves and each other as vessels for the imprint of God.

Devotees must be made aware of the entire story of Tonantzin Guadalupe with all of its implications to gain a greater sense of pride in their cultural and personal identity. Audre Lorde writes, "As we come more into touch with our own ancient, non-european consciousness of living as a situation to be experienced and interacted with, we learn more and more to cherish our feelings, and to respect those hidden sources of our power from where true knowledge and, therefore, lasting action comes."[62]

Just as Tonantzin Guadalupe affirmed Juan Diego in his moments of self-doubt and sense of unworthiness, devotees will find inner strength and conviction to make decisions outside of limiting spheres. Devotees have a unique opportunity to proclaim to the world the Guadalupan message of hope, love, and justice, a message of care and "connectedness" to the wider community that is fed through the theological aesthetics of narrative, image, and popular religion, including song, dance, altars, and fiesta.

---

62. Audre Lorde, "Poetry Is Not a Luxury," *Sister Outsider* (Berkeley, CA: Crossing Press, 1984), 37.

Käthe Kollwitz, *The* Pietà/*Mother and Son*, 1938. © 2011 Artists Rights Society (ARS).
New York/VG Bild-Kunst; Bonn.

Jayme M. Hennessy

Kollwitz
The Beauty and Brutality
of the *Pietà*

In 1938, Kaethe Kollwitz (1867–1945) cast a small bronze *Pietà* whose scene destabilized the sacrificial theme and significance of the *Pietà* within the militaristic culture of her day. Her small sculpture departed from the form and content of the traditional Christian *Pietà* in which Mary offers the body of her son Jesus to the viewer. In Kollwitz's *Pietà*, an "old, lonely, darkly brooding woman"[1] gazes into the face of her life-less son, tenderly touching his hand as his body collapses back into her own, back into her womb as if she could somehow hold him back from the destructive forces of the world. The bronze casting of the *Pietà*, the weight, and the earthen color of the metal combine to fill the sculpture with a strong sense of gravity and materiality as the bodies of both mother and son sink down into the dust of the earth. Here, in Kollwitz's *Pietà*, we face the horror of death rendered in cold, heavy bronze: the beauty and love of mother and child recast by human brutality into a crumpled figure of grief.

Known for "taking up symbolic imagery within a realist project,"[2] the artist brought her experience of the death of her youngest son, Peter, to her recasting of the *Pietà* motif. Peter volunteered to serve in the

1. Entry of December 1939, in Kaethe Kollwitz, *The Diaries and Letters of Kaethe Kollwitz*, ed. Hans Kollwitz, trans. Richard and Clara Winston (Evanston, IL: Northwestern University Press, 1988), 126.
2. Elizabeth Prelinger, *Käthe Kollwitz* (New Haven, CT: Yale University Press, 1992), 26.

German army in August 1914 and died later in October of that same year. Grieving Peter's death over the course of twenty-four years and witnessing a world wrapped in the destruction and death of two world wars, Kollwitz shaped a *Pietà*, nuanced by a sense of desolation in which the figure of the mother *does not* offer up the body of her son to the viewer. Reflecting, later in life, on her support of Peter's decision to volunteer for the war and his death on the battlefield, Kollwitz wrote, "We were betrayed then, at the beginning. And perhaps Peter would still be living had it not been for this terrible betrayal. Peter and millions, many millions of other boys. All betrayed . . . all is turbulence."[3]

A twentieth-century German artist-advocate, Kollwitz used her art to communicate ideas rather than beautiful ideals. Her drawings, prints, and sculptures prompted her audience to see the harsh realities of human experience, to feel some sense of sympathy and solidarity for this suffering humanity, and then to work to transform the social conditions that fostered this oppression and suffering. The power of her work and the excellence of her technique earned her an appointment, in 1919, as the first woman to teach at the Prussian Academy of Art.

Although she did not identify herself as a religious artist, Kollwitz occasionally employed motifs from the Christian tradition to structure her critique of social problems or to dignify the experience and suffering of her subjects. In her early work, the artist employed the visual motifs of the *Lamentation over Christ*, the *Visitation*, and the *Pietà*—not to spiritualize or to sentimentalize her art, but to transfer the affective content and prompting of these traditional images onto her subject: ordinary women, children, and men who struggled to survive the debilitating effects of harsh labor and poverty as well as the desolation of war.

Peter's battlefield death on October 22, 1914, plunged Kollwitz into a lifelong artistic process of mourning that would move her beyond the work of commemorating his death to create images that urged mothers to resist war and to protect the lives of their children. Commenting on the artist's eventual embrace of pacifism and its impact on her later work, Elizabeth Prelinger notes, "Spurred on by the death of her son, the artist began to comprehend the role of engaged art and its power. She began to accept the notion that, through her art, she could communicate social messages to the population and in so doing have an effect on her times."[4] While it is evident that Peter's death did confirm Kollwitz in her artistic

3. Entry of March 19, 1918, in Kollwitz, *The Diaries and Letters of Kaethe Kollwitz*, 87.
4. Prelinger, *Käthe Kollwitz*, 78.

mission of shaping social change, her experience of his death impelled her into a critical engagement with the symbolic images used to support the sacrificial *ethos* of the Prussian militaristic culture of her day, which socialized men and women to understand that the duties of motherhood included the will to sacrifice their sons for the good of the Fatherland.

Kollwitz's interpretative process is largely rooted in the critical and creative functioning of the analogical imagination—quite fitting, given the origins of the *Pietà* image and its imaginative movement into the passion of Christ. Following Kollwitz into the grief she initially believes is her share of the *Pietà*, I turn to the artist's diary entries to examine how she came to reconfigure or subvert the sacrificial significance of the symbolic image of the *Pietà*. Analogically engaging the image, she tested its exalted conception of sacrifice against her experience of grief and her intuition that maternal virtue does not demand sacrifice of one's children. Dwelling in this gap between the beauty of sacrifice exemplified in the *Pietà* and the embodied reality of violence and the desolation of war, Kollwitz came to affirm her maternal intuition, experience, and authority and to reject the sacrificial duty imposed on German motherhood. No small accomplishment for a woman artist in that day, for as she critiqued the symbolization of sacrifice in the *Pietà* image, Kollwitz began to subvert the masculine imaginary expressed through and reified in the symbolic images of her culture and world, an imaginary that continues to exert its power in our own time.

The *Pietà*: Sculpture of Compassion

The *Pietà* draws us into a moment when Mary receives the broken body of Jesus down from the cross and into her arms: a mother's final embrace of her child's body. The sculpture directs the viewer's attention across the dead body of Jesus to the grief of his mother, thus prompting the viewer to compassion, as beauty and brutality converge in the scene. We see the beauty of grace embodied in the deep and tender bond of human/divine love, and we see the disfiguring violence of sin that pulses through the world. Popularly known as *Pietà*, a title derived from the Italian word for "pity,"[5] the images originated in the early fourteenth century as *vesperbild*: devotional images used in Evening Prayer.[6] The scene of the sorrowing mother embracing her lifeless son is not found

5. William Forsyth, "Medieval Statues of the *Pietà* in the Museum," in *The Metropolitan Museum of Art Bulletin* 11, no. 7 (March 1953): 177–84, http://www.jstor.org/stable/3257594 (accessed October 11, 2009).
6. Ibid.

in the Scriptures but arises from an imaginative engagement with the passion of Christ. Drawing, analogically, on the experience of human relationships, love, grief, suffering, and vulnerability, the image aims to move the viewer into the mystery of the incarnation, to reflect on the vulnerable humanity of God become flesh, and to ponder the significance of this profound revelation of God's love for Christian life in history.

Now considered "traditional," the *Pietà* reflects a class of devotional images that were somewhat provocative in their day. According to Ewert Cousins, the twelfth and thirteenth centuries witnessed a new set of devotional images that emphasized the suffering humanity of both Mary and Christ and "functioned as a catalyst of a new devotion, bringing about a transformation of sensibility, which evoked a spectrum of human emotions, such as tender affection and compassion."[7] We see this appeal to the emotions in the scene of the *Pietà* as it engages the viewer with the suffering humanity of Mary and Christ. Here, in the *Pietà*, Mary is not an impassive royal figure but a very human mother who does what any mother would do when confronted with the brutalized and lifeless body of her son: she takes him into her arms and weeps. Here, in the *Pietà*, Christ no longer reigns triumphantly from the cross but is presented in the vulnerability of humanity to suffering and death. Through his wounds, through this visceral encounter with the humanity of Christ, the viewer is prompted to touch and to take his body through a visual or affective experience of communion, thus experiencing some sense of union with the divine.

The *Pietà* sculpture's prompting of compassion, its fourteenth-century dating, and the evident popularity of the image within the regions of the Rhineland and Lowlands have led Joanna Zeigler to propose that the early *Pietà* images were "Sculptures of Compassion" that may have originated with the early Lowland Beguine communities: a new form of Christian life, one in which women could live, pray, and work together without taking formal vows.[8] According to Zeigler, the *Pietà* may have served as a structuring principle for Beguines. Their manual labor, the touch involved in healing the sick or consoling those who were grieving, the practice of visual communion with the Body of Christ—all were drawn together in the tactile sense of the *Pietà*.[9] Summoning the

---

7. Ewert Cousins, "The Humanity and the Passion of Christ," in *Christian Spirituality of the High Middle Ages and Reformation*, ed. Jill Raitt, Bernard McGinn, and John Meyendorf (New York: Crossroad, 1988), 375.

8. Joanna E. Ziegler, *Sculpture of Compassion: The Pietà and the Beguines in Southern Low Countries, c. 1300–c. 1600* (Rome: Academia Belgica, 1992), 103.

9. Ibid., 103–4.

viewer into this scene of suffering humanity, the *Pietà* aims to draw the viewer into an affective union with the sorrow of Mary and the redeeming love of Christ and, from this affective union, to embrace and cultivate the compassion necessary to tend to the suffering humanity of their world.

The Will to Sacrifice and the *Pietà*

While the form of the *Pietà* has remained somewhat constant over the centuries, the same does not hold true for the meaning and significance of the image for Christian life. As with all Marian images, the *Pietà* has been interpreted and used in ways that have, at times, affirmed the subjectivity and spirituality of women and, at other times, in ways that have subordinated women to repressive social mores and religious idealizations. Viewed within the context of the Prussian militaristic culture that dominated German life from the eighteenth century through the end of the Second World War, the sacrificial aspects of the *Pietà* motif were brought to the fore to support the sacrificial ideology of the culture. Analyzing the ways in which the religious imagination is susceptible to manipulation, Albrecht Koschorke specifically addresses the transfer of the religious aspects of sacrifice embodied in the *Pietà* onto power of the state:

> Modern statecraft inherited and profaned the motif of the *Pietà* in two ways: first, with respect to what it chooses to depict and, second, with respect to what forms the unspoken margins of the depiction. For no matter how profound the silence that surrounds the grieving mother and the body that has sunk into her arms, no matter how intimately the curvature and folds of drapery of the two figures blend, an invisible observer is always attendant upon this scene of togetherness. It is the one at whose command the sacrifice was made, in whose will the mourning mother acquiesces; the one who imparts an element of devotion to even her most bitter pain. The image of the male corpse, which dominates the iconography of the West, and the corollary image of the grieving Madonna or its successor, the soldiers' mother, are defined by a third, external divine or godlike figure.[10]

Note the role of the "invisible observer" who has commanded the sacrifice and demands obedience: the German mothers—who saw the

10. Albrecht Koschorke, *The Holy Family and Its Legacy: Religious Imagination from the Gospels to* Star Wars (New York: Columbia University Press, 2003), 34.

Pietà housed in churches and chapels and serving as memorials to the soldiers who died in battle—understood that it was their duty to will the sacrifice of their sons to the wars of the Fatherland. The belief that maternal virtue should include the willingness to sacrifice one's child for the sake of the nation was not unique to Kollwitz's Germany. The poetry, art, and rhetoric of other Western nations at war evidenced a similar expectation;[11] however, Prussian militarism turned an expectation into an ideology.

Why this penchant for sacrifice, war, and glory in death? Why a concept of motherhood fused to an ideology of sacrifice? Grace M. Jantzen has proposed that this fascination with violence and death is foundational to Western culture. Look to the war memorials scattered across centuries and countries; gaze on the beauty and strength of sculpted bodies of young warriors—bodies that don't bear a mark of violence yet stand to honor those who have fallen in battle. This displacement of beauty onto death, Jantzen claims—quite provocatively—is best understood as a form of necrophilia. Analyzing this drive to violence, Jantzen expands the meaning of necrophilia to include a "cultural fascination and obsession with death and violence. A pre-occupation with death which is both dreaded and desired."[12]

Jantzen attributes this fascination with death and violence to the masculinist imaginary that has shaped and continues to exert its influence on the symbolic cultural reality of Western civilization. In its "silencing of the maternal body and natality," the masculinist imaginary has, according to Jantzen, "displaced beauty on to death,"[13] glorifying war and memorializing the beauty of the youths who marched off to battle. The militaristic culture of Kollwitz's Germany effectively socialized mothers to will the sacrifice of a son for the good or glory of the nation—and women did their duty. Angela Moorjani notes that "far from being limited to male acclaim, the will to sacrifice was approved and promoted by women across the political spectrum. . . . [M]others in particular understand and accept the necessity for one generation to shed its blood for the good of those to come."[14]

We may doubt the power of an image to so capture the imagination, but Georg Gadamer has observed how an image functions like a game,

---

11. Amy Bell, "Women's Politics, Poetry and the Feminist Historiography of the Great War," *Canadian Journal of History* 42, no. 3 (2007): 411–37.

12. Grace Jantzen, *Foundations of Violence* (New York: Routledge, 2004), 6.

13. Ibid., 39.

14. Angela Moorjani, "Kaethe Kollwitz on Sacrifice, Mourning, and Reparation: An Essay in Psychoaesthetics," *MLN* 101, no. 5 (December 1986): 1111.

in that it draws, holds, challenges, and changes the viewer.[15] Therefore, if a woman analogically participated in the motif, allowed its patterns and ideals to mold her imagination and shape her desires, she could be drawn into identifying with Mary. Like Mary, she would obey the Father/land; like Mary, she would do her duty and offer up her son to the Father/land; like Mary, she would grieve over her son's death; like Mary, she would experience God's approval and find herself exalted over all women. Or would she?

Whose Imagination? Critically Engaging the *Pietà*

It is evident that Kollwitz had a lifelong fascination with the motif of the *Pietà*. She saw the pattern of the *Pietà* in the sorrow of her mother, Katherine Schmidt, whose loss of three children left her with "the remote air of Madonna."[16] In 1903, we see Kollwitz, herself a young mother, turn to the motif in a series of drawings treating the theme of *Pietà/Mother with Dead Child*. Here, she tested the emotional range and pathos of the motif in a set of self-portraits depicting both Kollwitz and her son Peter locked in the embrace of the *Pietà*, an experience Kollwitz later interpreted as a premonition of Peter's impending death.[17] In the 1920s, we find the silhouette of the *Pietà* haunting Kollwitz's series on war as she juxtaposed scenes of suffering against a background that alluded to the form of the *Pietà*. Through these images, Kollwitz critically engaged the sacrificial dimensions of the *Pietà* and its beautiful representation/misrepresentation of suffering and death.

William Lynch has noted that "the task of the imagination is to imagine the real,"[18] and "imagining the real" is the challenge Kollwitz assumed during her years of mourning Peter's death. Situated in a militaristic culture that had repressed the maternal imagination, valorized death, and shaped the symbolizations of human experience,

---

15. Hans-Georg Gadamer, *Truth and Method* (New York: Continuum, 1993), 102. The work of art "has its true being in the fact that it becomes an experience that changes the person who experiences it."

16. Kollwitz, *The Diaries and Letters of Kaethe Kollwitz*, 18.

17. Entry of January 28, 1915, in Kollwitz, *The Diaries and Letters of Kaethe Kollwitz*, 145.

"In all this Peter and you are present. Loving and having to give up what one loves most dearly, and having it still—always the same. How is it for years, many years, the same theme was always repeated in my work? The premonition of sacrifice. But one is enough—Hans—one is enough."

18. William F. Lynch, *Christ and Prometheus: A New Image of the Secular* (Notre Dame, IN: University of Notre Dame Press, 1970), 23.

Kollwitz began from what Jantzen identifies as an "inevitably mascu-linized subject-position."[19] The images she engaged as she moved into mourning Peter's death are images that reflect and reinforce an exalted conception of the sacrifices of war and death on the battlefield. Lynch reminds us, however, that the analogical imagination is a *critical* faculty that tests images against *reality*; therefore, the striving for "likeness" with a particular image is *not* a matter of merely conforming to that image. On the contrary, the imagination—and its images—should challenge the truthfulness of the imagination and the images it produces.[20]

Identifying with the *Pietà*, testing its scene against the reality of her life and world, creating a new image transfigured by her own grief, Kollwitz critiques more than a beautiful religious image and its abil-ity to engage the truth of reality. She critiques the ideology of sacrifice embedded in her culture. Angela Moorjani and Regina Schutte have examined the psychological, symbolic, and aesthetic dimensions of Kollwitz's experience of mourning Peter's death.[21] Here, we focus on a question that Jantzen raised as she reflected on the difficulties faced by women in navigating the images of the masculine imaginary and creating symbols to offer new possibilities for understanding human life and obligation: "If the woman-subject does not yet exist, then how can she intervene in the symbolic? But unless there are shifts in the symbolic—and who but women will effect such shifts—how will the woman-subject ever become possible?"[22]

Turning to the artist's own words, we see a woman whose imagina-tion begins to emerge from its repressed state. Through her imagination, she engages the *Pietà* and "intervenes" in the symbolizations that mask violence and death with beauty. Testing the *Pietà* against her experience, Kollwitz broke, to some degree, with the masculine imaginary of her world. It was a move that effected a shift in the symbolic as Kollwitz took on the project of "imagining the real " and created images that presented possibilities for resisting the "love of death" that suffused her culture.

19. Grace M. Jantzen, *Becoming Divine: Towards a Feminist Philosophy of Religion* (Bloomington: Indiana University Press, 1999), 60.

20. William F. Lynch, *Images of Hope: Imagination as Healer of the Hopeless* (Notre Dame, IN: University of Notre Dame Press, 1965), 193.

21. Moorjani, "Kaethe Kollwitz on Sacrifice, Mourning, and Reparation," 1110–34. Regina Schulte and Pamela Selwyn, "Käthe Kollwitz's Sacrifice," *History Workshop Journal* 41 (Spring 1996): 193–22.

22. Jantzen, *Becoming Divine*, 60.

Turning to the artist's diary entries, we follow her mourning and transformation:

> *27 August 1914*: A piece by Gabriele Reuter in the Tag on the tasks of women today. She spoke of the joy of sacrificing—a phrase that struck me hard. Where do all the women who have watched so carefully over the lives of their beloved ones get the heroism to send them to face the cannon? I am afraid that this soaring of the spirit will be followed by the blackest despair and dejection. The task is to bear it not only during these few weeks, but for a long time—in dreary November as well, and also when spring comes again, in March, the month of young men who wanted to live and are dead. That will be much harder.[23]

Faced with the prospect of war and her duty to sacrifice her son for the good of the Fatherland, Kollwitz is ambivalent when she considers the prospect of mothers surrendering their children to the battlefield. Note, here, that it is considered an act of courage to will this sacrifice. What emerges in this reflection as a question will eventually evolve into an affirmation of her intuition and experience and an image of mother-hood that resists identification with sacrifice:

> *22 August 1916*: Made a drawing: the mother letting her dead son slide into her arms. I might make a hundred such drawings and yet I do not get any closer to him. I am seeking him. As if I had to find him in my work. And yet everything I do is so childishly feeble and inadequate. I feel obscurely that I could throw off this inadequacy, that Peter is somewhere in the work and I might find him. And at the same time I have the feeling that I can no longer do it. I am too shattered, weakened and drained by tears.[24]

The *Pietà* motif is imprinted on Kollwitz's art and mourning. Twenty months have passed since Peter was killed in battle, and Kollwitz has fully immersed herself in the motif of the *Pietà*: Peter has become the Christ figure, she the sorrowing Mother who seeks to embrace him. The exalted imagery of the sacrifice of the *Pietà* has not transfigured her motherhood; she is "shattered, weakened and drained by tears." He is lost to her, his body was lost to her, the body she birthed, nurtured, and loved—destroyed by war. Peter was never to be, again, seen or held.

---

23. Entry of August 27, 1914, in Kollwitz, *The Diaries and Letters of Kaethe Kollwitz*, 62.

24. Entry of August 22, 1916, in Kollwitz, *The Diaries and Letters of Kaethe Kollwitz*, 72.

> *30 October 1918*: response to Richard Dehmel. "There has been enough
> of dying! Let not another man fall! Against Richard Dehmel I ask that
> the words of an even greater poet be remembered: 'Seed for the plant-
> ing must not be ground.' "[25]

Germany had effectively lost the war, but Dehmel had called for
the remaining men and youth to sacrifice their lives for their country.
The ambivalence Kollwitz evidenced before the war started yielded to
confidence in her experience. She found a clearer voice and a sense of
her authority, as she said "No!" to the call for sacrifice. Here, we see
her imagination assert her vision of life, challenging and rejecting the
love of violence and death instantiated in the symbols of her militaristic
culture. We also find Kollwitz's appeal to the poet Goethe in a quote
often recognized as the impetus for her artistic mission that emerged
from Peter's death: "Seed for the planting must not be ground."

> *26 February 1920*: Sometimes it seems to me that the curtain is about to
> lift which separates me from my work, from the way my work must
> now be. I have a sense of something imminent coming closer. But then
> I lose it again, become ordinary and inadequate. I feel like someone
> who is trying to guess an object being described by music. The sound
> grows steadily louder; he thinks he is on the point of grasping it, and
> then the sound becomes weaker again and he has to look for another
> answer.[26]

Kollwitz offers a rather poignant, poetic, and somewhat mystical
reflection on an experience that she can't quite name. Her reflection begins with a vision of seeing the suffering of the world, through the eyes
of Jesus, and then through those of an older woman. At this point, she
has begun to create images that reveal the ugly reality and desolation
of war—images intended to subvert sacrifice and its sense of glory as
the viewer is plunged into the suffering of those on the home front and
their share of the war and its destruction.

> *21 April 1922 Good Friday*: My God, why hast thou forsaken me? . . .
> In my secret heart I had probably expected that I would not be for-
> saken. And perhaps Jesus was not prepared for his Father's refusing
> to send the legion of angels; and I too secretly expected there would

25. Entry of October 30, 1918, in Kollwitz, *The Diaries and Letters of Kaethe Kollwitz*,
88–89.
26. Entry of February 26, 1920, in Kollwitz, *The Diaries and Letters of Kaethe
Kollwitz*, 97.

be provided the ram for the sacrifice. Why was Abraham just taken at his word; why was it enough for him just to show he was willing?[27]

"Why hast thou forsaken me?" The agony of lament suffuses her diary entry as Kollwitz struggles through her sense of abandonment. Appealing to the narratives of the sacrifice of Jesus on the cross and the willingness of Abraham to offer up his son Isaac to God, Kollwitz struggles with the decision she made to will the sacrifice of Peter to the war. She had affirmed Peter's decision to volunteer for military service. She understood that the sacrifice of his life on the frontlines was related to her sacrifice on the home front. She had done what was expected of all German mothers: she had bent her will to the needs of the Fatherland, yet she was not consoled.

Kollwitz had embraced the sacrificial symbolism of the *Pietà* and found that it did not engage her in the reality of her son's death or the reality of her maternal grief. The beauty of the *Pietà* and its appeal to transcendence masked rather than engaged the ugly reality of war. Subverting the sacrificial theme of the *Pietà*, Kollwitz created lithographs, sketches, and bronzes that reoriented maternal virtue to the courage to resist war and destruction: *Mothers* (1921), *Tower of Mothers* (1938), *Mother and Two Children* (1938), and the final image of her career, *The Seed for Planting Must Not Be Ground* (1942). In these images, we see children wrapped in the protective embraces of mothers. *Mothers* and *Tower of Mothers* offer a vision of women united in the protection of children, their strong bodies and arms wrapping around the children, embracing them in fortresses of maternal love and the courage to resist. In *Mother and Two Children* and *The Seed for Planting Must Not Be Ground* we see the artist again subvert the form of the *Pietà*: a lone mother enfolds children in the sanctuary of her body.

The small bronze *Pietà* cast by Kollwitz in 1938 allows her to do, analogically, what she had not been able to do after October 1914: take Peter's body into her arms and weep. Her small *Pietà* sculpture may have been a personal expression of her continued mourning for Peter: regret for having supported his decision to sacrifice his life for the Fatherland and the sense of desolation, abandonment, betrayal that marked her life as she mourned his death.

The sculpture was created in the final years of her life, when her commitment to pacifism brought her the condemnation of the Nazi

27. Entry of April 21, 1922, in Kollwitz, *The Diaries and Letters of Kaethe Kollwitz*, 103.

Political Party. Her images depicting maternal courage and virtue as the will to resist war confronted "the will to sacrifice" and its intensification under Nazi rule. Kollwitz was eventually labeled a "degenerate artist" and forced to resign her appointment from the Prussian Academy of Arts in 1933. While she resigned her post, she did not resign her artistic mission: the images she created and let loose into the world continued to take her stand against the war and symbolize the obligation to protect and nurture human life.

But Mine Is Not Religious

In a diary entry of December 1939, Kollwitz compared her *Pietà* to one created by Freida Winckelmann, an artist-friend, and remarked, "But mine is not religious. . . . My mother is musing upon her son's failure to be accepted by men. She is a lonely, darkly brooding woman. The Winckelmann mother, however, is still the Queen of Heaven."[28] The declaration, "mine is not religious," gives rise to questions about Kollwitz's intentions for this image while also challenging some of the conventions and aesthetics of the religious *Pietà*. We can speculate that Kollwitz intended her *Pietà* as a secular image embodying the universal theme of maternal loss, or that her image is "not religious" because it is an expression of her personal sorrow. Her diary, however, offers another possibility: Kollwitz had undergone a personal and artistic "evolution" and could no longer tolerate the use of beauty to mask brutality. In an entry dated June 28, 1921, she recounts attending a drama of a peasant revolt, *The Weavers*, a play she once admired, but now she firmly critiques its appeal to violence and its attempt to "transform ugly reality into something grand."[29] Kollwitz, the artist, was a realist, and the reality of desolation and gross violence is undoubtedly in tension with the beauty and spiritualization of suffering in Winckelmann's decidedly religious *Pietà*, in which the appeal to beauty transforms the ugly reality of the death on the cross.

Representing the suffering and death of Jesus has always posed a challenge to Christian art: how does an artist present the ugly reality of the suffering and death in a way that evidences both the human and divine natures of the incarnate God? Treating aesthetic theology and the "beauty" of the cross (and, by extension, the *Pietà*), Richard

28. Entry of December 1939, in Kollwitz, *The Diaries and Letters of Kaethe Kollwitz*, 126.

29. Entry of June 28, 1921, in Kollwitz, *The Diaries and Letters of Kaethe Kollwitz*, 99.

Viladesau proposes that there is a specifically Christian sense of beauty: a "converted" sense of beauty that is not limited to worldly conception of beauty. Referring to Augustine on the beauty of the cross, Viladesau notes that one is capable of apprehending the "inner beauty, what we might call the 'moral beauty' of Christ, the beauty of God's incarnation for human salvation, a beauty that shines out even—and indeed, especially—in the cross."[30] Such a concept of beauty requires a new way of seeing reality and, accordingly, "challenges us to rethink and to expand our notion of the beauty of God, and indeed of 'beauty' itself."[31] It is this attunement to spiritual beauty that trains the vision of the Christian, who, in gazing upon the crucified body of Christ, apprehends the beauty of divine love mediated through his death on the cross; thus, the emphasis on beauty in some representations of the cross or *Pietà*.

Images of this beauty and suffering are, however, more ambiguous than textual representations allow. Margaret Miles addresses the hermeneutical concerns that surround the creation, reception, and interpretation of visual images and emphasizes their role in the cultivation of embodiment and comprehending physical existence.[32] Christian art, then, not only represents spiritual wisdom and divine beauty but also functions, according to Miles, as "visual symbols that interpret, actualize and enhance the life of the body."[33] With this in mind, we need to question whether these beautiful images of the cross and *Pietà* adequately engage the suffering humanity of the incarnate God, who shares in our bodily existence, or are they evidence of the drive to displace beauty onto death that Jantzen locates in the foundations of Western civilization?

Kollwitz's interpretation of the *Pietà* challenges Christian religious art to take embodiment seriously and to resist, as Jantzen notes, the tendencies of Western culture to displace beauty onto death. The externalization of her experience of loss and grief in her *Pietà* sculpture reminds us of the need for religious images to engage, more adequately, the embodied reality and emotional dynamics of human life, in order to draw us more fully into both the mystery of the incarnation and the gift and responsibility of our humanity. The critical impetus behind the

---

30. Richard Viladesau, *The Beauty of the Cross: The Passion of Christ in Theology and the Arts; From the Catacombs to the Eve of the Renaissance* (New York: Oxford University Press, 2006), 12.

31. Ibid., 9.

32. Margaret Miles, *Images as Insight: Visual Understanding in Western Christianity and Secular Culture* (Boston: Beacon Press, 1985), 35.

33. Ibid.

artist's image of the *Pietà* cautions us of the use of traditional Christian images—intentionally or unintentionally—to encourage the submission to suffering that should, instead, prompt resistance.

Kollwitz's reinterpretation of the *Pietà* is a first step in an ongoing process in which women bring their experiences to the *Pietà*, to test the image and to create its meaning for Christians in today's world. Toward that end, Jantzen reminds us, "we can succeed only insofar as we take up, correct, and build upon one another's new words and new constructions, doing together what it is impossible to do alone."[34] Let Jantzen's words, then, serve as both an inspiration and a caution: bringing women's experience to the process of interpreting images and creating new symbolizations is "impossible to do alone." For it is a matter of creating and preserving these new symbolizations in a world that is still the domain of the masculinist imaginary. In 1994 an enlarged version of Kollwitz's bronze *Pietà* was installed in the Neue Wache in Berlin, a guardhouse that has served as a memorial honoring those who have died in Germany's wars. The memorial is controversial, in commemorating both the soldiers who served the Third Reich and the civilian victims who perished in death camps. Kollwitz's *Pietà* stands, then, as a reminder of the opportunities and difficulties women face as they strive to symbolize their experience and preserve that symbolization as it disrupts and expands the symbolization of the religious imagination in our present world.

34. Jantzen, *Becoming Divine*, 61.

"Laundry" © Kristi Link Fernholz Photography. klfstudio.com

Colleen Mary Carpenter

Contemplating the
Landscapes of Motherhood
The Discovery of Beauty in
a Place We Thought We Knew

The western Minnesota prairie tends to strike outsiders as frighteningly vast, empty, and dull—a sea of monochromatic grasses. Minnesota artist Kristi Link Fernholz knows better, and her photographs capture the surprising beauty of the prairie. "Prairie Smoke" offers the viewer a close-up of a single, fragile prairie flower bending in a brisk summer wind; "Big Bluestem Field" steps back to show an endless field of deep brown grasses, divided from the empty sky by a strip of deep green at the horizon.[1] The colors are startling and anything but dull, the vastness of the prairie inspires awe rather than fear, and the delicate beauty of the flower gives lie to any notion we might have had of the prairie's emptiness. There is beauty here, wild and breathtaking beauty: we just need to learn to see it. Fernholz's work is not limited to wild landscapes, however. She also photographs the domestic landscapes of life on her family's farm, and here too viewers discover that what we thought we knew about the lay of the land is limited at best.

This essay considers three of her works, "Laundry," "Sister," and "Tutu Bike." Taken together, they provide the rough outlines of a landscape not of the prairie but of motherhood itself: the daily work, the

1. Both of these photographs can be seen at www.klfstudio.com, the first under the heading "Prairie Room" and the second under "Beyond Focus."

love and loss, and the encounter between our children and the wider world. Fernholz's perspective on each of these, like her perspective on prairie flowers and fields, startles the viewer into seeing what was once ordinary, dull, or even frightening as something else entirely—something beautiful.

I have used these photographs in introductory level undergraduate theology classes to spark discussion of mothers and motherhood. Whether the conversation is heading toward an analysis of different kinds of human experience as a source of theological reflection or toward an exploration of the idea of the motherhood of God, my students find much to comment on, wonder about, and simply notice in Fernholz's work. Different students are drawn to different aspects of a given photograph, and even a discussion of why some students are indifferent to or disturbed by an image adds depth to the larger picture of motherhood we are sketching together as a class.

The fact that these photographs were taken by a mother is important. The beauty of motherhood has been celebrated ad nauseam in Western culture, but usually that celebration takes mothers as objects, not as subjects. Here we have the opposite: it is a mother who is the *creator* of beauty through her photographic choices and skill, not merely the "symbolic icon" of someone else's idea of the beautiful.[2] I raise this point with my students through a question: Does it matter that these photographs were taken by a mother? The subsequent discussion of perspective, and how where we stand affects what we see, recurs throughout the course as we consider who is making an argument, what that person's assumptions are, and what blind spots or privileged information that person brings to the discussion. For the purposes of this essay, Fernholz's status as both mother and artist invites us as viewers to shift our perspective in considering the idea of motherhood, since it is both subject and object of these photographs. Instead of approaching the landscapes of motherhood "objectively," with a map and a tourist's mind-set, expecting to see the highlights and skip "the boring stuff," we can instead explore motherhood "subjectively." We are no longer tourists but have gained privileged access to an "inside view." We are invited to see the landscapes of motherhood as Fernholz does. We can learn from her point of view—and then take the time to think about why she chose to show us these things and not others, why she focused on things we might otherwise have ignored. We can, in short, expand our

---

2. Susan A. Ross, *For the Beauty of the Earth* (New York: Paulist Press, 2006), 4.

understanding and imagination through engagement with Fernholz's imagination.

Motherhood and the Metaphor of Landscape

Constructing an accurate, useful picture of what motherhood is like is extraordinarily difficult.[3] Too often, motherhood is presented in such a sentimentalized, unreflective way that it serves more to punish the women who are unable to meet the standards of perfection so glowingly described than to celebrate the actual struggles, joys, choices, and experiences of women who are in the midst of the daily work of caring for children. Moreover, motherhood is both overly valued and strikingly devalued at the same time: it is often understood both as the epitome of self-sacrifice and pure love and as mindless drudgery. Any attempt to pull the pendulum back from either extreme appears only to endorse the other, making a true picture of motherhood almost impossible to construct. In addition, as Irish theologian Anne Thurston points out, feminist theologians who seek to explore the experiences of motherhood as a resource for theology cannot ignore "the fact that motherhood was and to a very large extent still is for many women a role which confines and limits them, resulting in economic dependency and low social status."[4] Yet Thurston goes on to insist that theology must find a way through this dilemma, because no attempt to understand human experience can be complete without taking seriously the experience of women "as givers and sustainers of life."[5]

Fernholz and her photographs offer us a possible resolution to the dilemma Thurston presents. Instead of attempting to describe the experience of motherhood, we can use Fernholz's photographs to explore what it looks like to see the world from the point of view of a mother; instead of trying to see mothers, we will attempt to see what mothers see. This kind of shift has been used before in theological argument: in order to write about the complex reality of being a white South African during the apartheid years, theologian Denise Ackermann decided that the complexity of her situation demanded an entirely new approach. Rather than trying to describe what we might see if we looked at her and her life, she wrote about what she saw as she looked at South

---

3. This is especially true in a college classroom, where few students have personal experience of being mothers and most are in the midst of the young adult work of separating from their own mothers.

4. Anne Thurston, *Because of Her Testimony* (New York: Crossroad, 1995), 33.

5. Ibid.

Africa. In her book *After the Locusts: Letters from a Landscape of Faith*, Ackermann uses the metaphor of "sketching a landscape" to describe this method and choice of perspective.[6] Ackermann tells the reader that it is her intent to sketch "a giant picture with different landscapes and figures, swarms of locusts and fields of flowers, different colours and symbols; it requires imagination, even guesswork, and it is always provisional."[7] The imaginative, provisional aspect of her landscape is especially intriguing in a discussion of motherhood, as being a mother requires both imagination (to meet a child's ever-changing needs in an ever-changing world) and a recognition that today's answers are likely to be modified by whatever happens tomorrow.

As the reader moves through the book, Ackermann fills in her landscape, adding signs and markers to identify beauty, blight, and borders.[8] She "colors in sky, sun, bush, food, and people with different identities."[9] She uses "bright red" to mark "snares and traps," locates "obstacles and places of rest," signifies places of lament with "red flashes and plumes of smoke," and labels the work of justice with "signs of hope and new life."[10] She includes her children, her questions, and her sorrows; she includes what she has learned and what she longs to understand. The landscape she sketches is as beautiful and complex as her life experience, and by using the metaphor of landscape to frame the story of her journeys in faith, she is able to point to each element of that complexity without having to flatten, as it were, a lifetime of bumps and odd turns. Describing motherhood is equally as complex; for this reason alone it would make sense to borrow Ackermann's method. Nevertheless, using the metaphor of landscape turns out to be particularly apt in attempting to speak about motherhood for another reason: as Americans, our understanding of the vast and varied American landscape is marked by many of the same flaws and limitations as our understanding of motherhood.

Nature writer Barry Lopez points out that most Americans have very little experience with the American landscape and instead know it primarily through television, magazines, and calendar photographs. Notwithstanding the simply beautiful calendar portrayals, however, "the real American landscape is a face of almost incomprehensible depth

6. Denise Ackermann, *After the Locusts: Letters from a Landscape of Faith* (Grand Rapids, MI: Eerdmans, 2003), 2, xiii.

7. Ibid., 2.

8. Ibid., 16.

9. Ibid.

10. Ibid., 53, 109, 124, 132.

and complexity."[11] Motherhood too is marked by depth, complexity, and a superficial ubiquity (we all *have* a mother, but only some of us have experienced *being* a mother). Moreover, when Lopez points out that the American landscape is made up of uncountable smaller, particular geographies, the analogy to motherhood continues: no two women share the same experience. The difference can be as stark as that between the sand hills of Nebraska and the redwood forests of California. This fact brings up one of the most significant challenges to the methodology of this essay: I am presenting the landscape of just one mother. Just as the tallgrass prairies of Minnesota do not begin to comprise the fullness of the American landscape, so too it is clear that Fernholz's experience of motherhood does not constitute the fullness and variety of millions of women's experiences of bearing and raising children. On the other hand, to know the prairie is to know something real, and something important, about the greater American landscape. The same can be said in looking at Fernholz's photographs: to know the landscape presented here is to know something real, and something important, about the wider landscapes of motherhood.

Yet we cannot ignore those wider landscapes. The variety of combinations of race, class, religion, ethnicity, geographic location, and historic time period that are possible under the category "mother" is staggering and, for all practical purposes, infinite. Too often this variety has been neglected, dismissed, or ignored. Womanist and mujerista theologians have rightly condemned the blindness and arrogance with which white feminists have generalized their experiences to "all women," and as a white feminist writing about a white mother/artist, I would certainly appear to be making an all-too-familiar (and all-too-preventable) error. I am not, however, claiming Fernholz's experience as a norm. Instead, I am using it as a particular example to explore in its own unique depths, and I am doing that in the context of ongoing feminist scholarship about how we can speak about the particularity and universality of motherhood.

Recent years have seen feminist scholars become far more cautious about their universalizing tendencies and much more forthright about their limitations in vision, understanding, and insight.[12] Perhaps the best

---

11. Barry Lopez, "American Geographies," in *Finding Home*, ed. Peter Sauer (Boston: Beacon Press, 1992), 118.

12. See, for example, Bonnie Miller McLemore's discussion of the difficulties of discussing motherhood across class and racial lines in *Also a Mother* (Nashville, TN: Abingdon Press, 1994), 32–33. She states, "White middle class women have much to learn from the struggles of women in other racial and economic groups who

model for how to deal with the complexities of speaking of the varieties of motherhood is found in the work of Sara Ruddick, who begins her approach with the clear statement that "maternal practice responds to the historical reality of a biological child in a particular social world."[13] There is no universal, generic mother caring for a generic child: there is only the historical, the particular, the individual. On the other hand, Ruddick also argues that across time, class, and culture, some aspects of motherhood are "invariant and nearly unchangeable."[14] There are commonalities, in other words, despite the real differences.

For my purposes here, I would like to introduce one particular affirmation of the usefulness of speaking of commonalities across different experiences of motherhood. In a monograph comparing the maternal voice in the novels of Toni Morrison, Bobbie Ann Mason, and Lee Smith, literary critic Paula Gallant Eckard begins with a cautious survey of contemporary scholarship on the actual historical experiences of Southern women during the nineteenth century. Black and white, rich and poor, slave and free—Eckard delves into the experiences of women (as far as the historical record allows) and details the differences, the similarities, and the points of convergence. With this historical background as an anchor and reference point, she turns to the novels and examines how these different women construct their different narratives of motherhood:

> Their novels show significant divergences in the construction of motherhood and maternal experience—divergences that are profoundly shaped by differences in race, class, culture, and geographic region. However, enough intersections exist that I can "bind" these writers together to show how maternity serves as a vital substructure in their works and thus contributes to a collective female literary experience.[15]

---

have experienced [the ideal of motherhood] in different ways. . . . The burdens of motherhood and the dilemmas of work, love, and family of black women are different from those of white women. . . . Only in understanding the divergent forms that domination assumes will the exploitation of all women and mothers end" (33).

13. Sara Ruddick, "Maternal Thinking," in *Mothering*, ed. Joyce Treblicott (Totowa, NJ: Rowman and Allanheld, 1983), 214–15. Quoted in Paula Gallant Eckard, *Maternal Body and Voice in Toni Morrison, Bobbie Ann Mason, and Lee Smith* (Columbia: University of Missouri Press, 2002), 6. Ruddick develops these thoughts in greater depth in chapter 2, "Talking about 'Mothers,'" in her *Maternal Thinking: Toward a Politics of Peace* (Boston: Beacon Press, 1995).

14. Ruddick, "Maternal Thinking," in Eckard, *Maternal Body*, 6.

15. Ibid.

As Eckard makes the claim for a collective female literary experience, so I would like to attempt to speak of a collective female *visual* experience. If mothers construct written understandings of motherhood in ways that powerfully intersect with the writings of other mothers, then so too what very different mothers *look at* in their daily practice of mothering is likely to contain these intersections as well. What a given mother sees is often recognizable, familiar, and translatable to other mothers, even if it is not exactly the same. The landscapes of motherhood as pictured by Fernholz, then, can legitimately serve as a starting point for a wider discussion of those landscapes.

In fact, the particular nature of Fernholz's experience of her corner of the broad landscape of motherhood brings up an important peda- gogical point: in discussing the notion of the landscapes of motherhood in a classroom situation, Fernholz's work is most effectively presented along with images by another artist, preferably one very different from Fernholz in one or more significant ways (age, personal experience, race, ethnicity, geographic location, etc.). The artists featured in *Who Does She Think She Is?*—a documentary about women artists who "navigate some of the most problematic intersections of our time: parenting and creativity, partnering and independence, economics and art"—are espe- cially appropriate; they include Afro-Caribbean painter Camille Musser, New Mexican artist Maye Torres, and Japanese artist Mayumi Oda.[16] Another possibility is the work of Peruvian peasant women textile art- ists, whose "hand-stitched appliqued and embroidered pictures, called *cuadros*," represent not only their memories of life in the countryside (before they fled to the shantytowns of Lima in an effort to escape guer- rilla warfare) but also their current hopes and concerns with respect to unemployment, safety, health care, and education in their new homes.[17] My choice of Fernholz—an artist from Minnesota—was deliberate, as I wanted my students (nearly all of whom are Minnesotans) to have a solid connection with some aspect of these images. Learning to see from

16. "Educational Release," *Who Does She Think She Is*; http://www.whodoes sheetthinksheis.net/ educational (accessed August 8, 2011).

17. From the abstract of Rebecca Berru Davis, "Creative Acts of Survival, Con- scious Acts of Subversion: Textile Pictures by the Peruvian Women of the Pamplona Alta." For more information about these textiles and their creators, see Davis' essay in this collection as well as web sites describing exhibitions of this artwork at the Moreau Gallery, St. Mary's College, Notre Dame, Indiana, and at the Dominican School of Philosophy and Theology, Berkeley, California; http://www.moreauart galleries.com/?p=212 and http://www.dspt.edu/197810127171930310/cwp/view .asp?A=3&Q=275103&C=55783.

a new perspective is easier, after all, if one's first attempt is to see from a slightly different perspective, not a radically different one. If I were teaching elsewhere, I would hope to be able to use Fernholz as my "far from home" example and find a local artist (yet still one very different from Fernholz) to give students a chance to move into a perspective that is at least a little bit similar to their own.

Three Landscapes of Motherhood

Before discussing her photographs, a word of introduction about artist and photographer Kristi Link Fernholz is necessary. Fernholz is a native of Minnesota, a graduate of the University of Minnesota–Duluth, and currently lives on an organic farm in rural western Minnesota. "Most of my photographs are of native prairie plants and have been taken near my home," Fernholz states. That home is "tucked away in the tallgrass prairie along the ridges of the Minnesota River Valley."[18] She adds that she is now a "mom of three, Gavin, Anika, and Nora," and has no illusions that she is somehow the same artist that she was before Gavin's birth in 2002. In her description of a recent series of photographs, she explains:

> Most of these photos were taken pretty close to the driveway, with one child in a backpack and the other in a wagon, stealing brief moments to look for color and texture inspiration. Gone are the days of a two-hour leisurely excursion with just me and my camera. It seems hard to get much further than the driveway these days. And that is really OK.[19]

Clearly, being a mother has changed Fernholz's artistic methodology in ways that could well be judged as limiting, and perhaps even damaging, her commitment to an exploration of the beauty and mystery of the prairie. Doesn't a photographer *need* "leisurely excursions," not just "brief moments" stolen from the children? Isn't it preposterous to limit oneself to the driveway when the prairie rolls forth for miles in all directions? In fact, Fernholz's work reveals just the opposite: it is entirely possible to explore the beauty and mystery of both home and prairie from the perspective of a mother. It is, just as she says, "really OK." More than that, actually: it is really breathtaking.

18. All three photographs can be seen on Fernholz's web site. "Laundry," "Tutu Bike," and "Sister" are all part of the *Almost There/Farm Sketch* series.
19. From the artist statement for the 2006 show, "Beyond Focus: Photographs of the Western Minnesota Prairie."

"Laundry"

A double clothesline stretches across a yard; we can see neither its beginning nor its end. A round wicker laundry basket rests in the foreground; in the background, the forest looms. This is not what a viewer might expect for a prairie farm: Where is the wide open sky? Why not crops or fields in the background, or the edge of a barn, or a glimpse of a well-kept farmhouse with an inviting porch? No, this image does not conform to our expectations of farms, prairies, or laundry lines. Despite the fact that hanging out the wash seems rather old-fashioned, the laundry here is not old-fashioned at all. Instead, it is all brightly colored and rather playful: a bright red shirt, shocking yellow shorts, a red towel with a splash of orange along one edge—and, of course, the candy-pink bra. No crisp white sheets billowing in the wind; no sturdy work clothes. This is not your grandmother's laundry line.

On the other hand, it is not so different that she would fail to recognize it. "Laundry is universal," Kathleen Norris reminds us in *The Quotidian Mysteries*. "We all must do it, or figure out a way to get it done."[20] It is unending work: no matter how much is washed, dried, folded, and put away, there is always someone marching into the house wearing yet another outfit that will need to be washed tomorrow. The laundry line stretches out of the photograph in both directions, reminding us that laundry stretches through time in both directions. There was plenty to do yesterday; there will be more tomorrow.

Fernholz made many choices in constructing this image, but two in particular are of interest for our investigation of the landscapes of motherhood. The first lies in her use of color and the second in her use of light. The choice of a laundry line full of brightly colored and diverse items of clothing, rather than, for example, a stereotypical line of billowing white sheets, marked the image as contemporary and also gave it an unusual air of playfulness. Doing the laundry is typically seen as boring work, and hanging out the wash is old-fashioned—but those yellow shorts are neither boring nor old-fashioned, and the pink bra is somewhere between playful, teasing, and bold. In contrast, imagine this image in black and white or with the clothes hung in a strictly ordered fashion. Either of those choices would ask the viewer to see the difficulty, stress, and burden associated with a repetitive, never-ending task. Fernholz, however, invites the viewer to see her daily work colored with a slightly haphazard joyfulness—an artistic choice that demands further reflection on the role of play in a mother's work. Recall that most

20. Kathleen Norris, *The Quotidian Mysteries* (New York: Paulist Press, 1998), 16.

of Fernholz's photographs are taken with her children nearby and that a mother's daily work includes not just laundry, cooking, and cleaning but also educating her children. Hanging laundry is a perfect opportunity for teaching color and number; for identifying "washcloth," "towel," and "shirt"; and even for demonstrating the right way and the wrong way to hang clothes. And all of this can be a game: imagine a solemn mother saying, "Now here are the blue shorts—" whereupon the child squeals with laughter at her mother's "mistake" and happily cries, "Mama! Yellow!!" Fernholz may or may not have had this conversation with her children—but looking at her photograph reminds me of the times that I have had similar conversations with my children and of the stories my mother told about having that conversation with me.

Fernholz's use of light is even more significant than her use of color and adds complexity to our first impressions of play and cheerfulness. The forest in the background is dark, looming, and ominous—a rather grim background for such bright clothing. On the other hand, the grass under the laundry is sun-speckled and bright. Now notice that the bottom edge of the hanging laundry tracks the line where the grass meets the forest. The laundry thus serves as the barrier between light and darkness: the daily work of civilization that keeps the wilderness at bay. A mother's daily work not only keeps her children clothed but fends off chaos. It is a work of renewal, even of creation; the larger significance of such mundane tasks is usually invisible, but here we see it clearly. "There are days when it seems like a miracle to be able to make dirty things clean,"[21] Norris reminds us, and Fernholz's photograph adds that such a miracle is both a joy and a very serious business.

"Sister"

This black-and-white photograph shows a mirror image of a small girl leaning against a window or a mirror. We cannot see her face, just the curve of her cheek and her hair spilling down. Her pudgy toddler arm rests on the glass, and a line of shocking light divides each of her hands from its mirror image. Most of the photograph is the reflection, which takes up approximately two-thirds of the space: "reality" is relegated to a small section on the right. The viewer's initial reaction to this photograph is likely that it speaks of longing—a child reaching for something out of reach, either something beyond the window/door, or the strange world "inside" the mirror. There is an element of sadness here and an air of quiet watchfulness. It seems to be a familiar image—

21. Ibid., 15.

"Sister" © Kristi Link Fernholz Photography. klfstudio.com

perhaps because there are so many things children want that they cannot have—and over and over again I have heard as a first response to this work, "Oh, I remember that. My daughter used to do the same thing."

The photograph clearly evokes the idea of the double, mirror image—or twin. And it is here that Fernholz's landscape of motherhood differs radically from that of most other women who watch their daughters peer intently through a window or into a mirror. Most of us see simply the reflection of the child before us—but the title of this work is "Sister." As Fernholz explains on her website, "I am a mom of three, Gavin, Anika, and Nora. Anika's twin sister Nora passed away at the age of three days old. It is Anika and her reflection featured in 'Sister.'"[22] Suddenly it is not the world outside that is unreachable but the lost twin, the girl who might have been the mirror image of her living sister. The bright light that separates Anika's hands from the hands of the reflection suddenly becomes the bright line between life and death, between earth and heaven. Fernholz herself describes Nora, the baby

22. www.klfstudio.com/#about (accessed August 3, 2011).

who died, as someone who has returned to another place, a place we cannot quite touch, cannot quite reach:

> She was always wrapped in loving arms with a warm heartbeat near her. It comes down to that. She came, she lived, she felt love, and then she died. She smelled our farm and our house. She felt the sun and wind on her face. She opened her eyes and took us all in, but she was never far from the place from which she came. The spirit world. Heaven. From God in its many forms. And there she returned.[23]

Instead of two girls laughing about being mirrors for one another, playing games with their doubleness, we have a haunting photograph of a single child, doubled in reflection but not in life. The turn of her head, the press of her hands against the unyielding glass, the black-and-white tones: all these contribute to the subtle sorrow that pervades the image.

The landscape here is a landscape of love and loss. Neither can be separated from the other. "It was so good to hold my surviving baby in my grief," Fernholz wrote of the days after Nora's death, "and so hard to hold my surviving baby in my grief."[24] And while it is true that not many mothers have experienced the tangle of joy and grief that accompanied Nora's brief life, the broader landscape of grief is an inescapable part of the landscape of motherhood. The vast majority of mothers who have ever lived have experienced the loss of a child, and while such loss is less common in Western countries than it used to be, it is still something that shapes motherhood. Additionally, many mothers who have not experienced the death of an infant or child have experienced the loss of miscarriage. This does not seem comparable to the loss of a living child, but for some, perhaps many, it is. In the words of novelist Barbara Kingsolver:

> A miscarriage is a natural and common event. All told, probably more women have lost a child from this world than haven't. Most don't mention it, and they go on from day to day as if it hadn't happened, and so people imagine that a woman in this situation never really knew or loved what she had.
>
> But ask her sometime: how old would your child be now? And she'll know.[25]

---

23. Amy Kuebelbeck and Deborah L. Davis, *A Gift of Time: Continuing Your Pregnancy When Your Baby's Life Is Expected to Be Brief* (Baltimore: Johns Hopkins University Press, 2011), 339.

24. Ibid., 305.

25. Barbara Kingsolver, *Animal Dreams* (New York: HarperCollins, 1990), 52–53.

That simple assertion, "She'll know," is haunting to those of us who have not lost a child, because it tells us that the age and development of the dead child is as present to the mother as the age and development of her living children. From a mother's perspective, the separation between life and death, between living children and dead children, between who can be embraced and who can only be remembered, shines as brightly as the light shining on Anika's hand—and the children on both sides of that line are equally visible.

"Tutu Bike"

In this photograph, we encounter a true landscape: a wide expanse of earth and sky that reveals the character of a particular place. A key characteristic of a prairie landscape is that often its most interesting feature is not the land but the sky: swirling clouds tend to draw the eye more than the flat and seemingly static land. Fernholz here presents us with a mother's perspective of a child on the prairie—a child who appears almost ridiculously small in comparison to the scale of the world

"Tutu Bike" © Kristi Link Fernholz Photography. klfstudio.com

around her. As before, Fernholz uses the contrasts between light and dark, and playfulness and seriousness, to structure her work.

Like "Sister," this is a black-and-white image, which draws our focus to the startling inbreaking of light. The upper two-thirds of the photograph is sky, and the lower section is mostly prairie grasses. A gravel road begins at the bottom center and curves off to the right; we cannot see where the road originates or where it is going. Clouds gather at the center of the photograph, with a threatening, black, flat-bottomed cloud shading most of the prairie. Despite the menacing look of this cloud, however, it is only dark when viewed from below. From above—or in our case, from a sufficient distance—we can see that the darkness is but a part of an enormous cloud whose bulk is light. And that light is so powerful that at its center we can no longer see the shape of the cloud: it has been swallowed in glory.

This dance of light and darkness hovers over the head of a small girl, dressed in a tutu and walking her bike along the road, heading away from the viewer. The girl is looking straight out at the clouds, not at all toward the upcoming curve in the road, giving the viewer a strong sense of her determination to keep moving forward, regardless of what she runs into. From a mother's perspective, the child is heading out into a world framed by both darkness and light, danger and joy, risk and adventure. What child—especially a child in such whimsical dress—is prepared for such a world? Yet our children head out into it every day—and follow roads whose ends we cannot see. There is silliness and childish simplicity in this photo: the tutu, the bike and basket. There is also emptiness and darkness: the vast prairie, the lowering clouds. Finally, there is both light and hope, found both in the shocking glow in the sky and those isolated, mysterious places where that glow illuminates the earth.

Imagination and the World We Thought We Knew

In Fernholz's photos, we have seen both playfulness and sorrow, have faced both the threatening and the promising, and have wondered at both the ordinary and the extraordinary. Fernholz has shown us things we would not have noticed on our own; studying her photography has taught us something new about the world we thought we knew. We find ourselves looking at the world in a slightly different way and noticing the gaps between what we might see first and what Fernholz shows us through her art. Learning about the landscapes of motherhood in this way has taught us about mothers—and it has also been an exercise in perspective: that is to say, in broadening and deepening our imaginations.

The cultivation and critical analysis of our imaginations is a central task of education, even if it is rarely noted in the "course outcomes" section of a syllabus. This is especially true in the theology classroom, where a student's ability to sympathetically engage with both experiences and arguments from far outside his or her daily life is required. For example, christological debates from the fourth and fifth centuries seem boring and pointless to many students—unless they are able to find a way to enter into and eventually appreciate the concerns of people whose lives, passions, and even assumptions are terribly foreign to a twenty-first-century American. Further, the cultivation of the imagination is important not just for the work of academic theology but for spirituality as well. Scripture scholar Sandra Schneiders argues that the imagination is at the heart of religious experience, and thus "a healthy spirituality requires a healing of the imagination."[26] That is, it is more than likely that we have reached adulthood with an imagination that is at least somewhat limited, even damaged, by what we have experienced thus far. Sexism, racism, and the constraints of culture and class are among the damaging limitations we face; each of us must also confront the particular circumstances of our family, neighborhood, education, and work.

The imagination as discussed here is not to be understood in the colloquial sense of the ability to "make things up." It is instead far more important: Schneiders defines imagination as the "constructive capacity to integrate our experience into dynamic and effective wholes which then function as the interpretive grids of further experience."[27] In other words, the imagination is our capacity to build accurate frameworks through which we can understand and interpret our experiences. The imagination is dynamic because building those frameworks is "a neverending process," since each new experience modifies the framework we have constructed so far.[28] Theologian Bernard Cooke also emphasizes the human need to continually refine our ability to understand and interpret the world. He argues that it is the task of an entire lifetime to learn to interpret the world as accurately as possible and that in order to do so we must develop

---

26. Sandra Schneiders, *Women and the Word* (New York: Paulist Press, 1986), 19.
27. Ibid.,16.
28. Ibid.

the ability to encounter openly whatever comes into our lives—people, happenings, personal pain or joy—and to "read" the encounter with insight and accuracy, so that the experience we have correlates with what is actually occurring. . . . We are constantly learning more about ourselves and about what surrounds us; we are consequently correcting somewhat the interpretations we earlier placed on things. . . . All human progress . . . requires an advance in the capacity to interpret and to experience more deeply and more accurately.[29]

Following Schneiders and Cooke, then, we as teachers can recognize that the work of shifting and enlarging students' perspectives on the world is an extraordinarily important part of the work we do in the classroom. We also need to know, however, that this work is particularly significant for today's students. A recent study by psychologists at the University of Michigan, surveying thirty years of data about college students and empathy, concluded that today's students are far less likely to "report having empathetic concern for others " and that they are similarly disinclined to "take on another person's perspective."[30] The level of decline in student interest in and aptitude for empathy is shocking, and most of it has occurred within the past ten years. The study reports that students today are 48 percent less likely to be empathetic than their peers in 1979 and also shows a 34 percent drop in the practice of taking another's perspective.[31]

Given this data, it is clear that educating our students' imaginations today is more difficult and more important than ever. An understanding of the world that ignores the perspective of the stranger leads to a narrow and inadequate understanding of the depth and richness of human experience. Those who have never visited the prairie dismiss it as empty; those who do not bother to traverse the landscapes of motherhood are likely to fall into old traps of either glorifying or despising a mother's work. In the end, those who fail to question, reorganize, and reinterpret their experiences are doomed to a small and distorted understanding of themselves and the world around them. As a teacher, a feminist, and a

29. Bernard Cooke, *Sacraments and Sacramentality* (New London, CT: Twenty-Third Publications, 1994), 35.

30. Erik Hayden, "Today's College Students Lacking in Empathy," Miller-McCune; www.miller-mccune.com/news/todays-college-students-lacking-in-empathy/16642. Hayden relies on work done by Sara Konrath, Edward H. O'Brien, and Courtney Hsing, "Changes in Dispositional Empathy Over Time in American College Students: A Meta-Analysis," a paper published online in 2010 and in the *Personality and Social Psychology Review* in 2011 (May 15): 180–198.

31. Ibid.

theologian, I am convinced that the cultivation of a broad, deep, sympa-
thetic, and critical imagination is necessary for each of us in order to see
clearly, choose wisely, and act justly in the world. Careful contemplation
and lively discussion of the photographs of Kristi Link Fernholz can be
a significant part of this work of cultivating the imagination: her art is
a small and precious flower in the midst of the vast prairie, reminding
us that those who have the patience, attention, and vision to search for
beauty will, in the end, find it.

Part 2

She Who *Is Imagined*

M. Shawn Copeland

The Critical Aesthetics of Race[1]

My body was given back to me sprawled out, distorted, recolored, clad in mourning on that white winter day. The Negro is ugly, the Negro is animal, the Negro is bad, the Negro is mean, the Negro is ugly; look, a [Negro], it's cold, the [Negro] is shivering, because he is cold, the little boy is trembling because he is afraid of the [Negro], the [Negro] is shivering with cold, that cold goes through your bones, the handsome little boy is trembling because he thinks that the [Negro] is quivering with rage, the little white boy throws himself into his mother's arms [in fear]. . . . I sit down at the fire and I become aware of my uniform. I had not seen it. It is indeed ugly. I stop there, for who can tell me what beauty is?[2]

This passage by the controversial psychiatrist and activist Frantz Fanon from his *Black Skins, White Masks* provides an entry point in probing the relation between race and aesthetics. In this work, Fanon takes the Algerian experience of French colonial violence as a point of departure from which to analyze the alienation from self and society of black and other peoples of color around the world. White colonial racial gaze has racialized the "others," imprisoning them into blackness or brownness or yellowness or redness, sealing the "others" into what

1. This article previously appeared in *The Journal of Catholic Social Thought* 3(1):17–27.
2. Frantz Fanon, *Black Skin, White Masks* (New York: Grove, 1967), 114.

Nigel Gibson has called "a crushing objecthood."[3] What Fanon seeks is "disalienation,"[4] a liberation at once biological, social (i.e., political, economic, technological), aesthetic, existential, intellectual, and religious.

Fanon does not employ the formal terms "race" or "racism"; rather, he illustrates them to bristling effect. Anxiety and fear, shock and shame spill over the page to signify social, aesthetic, and moral conflict as personal anguish in the contrast and differentiation of human bodies. This disquieting meditation not only incriminates our most noble social, existential, moral, and religious aspirations but judges as well our efforts toward their realization. This passage leads us onto a field mined with shards of memory (*Geschicte*) and history (*Historie*), furrowed by conceptual models and practices spawned by modernity's arrogance and the failure of the European Enlightenment, and hemmed in by the disturbing aesthetics of race.

A brief overview of the discussion: Because I take race and racism seriously, I begin with the concept of race. In order to oppose racism, it is crucial to understand the continuing significance and shifting meanings of race, particularly in the United States of America. Accordingly, the *first section* explores three conceptions or theories of race. The idea that the meaning of race or racial identity can change is a relatively new one. Even as recently as forty years ago, race was considered something fixed that denoted a group of persons who were connected by common origin and marked by distinct physical characteristics. Hence, race implied a natural, even essential, characteristic that could determine the person. During the past twenty-five years, however, a body of theoretical analysis has developed to destabilize and problematize the concept of race. To this end, we discuss three theories of race—race as an ideological construct, as an objective condition, and as a social construct or, what sociologists Michael Omi and Howard Winant call, racial formation process.[5]

3. Nigel C. Gibson, *Fanon: The Postcolonial Imagination* (Cambridge: Polity/ Blackwell Publishing, 2003), 16.

4. Ibid., 22.

5. Michael Omi and Howard Winant, *Racial Formation in the United States: From the 1960s to the 1990s*, 2nd ed. (New York and London: Routledge, 1994). Racial formation process is a variant of what, arguably, is the most dynamic rethinking of race: critical race theory. Critical race theory (CRT) got its start among academic lawyers in the mid-1970s. It uncovers the complicity of legal discourse and legal institutions in maintaining and defending white racist supremacy. Early theorists of this movement include Derrick Bell, Alan Freeman, and Richard Delgado. These thinkers drew inspiration from the reservoir of intellectual energy, imagination, and courage created by African liberation struggles, resistance to anti-Semitism, the

The *second section* provides a definition of racism and reviews ways in which the practice of racism exploits the limitations of the concept of race as an ideology and an objective condition. Racism is a complex and opportunistic social phenomenon that distorts everyday human living. While a casual outing in the park may risk nothing more than boredom, the probability of random, xenophobic violence is real. And concrete experience frequently betrays the best theory.

In the *third section*, I should like to try to say something from the point of view of a political theologian about race, racism, and Catholic social teaching. I should like to do this by attempting to reply to the question that concludes the passage from *Black Skins, White Masks* with which I began. "Who," Fanon asks, "can tell me what beauty is?" I answer that beauty is consonant with performance—that is, with ethical and moral behavior, with habit or virtue. In other words, beauty is the living up to and living out the love and summons of creation in all our particularity and specificity as God's human creatures. Finally, this essay concludes with some suggestions about how Catholic social teaching might disturb the aesthetics of race and racism, which have so deformed our Christian living.

Defining and Theorizing Race

Race as an Ideological Construct

To explain race as an ideological construct or the result of biased thinking (what Marx called false consciousness) reduces race to an illusion. Proponents of this view deem race as unscientific and, therefore, fictitious. The position as it stands is partly correct. But race as an ideological construct cannot respond rationally and well to instances of discrimination or hate speech. These proponents are likely to reject such maliciousness, but since race is an illusion, there is little that can be done. After all, they declare that "race has taken on a life of its own." But a curious and pathetic set of syllogisms emerges: If race is an illusion, then racial prejudice and racism are illusions. If race is an illusion, then the memories and narratives of slaves, of survivors of attempts at genocide, of the dispossessed, of the despised, of the wretched of the earth can only be illusory. If race is an illusion, then those who oppose racism unwittingly perpetuate race thinking. Yet, what are we to make

---

modern US civil rights movement, and opposition to colonialism. CRT spread to many disciplines, including education, cultural studies, English, sociology, political science, history, and anthropology.

of the brutal social facts of racism and racial prejudice? What are we to do with suddenly falsified accounts of conquest, colonialism, and empire? What are we to do with the witness of memories, cemeteries, and decaying ovens? Such a position sanitizes and reframes the perspectives of the victims of history into an evasive narrative. Such a position dodges the field of experience, which is the ground of good theory, and suppresses questioning, the most basic act of human intelligence.

Race as an ideological construct dissatisfies on two accounts. First, it fails to address the resilience and geographic irreverence as well as the effects produced by "race-thinking and race-acting."[6] Second, as an illusion race can neither explain nor connect to human experience, to human bodies and their particular situatedness in social and historical circumstances. But, as Omi and Winant argue so trenchantly, our societies are "so thoroughly racialized that to be without racial identity is to be in danger of having no identity. To be raceless is akin to being genderless. Indeed, when one cannot identify another's race, a micro-sociological 'crisis of interpretation' results."[7]

Race as an Objective Condition

To attempt to explain race as an objective condition seems highly problematic. With its allusion to scientific objectivity, such a definition admits biological racial and eugenicist theories. This approach can be traced through the empirical taxonomies of eighteenth-century physician François Bernier and naturalist Carolus Linnaeus to nineteenth-century proponents of so-called scientific racism such as Louis Agassiz and Paul Broca to Charles Yerkes and Lewis Terman in the early twentieth century (Gossett, 1963, 1997) up to Richard Herrnstein and Charles Murray's *The Bell Curve* (1994). In the name of scientific objectivity, these thinkers detached race from social and historical conditions and treated it as "an independent variable."[8] Because race thinking took on the mantle of objectivity, race came to function as a universal evaluative tool to measure human hierarchy—whites placed at the top of the scale, blacks at the lowest rung, and brown, yellow, and red women and men ranked in between. In Europe, right into the mid-twentieth century, this racial scale was used to exclude and represent Jews and Irish as

---

6. Omi and Winant, "On the Theoretical Status of the Concept of Race," in *Race, Identity, and Representation in Education*, ed. Cameron McCarthy and Warren Crichlow (New York and London: Routledge, 1993), 5.

7. Ibid.

8. Ibid., 6.

inferior others.[9] In the United States, this scale "was combined with an argument that human intelligence was a fixed and hereditary characteristic" that allowed not only the measurement of enslaved Africans and their descendants but also a chart of "acceptable and unacceptable immigrants."[10]

If the allusion to objectivity makes a convincing appeal to so-called conservatives, it also works well with so-called liberals. Liberals reject the biological argument but fall short of grasping the "variability and historically contingent character" of race and racial meanings. Their arguments fail to problematize individual relations to racial group identities and likewise ignore the "constantly shifting parameters through which race is understood, group interests are assigned, statuses are ascribed, agency is attained, and roles performed."[11]

Race as an objective condition also fails as an explanatory strategy. Inasmuch as this approach accepts as objective fact that one *is* one's race, it remains ahistorical. This position endorses, however unwittingly, a notion of "fixed" racial identity and, thereby, subordinates that identity to criteria that depart from *real* human experience. In other words, although there is a performative dimension to race, no performance need be fixed or prescribed. One way to get at this is to ask, "What does it mean *to act* white or *to act* black?" To push the issue, we might ask, "Does *acting* white in the Southern United States mean the same thing in 2004 that it did in 1937?" To treat race as an objective condition fails to appreciate the "historicity and social comprehensiveness of the race concept."[12]

The concept of race as an objective condition also fails to appreciate the way in which individuals and groups are pressed to work out conflictual racial meanings and identities in everyday life. To concretize this point, we might try a few thought experiments. We might imagine a young woman whose parents are of different races: How should she identify her racial heritage? Or consider that Latinos report ambivalence at ticking off the racial boxes black or white. They protest that neither of these descriptions represents their concrete reality. Finally, we might conjecture the dilemmas that the race concept posed for individuals and groups who endured and participated in ethnic cleansing in the

---

9. Robert Miles, *Racism* (London/New York: Routledge, 1989); Neil MacMaster, *Racism in Europe, 1870–2000* (Basingstoke, Hampshire, and New York: Palgrave, 2001).

10. Miles, *Racism*, 36.

11. Omi and Winant, "On the Theoretical Status of the Concept of Race," 6.

12. Ibid.

Balkans or genocide in Rwanda. The differing textures and densities of these experiments lead us to engage a third definition and approach to theorizing race, that is, race as a social construct or racial formation.

Racial Formation Process

Michael Omi and Howard Winant argue that race is "a concept which signifies and symbolizes social conflicts and interests by referring to different types of human bodies."[13] Omi and Winant contend that race is "an element of social structure rather than an irregularity within it . . . a dimension of human representation rather than an illusion."[14] They argue that race is a socially constructed form of human categorization.

Omi and Winant use the sociological term "racial formation" to denote the complex historically situated process by which human bodies and social structures are represented and arranged and how race is linked to the way in which society is organized and ruled. From this perspective, "race is a matter of both social structure and cultural representation."[15] Racial formation process accounts for a cluster of problems regarding race, including the dilemmas of racial identity and the relation of race to other forms of difference, for example, gender and nationality, and it clarifies the nature of racism and its relation to social oppression as this is expressed, even in so-called first world or developed nations, as economic exploitation, marginalization, powerlessness, cultural imperialism, and systemic as well as random violence.[16] While this perspective grasps the brutality of race on global and personal levels, it discredits the romanticization of race as essence and its misrepresentation as illusion. Racial formation process maintains that race is not a deviation within a given social structure but a constant feature embedded within it.

The explanatory power of racial formation process functions to account for both macro and micro levels. On the *macro level*, racial formation process adequately interprets contemporary social relations, the shifting meanings and relevance of race in a global context as well as "across historical time." Here, race as a social construct demonstrates considerable flexibility. Given the increasingly complex and globalized concept of race, racial formation process manages the "competing racial projects" or "efforts to institutionalize racial meanings and identities

13. Omi and Winant, *Racial Formation in the United States*, 55.
14. Ibid.
15. Ibid., 56.
16. See Iris Marion Young, *Justice and the Politics of Difference* (Princeton, NJ: Princeton University Press, 1990), 41–59.

in particular social structures, notably those of individual, family, community, and state."[17] The desire of women and men of mixed racial parentage to name themselves, the struggles of egalitarian movements against racial backlash, the postcolonial interrogations of empire, the decentering of powerful binary logics—for example, white/black, colonizer/colonized—as well as the sly concealment of discourses and exercises of racial domination: these sometimes contradictory enterprises reinforce the protean character of race.[18] Moreover, these enterprises generate both new forms of social oppression and responses that deploy race not only to expose its toxic limitations but also to reimagine and reconfigure social matrices to evoke the achievement and flourishing of authentic humanity.[19]

On the *micro level* racial formation process spells out how the most mundane as well as the most important tasks can be grasped as racial projects—voting, banking, health care, registering for school, inquiring about church membership. We have been taught to *see* race, and we do—and we see it most vividly when we insist that we are color-blind. Race is one of the first things that we notice about people (along with their sex) when we meet them. Further, the ability to read race accurately, to categorize people (black or white, red or brown, Mexican or Indian, Chinese or Vietnamese) has become crucial for social behavior and comfort. The inability to identify accurately a person's race spells crisis, and even as we question such interpretation, we continue to analyze and interpret our experience in racial terms. As Omi and Winant observe, "We expect differences in skin color, or other racially coded characteristics, to explain social differences."[20] This affects not only our relations to various social institutions, cultural activities, and religious rites and rituals but our relationships with other human persons as well as the constitution of our own identities. The very stereotypes we profess to abhor and repudiate break in on our encounters with physicians, professors, musicians, law enforcement officers, and elected officials of races different from our own. Critical interrogation of racial formation process, however, can uncover social conditioning for what it is—a set of learned behaviors and practices. At the same time, that

17. Omi and Winant, "On the Theoretical Status of the Concept of Race," 7.

18. Richard Rodriguez, *Brown: The Last Discovery of America* (New York: Viking, 2002); Frank H. Wu, *Yellow: Race in America beyond Black and White* (New York: Basic Books, 2002).

19. Emmanuel Eze, *Achieving Our Humanity: The Idea of the Postracial Future* (New York: Routledge, 2001).

20. Omi and Winant, *Racial Formation in the United States*, 60.

critical interrogation can identify and support strategies to overcome the debilitating legacy of race.

Race and Racism

Although race is not an ideology, racism certainly is. Because racial formation process accords critical attention both to social structures and to social signification, it can account for racism as ideology. Racism is the product of biased thinking, an ideology that willfully justifies, advances, and maintains the systemic domination of certain race or races by another race. Racism goes beyond prejudice (feeling or opinion formed without concrete experience or knowledge) or even bigotry (doctrinaire intolerance) by joining these feelings or attitudes to the putative exercise of legitimate power in a society; in this way, racism never relies on the choices or actions of a few individuals but is institutionalized.

Racialized subjects sustain and transmit racism as an ideology through their uncritical acceptance of standards, symbols, habits, assumptions, reactions, and practices rooted in racial differentiation and racially assigned privilege. There is no intent to "blame" but rather to shake us from our drowsing. Racism penetrates the development and transmission of culture, including education and access to it, literary and artistic expression, forms of communication, representation, and leisure; the participation and contribution to the common good, including opportunities to work and to engage in meaningful political and economic activity; the promotion of human flourishing, including intellectual, psychological, sexual, and spiritual growth; and the embrace of religion, including membership and leadership, catechesis and spirituality, ritual, doctrine, and theology. Thus, as James Boggs concludes, racism permeates every sphere of social relations.[21]

As an ideology, racism envelops the "normal" and "ordinary" social setup and spawns a negatively charged context in which flesh-and-blood human beings live out their daily lives and struggle to constitute themselves as persons. Racism is no mere problem to be solved but a construal of reality, a distorted way of be-ing human in the world. Racial formation process alerts us to the fact that racism is not something *out there* for us to solve; rather, it is in *our* consciousness, shapes *our* discourse and practices.

21. James Lee Boggs, *Racism and the Class Struggle* (New York: Monthly Review Press, 1970), 147–48; see also, David Theo Goldberg, *Racist Culture: Philosophy and the Politics of Meaning* (Oxford: Blackwell Publishers, 1993).

To speak about a culture with racism or *racist culture* is to grasp culture as "both, and interrelatedly, a signifying system and a system of material production."[22] Although race cannot be explained as an objective condition, in racist culture this idea obtains. Insisting on the empirical aspect of race, racist culture requires racial apprehension, conception, and judgment of each human being. Each human being is reduced to biological physiognomy; innocuous physical traits—skin color, hair texture, shape of body, head, facial features, blood traits—identified, ordered, exaggerated, evaluated. Each human being is assigned a racial designation that orders her or his relations to other women and men of the same and of different races. Finally, in this arrangement, one racial group is contrived as "the measure of human being" and is deemed normative. Meanings and values have been embedded in those differences so as to favor the group that has been contrived as "the measure of human being." Virtue, morality, and goodness are assigned to that racial group, while vice, immorality, and evil are assigned to the others. Entitlement, power, and privilege are accorded that racial group, while dispossession, powerlessness, and disadvantage define others.

Racist culture or a culture based on racial privilege and preference absolutizes racial differences "by generalizing from them and claiming that they are final." Thus, Albert Memmi maintains that when the difference is totalized, it "penetrates the flesh, the blood and the genes of the victim [and] is transformed into fate, destiny, heredity."[23] When the difference is transformed into fate or destiny or heredity, then that constructed difference is naturalized. Whatever the difference, it is made to penetrate profoundly and collectively; it is final, complete, and inescapable. Thus, those who are racially different diverge not only from a set of norms but from what it means to be a human being and, hence, from being human.

In a racist culture, definition and displacement, control and mastery, violence and power obtain. For racism will not allow us to overlook race; it demands that we see race and see it in specified and fixed ways. For example, raw reactions of various individuals to a fifty-year-old black man sitting in a tavern will certainly vary, but we cannot predict the outcome of such an ordinary racialized encounter. At the same time, that man's father or grandmother, having endured racial threat and suffered racial assault, quite probably can anticipate a range of scenarios, one

---

22. Goldberg, *Racist Culture*, 8.

23. Albert Memmi, *The Colonizer and the Colonized* (Boston: Beacon Press, 1967), 185, 189.

of which might well include the risk of death. But, in spite of the enervating irrationality and unpredictability of random violence in racist cultures, marginalized and excluded individuals and groups continue to struggle with integrity against invisibility, indifference, and resignation. For, despite a seeming permanence, Fanon insists, "racism is not a constant of the human spirit."[24]

Beauty and Justice

I repeat the question with which I began: "Who," Frantz Fanon asks, "can tell me what beauty is?" I answer that beauty is consonant with performance—that is, with ethical and moral behavior, with habit or virtue. In other words, beauty is the *living up to and living out* the love and summons of creation in all our particularity and specificity as God's human creatures. If the question is situated within a white supremacist horizon, however, then it challenges and contests any so-called objective or neutral approach to aesthetics and ethics. In such a context, Fanon's disquieting passage incriminates practices and speech regarding bodies, sexuality, gender, and race and power. Any response to Fanon's question ought to begin by acknowledging that any appeal to the empirical or visual in the effort to understand human being is never innocent, never ahistorical, and never divorced from power.

As the adage would have it, "Beauty is in the eye of the beholder," but the eye must be tutored to see, coached to attribute meaning to line and curve. Elaine Scarry distinguishes four key features of beauty: beauty is sacred, unprecedented, salvific, and intelligible.[25] What is beautiful commands awe and reverence; such is the response to an encounter with the divine, with the wholly Other. Beauty is singular, even as it generates creativity and mimesis. Beauty nourishes and restores interiority and incites a longing for what is true, what is good, what is just. What is beautiful evokes astonishment, delight; beauty, quite literally, takes our breath away. Yet, within a white supremacist horizon, depictions of beauty erase different and dark bodies; such bodies *cannot* be beautiful. In this horizon, different and dark bodies are repulsive, hideous; these bodies encode negativity, even evil.

---

24. Fanon, "Racism and Culture," in *Toward the African Revolution: Political Essays* (New York: Grove Books, 1967), 41.

25. Elaine Scarry, *On Beauty and Being Just* (Princeton, NJ: Princeton University Press, 1999), 22–23, 46, 47. I do not quote Scarry in order to argue against her but rather to point out some recognizable notions of beauty.

"Who can tell me what beauty is?" The reply, "Black is beautiful!" "Brown is beautiful!" defies the hegemony of white racist supremacy, shakes the foundations of its unethical deployment of aesthetics and power. The insistence, "Black is beautiful!" "Brown is beautiful!" shouts a disregarded theological truth, nourishes and restores bruised interiority, prompts memory, encourages discovery and recovery, stimulates creativity, acknowledges and reverences the wholly Other. To assert, "Beauty *is* black!" exorcises the "ontological curse"[26] that consigns the black body to the execrable and claims ontological space: space to *be*, space to realize one's humanity authentically.

"Who can tell me what beauty is?" Any reply to Fanon's question requires a response that transcends sexuality, gender, race, class, and culture yet neither shelves nor absolutizes the thorny ontologizing potential of these dimensions of concrete human existence. Beauty is consonant with human performance, with habit or virtue, with authentic ethical performance and action. Beauty is the living up to and living out the love and summons of creation in all our particularity and specificity as God's human creatures, made in God's own image and likeness.

Catholic Social Teaching and Disturbing Racism

How might Catholic social teaching be brought to disturb aesthetics of race? How might it disrupt the powerful racism that has deformed concrete vital living and expressive culture in the United States? How might it disturb the moral, spiritual, and spatial sensibilities generated by racist reactions and behaviors? At the very least, Catholic social teaching can provide resources to promote responsibilities of resistance and engagement. The resources of Catholic social teaching challenge those (dis)values, criteria, and practices that marginalize groups and persons from participation in society and thereby distort the common human good. At the same time, Catholic social teaching augments the promotion of solidarity, the articulation of appropriate values, new criteria, new practices for a life of human flourishing.

26. Paul Anthony Farley, "The Black Body as Fetish Object," *Oregon Law Review* 76 (1997): 527; cf. Michel Foucault, who writes: "The critical ontology of ourselves has to be considered . . . as an attitude, an ethos, a philosophical life in which the critique of what we are is at one and the same time the historical analysis of the limits that are imposed on us and an experiment with the possibility of going beyond them" (Michel Foucault, "What Is Enlightenment ? ["*Qu'est-ce que les Lumières?*"], in *The Foucault Reader*, ed. Paul Rabinow [New York: Pantheon Books, 1984], 32–50; http://foucault.info/documents/whatIsEnlightenment/foucault.whatIsEnlightenment).

First, to resist the powerful racism that has deformed humanity, those of us who are students and proponents of Catholic social teaching must take race and racism seriously. To take race and racism seriously is to reject liberal modernity's reduction of race to a morally indifferent category and racism to individual prejudices. This entails a repudiation of modernity's consideration of the use of racist epithets and racist discourse merely "as irrational appeals to irrelevant categories, to distinctions that delimit universal liberal ideals" or rights.[27] Taking race and racism seriously also means being willing to expose the church's racialized history of exclusions and rejections.

Second, to resist the powerful racism that has shaped us as a people and our culture, Catholic social teaching, with its promotion of justice as equalizing, voluntary, and rooted in love, provides a standard by which we may be tutored to open ourselves to other cultures and peoples. Certainly, in a historical and social matrix dominated by racism, genuine openness to "others," to strangers, to different cultures may never be easy. On the one hand, we need to be wary of superficial approaches to "others." Too often, we find ourselves enthralled with—what for us is—new, different, exotic, simply because it is new, different, and exotic. When we do this, how easy it is to slip into a relativism that shifts position, not to gain perspective, but to gain relative distance. From that distance, we can move on to seek out the next novelty, the next people, the next culture. We culture hop. We are easily distracted; our understanding is shallow, our judgment perfunctory, and our criticism superficial. Too often, with little or no historical understanding, we simply imitate values, norms, and practices that are constitutive and communicative of a particular culture. Lacking critical understanding, we fail to recognize that such inclusion, on our part, too often, is sheer tokenism and arrogance. Lacking authentic judgment, we omit criteria crucial in grasping the internal coherence and relation of various practices or values one to another. Lacking authentic commitment to the "hard" habitual work of daily living and incarnating a culture, we have little appreciation for the particular demands of sustaining those meanings, values, norms, institutions, and practices.

On the other hand, we cannot simply retreat from the challenges of engaging other and different cultures or peoples simply because such engagement is difficult and fraught with negative possibilities.

27. Fanon, "Racism and Culture," 41; see also Cornel West, *The American Evasion of Philosophy: A Genealogy of Pragmatism* (Madison: University of Wisconsin Press, 1989), esp. 92–93.

Rather, we must risk not only engagement but also the conversion that such engagement may bring about. For resisting racism should bring about change in us: change in our attentiveness, in our questions, in our reflection, in our judgments, in our decisions, in our choices, in our living, in our loving.

Third, those of us who are students and proponents of Catholic social teaching must promote human flourishing as a work for justice. We human beings are never reducible to atoms or statistics or social problems; nor are we reducible to attributes, stereotypes, or taxonomies. We women and men are instances of incarnate moral and ethical choice in a world under the influence of sin, yet we stand in relation to a field of grace.[28] To promote human flourishing emphasizes and engages humanity's essential humanness. Catholic social teaching reminds us that our resistance to racism is rooted not in the arrogance of triumph over evil but in love. Catholic social teaching offers us a compelling notion of the person—one that acknowledges and witnesses to the oneness of human creatures and honors the richness of our diversity as a basic feature of our unity and at the same time situating human creatures within the fragile, beautiful, *fractal* order of creation.[29]

28. Bernard Lonergan, "Finality, Love, Marriage," in *Collected Works of Bernard Lonergan*, vol. 4: *Collection*, 2nd ed., rev. and aug., ed. Frederick E. Crowe and Robert M. Doran (Toronto: University of Toronto Press, 1998), 205–21.

29. The term "fractal" refers to an irregular or fragmented geometric shape that can be repeatedly subdivided into parts, each of which is a smaller copy of the whole. Fractals are used in computer modeling of natural structures that do not have simple geometric shapes, for example, clouds, mountainous landscapes, and coastlines.

Michelle A. Gonzalez

The Jennifer Effect
Race, Religion, and the Body

I need to begin my essay with a few disclaimers. First of all, I love Jennifer Lopez. I don't always understand what she is doing, and I don't always get her fashion choices, but she is someone I admire for her style, her business savvy, and her perseverance. Second, I love popular culture and I enjoyed this opportunity to reflect critically on what I usually think about on my "down" time. My last disclaimer is that this essay will not be a theology of J.Lo. I tried, but Ms. Lopez can offer a lot for us to think about in terms of the context in which we claim to do theology, but not so much on constructive theological reflection. In my concluding comments, however, I hope to offer some hints at constructive theological avenues emerging from this study.

This essay examines the implications of a serious consideration of the construction of the persona of Jennifer Lopez on the discourse of Latino/a theological aesthetics. My emphasis is on how a study of Lopez and her influence on global popular culture forces us Latino/a theologians to scrutinize the nature of the Latino/a people we have constructed in our books, articles, and presentations. Unlike other scholars working in aesthetics within Latino/a theology, I want to place popular culture as a fundamental source for our theological reflection. Studies of religion and popular culture abound, yet often these focus on the role of religion within popular culture, both negative and positive. My hope is to also talk about the theological insights one can glean from popular culture. One may ask, what is theological about Lopez? Not a lot, I would admit. Nevertheless, contextual theologians spend a significant amount of time outlining the context and culture from which their theological elaborations emerge. Lopez as an entry point into theological reflection allows us to enter into Latino/a culture from a more mainstream, though admittedly less theological, starting point. I think we will find that J.Lo. challenges and affirms the work we have done and pushes us into a serious consideration of popular culture in our future theological collaborations.

I divide my study of Lopez into four sections. The first and lengthiest examines the construction of Latinidad that Lopez has created in her public persona. I will consider the shifts in this persona: at times J.Lo. presents herself as a Latina with little reference to her Puerto Rican roots, at other times a Nuyorican, and occasionally she has even been able to erase her "ethnic" identity through her acting roles. I then focus on Jennifer Lopez's most discussed body part, her butt. This section looks at an erotics and celebration of the body that Lopez has embodied throughout her career yet also problematizes the sexualization of her and consequently all Latinas. Does Lopez offer Latinas empowered celebration of our bodies and sexuality? Or does she merely affirm white Anglo constructions of Latinas as the exotic, erotic, other? The third section examines Lopez's relationship with the African American community. Lopez, I argue, began her career in the hip-hop community, yet the highs and lows of her relationship with the black community reflect a broader ambiguity within black–Latino/a relations. I conclude in the final section with the theological implications of this study, focusing on theological aesthetics.

Jennifer Lynn Lopez was born on July 24, 1969. She grew up in the Castle Hill neighborhood of the Bronx. While both parents are from Ponce, Puerto Rico, it is interesting to note that many of her bios emphasize that her grandparents were from Spain. Lopez first entered the pop culture scene as a Fly Girl dancer on the show *In Living Color*. Executive producer Keenan Ivory Wayans managed this groundbreaking black sketch comedy show from which actors Jim Carrey, Jamie Foxx, and Lopez emerged. Lopez's first significant film roles were in Gregory Nava's Hispanic epic *Mi Familia* and *Money Train* in 1995, but it was not until her 1997 starring role in *Selena* that the full force of Lopez exploded onto the pop culture scene. She was nominated for a Golden Globe for her performance. Lopez is the first Latina actress to be paid over one million dollars. She released her first pop album, *On the Six*, in 1999. In 2001 she made history when her movie *The Wedding Planner* and her album *J.Lo.* were simultaneously in the number one slot, making her the first singer-actress to achieve this. Her first fashion line, J.Lo., was launched in 2003. Lopez is a singer, dancer, songwriter, record producer, television producer, and fashion designer, arguably the most influential Hispanic entertainer in the world.

Jennifer's Latinidad

Part of Jennifer Lopez's tremendous success as a Hollywood actress is her ability to play multiethnic roles. She has played an Italian American, a Cuban, a Mexican American, a *mestiza*, a Puerto Rican. Lopez has even done what few other Latino/a actors have been able to do, that is, play characters where her ethnicity is entirely erased.[1] Part of her ability to morph into these different personas is her cinnamon skin, her ever-changing hair color and texture, and her lack of an accent. Her casting as Selena, which I will discuss shortly, was not the first time a Puerto Rican has been cast as a Mexican American.[2] This multiplicity of ethnicity is mirrored in Lopez's personal life, where Lopez has had high-profile relationships with Ojani Noa (Cuban American), Sean Combs (African American), Cris Judd (Filipino American), Ben Affleck (Anglo American), and Mark Anthony (Nuyorican). Lopez presents an interesting case study for us, because while she has consistently emphasized her Latina and/or Puerto Rican roots, she is not contained by her ethnic identity.

Lopez's music career began at the exact moment that the Latin explosion, as labeled by the music industry, thundered onto the pop scene. Ironically, the heart of the Latin explosion was, in fact, a Puerto Rican explosion. At the core of the Latin boom were Lopez, Ricky Martin, and Mark Anthony. It was only later that Shakira and, to a certain extent, Christina Aguilera jumped aboard the Latin music tidal wave. This Latin music boom, which many heralded as a belated recognition of Latino/a pop music by mainstream Anglo culture, was far from it. In fact, the Latin music boom only contributed to sexualized stereotypes about Latinos and Latinas, shaking their "bon bons" all over the United States. This boom also contributed to the homogenizing of Latino/a identity and the erasure of the majority of Latino/a culture and music. As Frances R. Aparicio has noted, the Latin music boom was constructed through Anglo eyes. "The Latin music boom, while specifically constituted by Caribbean and Puerto Rican, East Coast figures—Jennifer Lopez, Ricky Martin, Mark Anthony—was never articulated as a Boricua boom, but

---

1. Cuban: *Blood and Wine* (1996); Mexican American: *Selena* (1997) and *Bordertown* (2007); Italian American: *Wedding Planner* (2001); Puerto Rican: *El cantante* (2007); *mestiza* of Native American and white/Anglo: *U Turn* (1997); ambiguous ethnicity: *The Cell* (2000) and *Enough* (2002).

2. The list includes Freddie Prinze in *Chico and the Man*, Essai Morales in *La Bamba* and in the PBS show *Familia*, Jimmy Smits in *Mi Familia*, and Benicio del Toro as a cop in *Traffic*.

rather as a Latin music boom."[3] Aparicio argues that this Caribbean face ignores the realities of the majority of Latino/as in the United States and systematically ignores Mexican American music. Also at work here, she contends, is the Miami-based, hegemonic Latino/a music industry.

Lopez was distinct within this Latin boom in that she was a woman and that her music embodied a fusion of sounds, both Latin American and not. This is opposed to Martin and Anthony, who emphasized both Puerto Rican music and their Puerto Rican identity. Ironically, Martin's and Anthony's identifications as Puerto Rican accompany a rejection of their birth names: Enrique Martin Morales and Marco Antonio Muñiz. In spite of pushing what many describe as a homogenized notion of Latinidad, Lopez herself felt uncomfortable with the categories of Latino pop explosion and crossover. "I didn't like the way they used 'crossing over' because it made it sound like we just came over to this country."[4] Lopez makes a good point. Often the artists associated with the boom were labeled "crossover." This implies that the artist crosses over from Latin America, which would apply only to Shakira. In spite of her criticism of the Latin music boom, Lopez milked it for everything that it was worth, becoming the most high-profile Latina pop artist. Her use of hip-hop and rap was a means of expanding her musical audiences, and popular rap artists were featured prominently in various remixes of her songs. Ironically, this was a tactic used by her alter ego Selena, who incorporated cumbia into her musical repertoire as a way to tap into African music and broaden her Latina/Latin American appeal.

Most cultural studies and Latino/a theoretical texts on Lopez focus on her role as Selena. Lopez's much celebrated depiction of Selena is a point of praise and contention. It is interpreted as a case study for understanding Latinidad and is often couched in a critique of hegemonic constructions of Latino/a identity. Interestingly, it is an appeal to universal Latina identity that Lopez used to justify her role as Selena. Lopez argued that her common experience as a Latina was "enough" for her to play Selena. She did not need to be Mexican. Her shared Latinidad legitimized her role as Latina. The construction of Latinidad that emerges from the Selena/Lopez dyad is one that emphasizes bilingualism, the arts, and a close connection with "the people." In her article on Lopez as Selena, Aparicio argues that Latinidad does not have to be constructed as either a means of homogenization or a site for cultural

3. Frances R. Aparicio, "Jennifer as Selena: Rethinking Latinidad in Media and Popular Culture," *Latino Studies* 1 (2003): 92.

4. "J.Lo.: Success Makes the Best Revenge," *Hispanic* (June 2002): 40.

wars. Instead, she understands Latinidad "as a concept that allows us to explore moments of convergences and differences in the formation of Latino/a (post)colonial subjectivities and in hybrid cultural expressions among various Latino national groups." For Aparicio, Latinidad becomes a "decolonial imaginary," where

> we are constructing interlatino knowledge that allows Latino/as from various groups to understand their Latino counterparts, a knowledge that itself represents an alternative discourse given the silenced knowledge about each other that has been our educational legacy; secondly, an approach to "Latinidad" that searches for the analogous (post)colonial conditions and experiences among the various national groups allows us to appropriate the exhausted term to reinvigorate it with an oppositional, decolonizing ideology that will be much more liberatory than previous approaches to the term have yielded.[5]

In her response to Aparicio's article, Alicia Gaspar de Alba agrees, arguing that J.Lo. as Selena is not hegemonic but instead embodies "the very cultural, linguistic, and racial affinities the historical realities of colonialism, mestizaje, linguistic terrorism, cultural schizophrenia, territorial displacement, and organic feminism that connect not just the bodies of these two women, but Chicanas and Latinas at large."[6]

As her fame grew, Lopez moved away from her pan-Latina identity to a more Puerto Rican/Nuyorican sense of self. Her 2003 J.Lo. clothing line prominently featured the Puerto Rican flag on various tank tops and shirts. She was grand marshal of the New York Puerto Rican parade along with her fellow Nuyorican husband at the time, Mark Anthony. This shift to emphasize her Puerto Rican roots parallels her marriage to Anthony (who was born in 1968 in NYC and grew up in Spanish Harlem). Also, one of her most recent films, *El Cantante*, focuses on Puerto Rican singer Hector Lavoe and premiered in San Juan.[7] In a 2002 interview Lopez emphasized her connection to her Puerto Rican, working-class, Bronx roots: "People ask me all the time how do I stay connected, and I always tell them, 'How could I not?' It's who I am, and it manifests itself in everything I do. It's something you can't leave behind. I'm Jennifer Lopez, and I am a Puerto Rican from the Bronx."[8] Lopez's celebration of

5. Aparicio, "Jennifer as Selena," 93–94.

6. Alicia Gaspar de Alba, "The Chicana/Latina Dyad, or Identity and Perception," *Latino Studies* 1 (2003): 106–14.

7. Licia Fiol-Matta, "Pop *Latinidad*: Puerto Ricans in the Latin Explosion, 1999," *Centro Journal* 14, no. 1 (Spring 2002): 27–51.

8. "J.Lo.: Success Makes the Best Revenge," 40.

her Latinidad is a double-edged sword, however, for at times she feeds into what Frances Aparicio and Susana Chávez have labeled the *hegemonic tropicalization* of Latino/as. This term refers to the hegemonic construction of Latino/as as exotic other, constructing Latinas as brown, voluptuous women.[9] Lopez presents a mixed bag, simultaneously affirming and challenging stereotypes about Hispanic culture and Latina social roles.

Jennifer's Butt

When she first entered the scene, it seemed like the only thing people could talk about was Jennifer's butt. Her body mattered—not her talent; not her ability to dance, act, and sing; not even her face mattered. All everyone wanted to talk about was her body, more specifically, her butt. Lopez's body is a public site where Latina sexuality and Latina bodies are constructed, exploited, and celebrated. Even though Lopez has undergone a radical transformation since her earlier career, appearing much leaner and blonder than she did in the mid-1990s, her body remains foundational for her success.

Lopez made a name for herself in her adamant rejection of idealized Hollywood body types and her very public celebration of her buttocks. When promoting *Selena*, the actress famously stood up during an interview when asked if she padded her clothing, did a 360, patted her rear end, and stated, "*Todo es mio.*" In a 1998 *Time* magazine interview with Joel Stein, Lopez is quoted as saying, "In general, ethnic men like big butts."[10] Jennifer spent the first years of her career not only presenting the world her butt, shaking it, posing in magazines with it in our faces, but also arguing that men of color are, essentially, "ass men." The media had a field day. In her study of Jennifer Lopez, Mary C. Beltrán notes that the English media or *gringolandia* presentation of Lopez was much more sexualized than the Spanish-language version. While in English publications Lopez often appeared in overtly sexual poses, a more demure Lopez graced the covers and pages of publications such as *People en Español*.[11] Aparicio argues that both Selena's and J.Lo.'s bodies are sites of struggle where hegemonic constructions of beauty are created.

9. Frances Apiricio and Susana Chávez, "Introduction," in *Tropicalizations: Transcultural Representations of Latinidad* (Hanover, NH: University Press of New England, 1997), 1–17.

10. Joel Stein, "Jennifer Lopez," *Time* (October 5, 1998).

11. Mary C. Beltrán, "The Hollywood Latina Body as a Site of Social Struggle: Media Constructions of Stardom and Jennifer Lopez's 'Cross-over Butt,'" *Quarterly Review of Film and Video* 18 (2002): 71–86.

"Both bodies were public enactments and physical embodiments of simultaneous colonial desire and subaltern resistance."[12] Both women rejected anorexic, Anglo, white stereotypes about beauty yet at the same time struggled to accept and embrace their own bodies.

Big or not, Jennifer's butt is before us and she is, unquestionably, a "trend setter in early twenty-first century body politics."[13] I don't know if Shakira and Beyoncé would have been able to shake it in our faces had Lopez not done so first. To embrace the butt and the body is an empowering act. As bell hooks notes, the celebration of the butt is fundamental to African American hip-hop culture. "It was really the song 'Doin' the Butt' that challenged dominant ways of thinking about the body which encourage us to ignore asses because they are associated with undesirable and unclean acts."[14] In other words, in celebrating the butt, one rejects the demonization of the butt. As Frances Negrón-Muntaner notes, Jennifer's celebration of her butt is a celebration of Latino/a culture:

> I would take Jennifer's praise of the ass further, and propose it as a way of popularizing an "attitude" in relation to dominant culture, more like "kiss my ass" after having one's "ass kicked" for being Puerto Rican and/or Latino. . . . A big culo does not only upset hegemonic (white) notions of beauty and good taste, it is a sign for the dark, incomprehensible excess of "Latino" and other African diaspora cultures. Excess of food (unrestrained), excess of shitting (dirty), and excess of sex (heathen) are its three vital signs.[15]

Ultimately, however, big or small, celebrated or hidden, the emphasis on Jennifer's body still reduces her to the sexualized male gaze. She is still an object of male sexuality.

Do Latinas want to be reduced broadly to our bodies and, more specifically, to our butts? While this liberates me from my morally repressed Catholic upbringing in a household that pretended that sexuality was nonexistent, do I become imprisoned in a more dangerous stereotype? As Sandra Cisneros so wonderfully begins her essay "Guadalupe Sex Goddess," "In high school I marveled at how white women strutted

12. Aparicio, "Jennifer as Selena," 99.

13. Angharad N. Valdivia, "The Location of the Spanish in Latinidad: Examples from Contemporary U.S. Popular Culture," *Letras Femininas* 31, no. 1 (Summer 2005): 66.

14. bell hooks, "Selling Hot Pussy," *Black Looks: Race and Representation* (Boston, MA: South End Press, 1992), 64.

15. Frances Negrón-Muntaner, "Jennifer's Butt," *Aztlan* 22, no. 2 (Fall 1997): 187 and 189.

around the locker room, nude as pearls, as unashamed of their brilliant bodies as the Nike of Samonthráce. . . . You could always tell us Latinas. We hid when we undressed, modestly facing a wall, or, in my case, dressing in a bathroom stall. . . . In the guise of modesty my culture locked me in a double chastity belt of ignorance and *vergüenza*, shame."[16] Or, as bell hooks argues, is drawing attention to the body subverting the white gaze for a Latina gaze a form of empowerment?[17]

Jennifer's Hair

Lopez cemented her identity as J.Lo. with the release of her second album. This was the culmination of her hip-hop persona. In the late 1990s Lopez appeared as the ultimate crossover artist. I do not mean "crossover" in the sense of from Anglo to Latino/a; I mean "crossover" as in Latino/a to African American. She bridged both worlds through her music, fashion, and personal life. Then came the song "I'm Real," where Lopez, a nonblack woman, dared to say "nigga." The elevated status she had within the black community left her when her relationship with rapper Sean Combs ended, and while she is Latina, she is not black. As Karen Grigsby Bates thoughtfully points out, "Although she is a woman of color, she is not black, and whatever NBA status that had been conferred upon Lopez by her relationship with rap impresario Sean Puffy Combs was rescinded when she and P. Diddy went pfftttt!"[18] In an interview on the *Today* show, Lopez expressed confusion and hurt for being singled out.

After her breakup with Combs and the incident with the N-word, Lopez began to slowly ease herself out of the hip-hop world and find a home in a more Anglo environment. This is exemplified by her movie roles and her love life. It is also exemplified by her hair. When she was a Fly Girl, Lopez sported a short curly boy cut. Early in her movie career she sported dark hair, often worn curly. During her relationship with Combs, she began to add caramel highlights, though her hair remained

16. Sandra Cisneros, "Guadalupe the Sex Goddess," in *Goddess of the Americas*, ed. Ana Castillo (New York: Riverhead Books, 1996), 25.

17. "There is power in looking. . . . The 'gaze' has been and is a site of resistance for colonized black people globally. . . . In resistance struggle, the power of the dominated to assert agency by claiming and cultivating 'awareness' politicizes 'looking' relations—one learns to look a certain way in order to resist" (bell hooks, "The Oppositional Gaze," *Black Looks*, 115–16).

18. Karen Grigsby Bates, "Review of *Nigger: The Strange History of a Troublesome Word; The Filthiest, Dirtiest, Nastiest Word in the English Language*," *Journal of Blacks in Higher Education* 35 (April 2002): 128–29.

dark. In fact, in the video for "Love Don't Cost a Thing" she sports cornrows, and she then made several media appearances with them in her hair. After her breakup with Combs, however, we saw a definite lightening of her hair, which is now always ironed straight.

Hair is just hair, right? Only fashion? Wrong. Hair, especially for Puerto Ricans, is a, if not *the*, marker of racial identity. Negrón-Muntaner argues that, for Puerto Ricans, it is hair texture and not skin color that is the primary racial designator. Her article centers on the outrage that ensued on the island of Puerto Rico when Puerto Rican Barbie came out—a doll with straight hair.[19] Puerto Ricans did not react to the doll's skin tone or outfit; instead, they were insulted that a Puerto Rican Barbie would have straight hair, thus encouraging young Puerto Rican girls to iron their hair. It is, therefore, quite significant that the more famous Lopez became, the blonder she became. Similarly, Shakira dyed her hair blonde when she released her English-language "crossover" album. Since Lopez has married Anthony, released a Spanish language album, and toured with her now-ex-husband, a more Puerto Rican, darker-haired Latina Lopez has reemerged.

Aesthetics from the Block

Theological aesthetics is a growing area in contemporary theology. Though not necessarily a theological "school" or "field" per se, those authors working on theological aesthetics constitute a conversation or particular theological style grounded in their concern for beauty.[20] An emphasis on the aesthetic is grounded in the belief that within the realm of symbol, imagination, emotion, and art one finds a privileged expression

19. Frances Negrón-Muntaner, "Barbie's Hair: Selling Our Puerto Rican Identity in the Global Market," in *Latino/a Popular Culture*, ed. Michelle Habell-Pallán and Mary Romero (New York: New York University Press, 2002), 44. Here, she is building on the work of anthropologist Sidney Mintz, who states, "Puerto Rican cultural standards for racial identity appear to place the most weight on hair type, less on skin color" (see Sidney Mintz, "Cañamelas: The Subculture of a Rural Sugar Plantation Proletariat," in *The People of Puerto Rico: A Study in Social Anthropology*, ed. Julián H. Steward et al. [Urbana: University of Illinois, 1956], 410).

20. Theological aesthetics holds that in the encounter with beauty there is an experience of the Divine. As defined by Richard Viladesau, "What is meant by 'theological aesthetics' in its wide sense is the practice of theology, conceived in terms of any of these three objects, in relation to any of the three objects . . . God, religion, and theology in relation to sensible knowledge (sensation, imagination, feeling), the beautiful, the arts." See *Theological Aesthetics: God in Imagination, Beauty, and Art* (New York: Oxford University Press, 1999), 11.

of the encounter with the Divine and its articulation.[21] Latino/a theologians have been at the forefront of this movement. Roberto S. Goizueta sees the role of aesthetics as integral and organic to Latino/a theology: "If Tridentine Western theology stressed the fact that God is known in the form of the True (Doctrine), and liberation theology that God is known in the form of the Good (Justice), U.S. Hispanic theology stresses the fact that God is known in the form of the Beautiful."[22] Through their work on aesthetics, these theologians transform the methodology of Latino/a theology and broaden the dialogue partners of Latino/a theologians.[23]

For the scholar of Latin American and Caribbean religion the arts are a fundamental starting point. This is not because there is not a rich intellectual tradition. There is. Nevertheless, this intellectual and ecclesial tradition emerges primarily from the eyes of the conquerors, the missionaries, the Europeans. In order to uncover the history of African and indigenous religions in the Caribbean and Latin America, other sources must be utilized. Indeed, even to uncover the authentic history of the Latin American church one cannot rely exclusively on intellectual and ecclesial history. We also need to tap into the lived religious history of

21. Margaret Miles argues that the textual history of Christianity must be recognized for its elitism as it is written by culturally privileged, male, and upper-class authors. Margaret R. Miles, *Image as Insight: Visual Understanding in Western Christianity and Secular Culture* (Boston: Beacon Press, 1985), 9. In the area of Latino/a theology, Orlando Espín argues that study of Latino/a popular Catholicism is an avenue for retrieving the theology of the masses excluded from the canons of textual theological history. Orlando O. Espín, *The Faith of the People: Theological Reflections on Popular Catholicism* (New York: Orbis, 1997).

22. Roberto S. Goizueta, *Caminemos con Jesús: A Hispanic/Latino Theology of Accompaniment* (Maryknoll, NY: Orbis Books, 1995), 106. For more on Latino/a theological aesthetics, see Peter J. Casarella, "The Painted Word," *Journal of Hispanic/Latino Theology* 6, no. 2 (November 1998): 18–42; Alejandro García-Rivera, *The Community of the Beautiful: A Theological Aesthetics* (Collegeville, MN: Liturgical Press, 1999); Jeanette Rodríguez-Holguín, "La Tierra: Home, Identity, and Destiny," in *From the Heart of Our People: Latino/a Explorations in Catholic Systematic Theology*, ed. Orlando Espín and Miguel Díaz (Maryknoll, NY: Orbis Books, 1999), 189–208.

23. Linked to the body is the role of the aesthetic within Latino/a theology. Through the work of García-Rivera, Goizueta, Casarella, and me, theological aesthetics has become a vital component of Latino/a theological reflection. The theological aesthetics of Alejandro García-Rivera combines Hans Urs von Balthasar, North American philosophy, and semiotics. García-Rivera understands the true, the good, and the beautiful in terms of communities. Charles Sanders Peirce and Josiah Royce provide the philosophical framework for this task. The aesthetic principle that emerges from this interweaving of voices is the lifting of the lowly, a subversive aesthetic norm with ethical implications. García-Rivera's publication on a theology of art furthers his aesthetics and expands his sources to include the visual arts.

Latin Americans and Latino/a peoples. As noted by Alejandro García-Rivera, "Theology lives in the music, imagery, and cultural symbols of those who must live out that which 'textbook theology' attempts to understand. . . . Textbook theology dissects while living theology appreciates. Textbook theology provides understanding of the parts; living theology lets us appreciate the whole."[24] The word "living" is fundamental here. Too often, the study of religion has focused on the texts of religious traditions versus the lived religious practices. This lived religion is found in the symbols, rituals, and everyday practices of devotees. García-Rivera's insight, one that I wholeheartedly agree with, is that we must expand our theological sources and conversation partners in order to get at the heart of living religion.

Studies of popular culture as a starting point for theological reflection shift us away from what I would argue is the excessively ecclesiological emphasis of Latino/a theology. While I realize that Catholic theology must be rooted in Catholicism and that the ecclesial context must be central to our work, it does not need to be the only center. It concerns me that many excellent Latino/a theologians are not relevant dialogue partners outside of the discipline of theology. I am also worried about our ability to address the issues and concerns of those Latino/as who do not fall neatly into the ecclesiological realm. Similarly, popular culture is an important resource for Latino/a theological aesthetics. The fusion of African American and Latino/a culture is a reality in the popular realm, and yet there is this standstill in the theological world. If we are going to take aesthetics seriously, we must not only incorporate high art and religious ritual but also admit that the appeal of popular culture to the masses is something worthy of our theological speculation.

As I mentioned in my introductory comments, this is not a constructive theological reflection on Jennifer Lopez. Lopez and religion are rarely uttered in the same breath. Her father is a Scientologist, but she has always claimed and embraced her Catholic upbringing. She does not, however, use religious imagery in her music videos, lyrics, or as an element of her public persona. There were rumors during her breakup to Ben Affleck that she was visiting a *sanetera* for spiritual advice, but these were never substantiated. Unlike other pop artists who at times interweave religion into their image, lyrics, and personas, Lopez does not go that route.

24. García-Rivera, *A Wounded Innocence: Sketches for a Theology of Art* (Collegeville, MN: Liturgical Press, 2003), viii.

In spite of the lack of a strong religious presence associated with Lopez, I do contend that a serious study of Lopez in light of Latino/a cultural studies and theory can help nuance our theological discourse. In the first area discussed in this paper, Latinidad, it is clear that Lopez as Selena pushed and continues to push the question of authentic Latinidad. This is a lingering question for Latino/a theologians, who continue to struggle to articulate a sense of Latino/a identity without eclipsing the particularity of distinctive Latino/a communities. I would like to return to the question of whether an authentic Latino/a or Hispanic actually exists ontologically, or if Latino/as are merely a socio-political construction.

In her article on Lopez as Selena, Aparicio presents the dyad as a site for constructive Latino/a identity construction. She presents two extremes in which Latinidad is often depicted. First, Latinidad is often constructed as a site of struggle between Latino/a groups fighting over attention, resources, and voice. The second manner in which Latinidad is critiqued is as a homogenizing force that negates the diversity of Latino/a peoples. Again, this is not new to Latino/a theologians. Latino/a theology is dominated by the heavy influence of Mexican American religious expressions. In my own scholarship I have described this as the "Mexicanization" of Latino/a theology, where Our Lady of Guadalupe, *mestizaje*, and the border have become normative concepts.[25] This is ironic, given that a significant number of Latino/a theologians are of Caribbean descent. Latinidad becomes a site of contention when one national group among Latino/as becomes the overwhelming face of Latino/a identity and religion as a whole. What is important for us to consider, however, is a positive construction of Latinidad that creates a space for us to learn about our communities and dialogue among each other, creating what Aparicio describes as "interlatino knowledge," which can infuse our theological, political, and social commitments.

Once upon a time I am pretty sure I wrote that Latino/as do not exist ontologically. If I didn't write it, I certainly taught it. Now I am not so sure. As the mother of two Guatemalan Cuban Americans who live in Miami, I am starting to think Latino/as do exist. Not to diminish our culture to food, but in my house we eat *picadillo* and *tortillas*, and my sons will understand their culture and identity not as one part Cuban and the other Guatemalan but as a whole that is the world in which they inhabit. They will be, essentially and ontologically, Latino. I also would argue that, for better or worse, Latino/a culture and perhaps

25. Michelle A. Gonzalez, *Afro-Cuban Theology: Race, Religion, Culture, and Identity* (Gainesville: University Press of Florida, 2006).

even Latino/a religion do exist. Yes we have rituals and devotions that are quite specific to our national roots. We are, however, also starting to see a level of hybridity within Latino/a religious practices that must be addressed in our scholarship.

Theological reflections on embodiment and sexuality also emerge from a study of Lopez. Catholic theologians must engage the extremely twisted, hypocritical, and misogynistic historical tradition when it comes to bodies in general and women's bodies in particular. We are part of a religious tradition that celebrates sacramentality and the incarnation, yet through the centuries the body is presented as an impediment to our relationship with the sacred. For women, our bodies are the barrier to the priesthood and, in the words of some theologians, such as Augustine, our ability to authentically reflect the *imago Dei*. Whether it is reducing women to mothers or to objects of sexual and moral temptation, Catholicism does not often promote a healthy understanding of the body and sexuality.

Feminist theologians highlight the body as a site and expression of their relationship with God. Recovering the body is a central feminist theological task. This recovery is nuanced by an acknowledgment that when the female body is the focus of theological reflection, this body is often reduced to sex. So the female body is emphasized in terms of biological reproduction and, consequently, motherhood, or the body becomes sexual temptation. Feminists, therefore, want to overcome this dualism and present female bodies as an authentic reflection of women's image of God and a means of expressing their relationship with the sacred. A study of Lopez puts the body, and specifically the butt, right in our faces. This other extreme is to some just as unsettling perhaps as the more traditional understandings of the body. Lopez and her butt celebrate the Latina body as beautiful. Lopez's emphasis on her curves undermines a white Anglo aesthetics that constructs beauty in terms of fair skin, painfully thin bodies, and blonde hair. Lopez's celebration of her body can also be seen, however, as a reduction of Latinas to their bodies, a common stereotype operating in Anglo popular culture. Lopez challenges us to examine the construction of Latina sexuality in a serious and theological manner. I am not content with and am extremely critical of the construction of sexuality in the dominant Catholic theological and ethical tradition that is operative in many Latino/a communities. An alternative must be offered.

Theological aesthetics offers a rich entry point into embodiment through its emphasis on the materiality of life. This, in turn, reveals a Roman Catholic sacramental imagination concerning the organic unity of the material and spiritual worlds. The material world participates in the sacred and is not merely an impediment to it (as is often the case when the body is discussed). It is ironic that a religion that emphasizes the importance of the historical embodiment of its savior is so ambiguous about women's bodies. Women's bodies are often reduced to objects of desire, lust, and temptation that must be controlled by male authority. Through their retrieval of the body, feminist theologians transform a dimension of our humanity that was once the source of women's marginalization into a site of the *imago Dei*.

In her overview of the feminist theoretical concerns that inform feminist theology, Mary Ann Zimmer notes that the body has always been a central concern for feminist theorists: "This is true partly because women have often been identified with the bodily aspects of being human while men have been assigned the project of transcending the body through culture and thought."[26] The body, feminists note, is always devalued, and reason comes to symbolize the essence of humanity. Because of women's historical and contemporary association with the body, this is of vital concern for feminist theologians. Questions that plague feminist writings on this topic are: What difference does it make that human persons are embodied? What difference does it make that bodies are gendered? Ultimately, as Lisa Cahill points out, "The issue for contemporary feminists is whether, in a nondualistic perspective, the differential embodiment of men and women must be assumed to make a difference in their way of being in the world, even if not a difference which implies hierarchy, or even very extensive or firmly demarcated role allocation."[27] Feminist theologians must wrestle with the theological value of the body and the role of distinctive embodiment as male or female within theological anthropology.

Susan Ross argues that one can have neither an essentialist nor an engendered understanding of the body. Through their scholarship, feminists challenge three interpretations of the body: the dualistic construction of the body and mind; the liberal emphasis on the universality of humanity and insignificance of the body for this position, which ignores

---

26. Mary Ann Zimmer, "Stepping Stones in Feminist Theory," in *In the Embrace of God: Feminist Approaches to Theological Anthropology*, ed. Ann O'Hara Graf (Maryknoll, NY: Orbis Books, 1995), 17. For an excellent study of the relationship between embodiment and holiness within historical Christianity, see Peter Brown, *The Body and Society: Men, Women, and Sexual Renunciation in Early Christianity* (New York: Columbia University Press, 1988).

27. Lisa Cahill, *Sex, Gender, and Christian Ethics* (Cambridge: Cambridge University Press, 1996), 84.

concrete contexts and inadvertently normalizes male experience; and essentialist constructions of masculine and feminine nature. She explores the ambiguity surrounding the body within Christian theology:

> The understandings of the body that have emerged over two thousand years of Catholic tradition's history are complex. On the one hand, the Christian tradition has affirmed the goodness of creation and, in the doctrine of the incarnation, has declared that God's very being has become inevitably connected with embodiment. . . . But on the other hand, the tradition's ambivalence toward, and sometimes even hatred of, the body is as much a part of its history as is its reverence of it.[28]

The body is both vilified and glorified within the Christian tradition. When it is vilified, however, it is most often linked to women. The ambiguity surrounding the body mirrors, in many ways, the ambiguous views of women throughout Christian theology, where they are both celebrated and disparaged.

Conclusion

Jennifer Lopez provides an ideal locus for my ongoing research on the significance of black culture for understanding Latino/a religion and the fact that we need increased dialogue and collaborations between black and Latino/a theologians. This is a dynamic element of Latino/a popular culture.

A serious consideration of pop culture icons such as Lopez opens up new conversations for feminist theological aesthetics. The reduction of Lopez to her body is a point of tension for Latinas who are often reduced to their bodies. Similarly, the introduction of hair, in addition to skin tone, as a racial marker expands narrow constructions of race and also highlights the fluidity of racial identity for Latino/as in the United States. Lopez's body, at the intersection of theology, the media, and racial politics, challenges reductionist constructions of identity. In addition, topics such as the theology of hair, clothing, and popular culture are exciting new possibilities for feminist theological aesthetics, ones that could push us to more deeply understand the theology of the body in its contemporary ethno-political context.

28. Susan A. Ross, *Extravagant Affections: A Feminist Sacramental Theology* (New York: Continuum, 1998), 102–3.

Laurie Cassidy

Picturing Suffering
The Moral Dilemmas in Gazing at Photographs of Human Anguish[1]

In contemporary North American culture the knowledge of human suffering is often dependent solely on visual images. Photographs present a problem for Christian social ethics because their function in relationship to suffering human beings is often ambiguous.[2] These images can bring much-needed attention to persons in anguish while sometimes simultaneously exploiting these persons. The popular assumption is that photographs document an "on-the-spot eyewitness account" of reality. To accept these images as simply "pictures of the real" ignores the institutions of power and systems of oppression that condition how photography mediates this reality.[3] I argue that photographs are

1. This essay is a version of my article, "Picturing Suffering: The Moral Dilemmas in Gazing at Photographs of Human Anguish," *Horizons* 37, no. 2 (Fall 2010): 195–223, which is reprinted here with the kind permission of the journal.

2. "When a situation is marked by ambiguity, its resolution is unclear: there is more than one possible solution, more than one meaning. It is often marked by tension, as competing resolutions are suggested by those involved. In between order and chaos, ambiguity demands further reflection, consideration of new and different outcomes, decisions on what issues are at stake in its resolution" (Susan Ross, *Extravagant Affections: A Feminist Sacramental Theology* [New York: Continuum, 1998], 69).

3. "[T]he institutional uses of photography makes us think photographs are truthful pictures, not photographic techniques themselves. . . . Foucault's emphasis on institutions and power/knowledge is crucial for understanding the belief that photography pictures the real" (Gillian Rose, *Visual Methodologies: An Introduction to the Interpretation of Visual Materials* [London: Sage Publications, 2001], 167).

cultural texts whose assumptions and meanings are often unclear in regard to what they say about suffering human beings and what they imply about the causes of and responses to their plight. To ignore these deeply imbedded meanings may be to erase the suffering subjects of history and their claim upon us.

My major thesis is this: *Photographs of suffering human beings must be questioned in order to determine what they imply about the causes and responses to human anguish.* The necessity of questioning photographs of suffering is grounded in Christianity's root metaphor of *imago Dei*, which holds out an imperative to realize the dignity and radical sociality of viewer and viewed.

My essay proceeds as follows. First, I will introduce the moral problem of viewing a photograph of human suffering by exploring the complex process of viewing from the standpoint of the viewer. A fundamental assumption of my work is the powerful and provocative way that photographs offer knowledge of human suffering to the imagination, not directly to rational thought. The image and the complex process of viewing are often unconscious and taken for granted because we see the picture as a window on reality, not a constructed image communicating a message about reality. The experience of viewing a photograph is assumed to offer a new factual account or documentation of reality, but rather this process of viewing can reinforce commonsense understandings of people and situations.

Second, I will draw on visual-cultural studies to demonstrate the morally ambiguous character of photographs of human suffering. This field of study offers Christian social ethics a variety of tools to interrogate how photographs are part of processes of cultural representation, which deeply condition the knowledge of human suffering. Here, my purpose is limited: I utilize these resources to analyze Kevin Carter's 1994 Pulitzer Prize–winning photo of a Sudanese child. Through my analysis of this image I will illustrate that photographs are not a literal depiction of suffering but rather a "reflection of or response to—social, political and economic processes."[4]

Third, drawing upon the fundamental principle of *imago Dei*, I will argue that questioning photographs of suffering human beings functions to deconstruct the moral character of the representation in relationship to the imperative of human dignity and to reconstruct the ties that bind the viewer to the viewed as a human being with a claim on the viewer's shared humanity. Questioning photographs of suffering human beings

---

4. Margaret Dikovitskaya, *Visual Culture* (Cambridge, MA: MIT Press, 2005), 1.

creates the possibility of realizing the dignity and radical sociality of being made in the image and likeness of God.

The Power of Gaze

The dynamics of power involved in gazing and being gazed upon may be the most difficult element of vision of which to be consciously aware. Visual-cultural studies points out that to look, to gaze, at photographs suggests that the viewer is a spectator. In many cases, particularly in relationship to photographs of suffering, being a spectator implies more power than being the object of the gaze.[5] The person who gazes is the subject of agency, one who can act. The one who is gazed upon is captured in the frame of the photograph as the object.

In the case of photographs of suffering, the one who gazes is never seen, never in the "picture." The person suffering, however, never leaves the frame of reference of suffering:

> In other words . . . as a member of a community whose primary relationship to suffering is as a *spectator*, as those whose relationship to suffering might be summarized as: we can take it for granted that our life does not include certain kinds of suffering; we are at a distance from those who suffer; the visible suffering of others is available to us as a means to reflect on our own lives and subjectivities?[6]

This provocative question by Anna Szorenyi orients my inquiry into gaze. In this section I will explore how this often barely conscious role as a spectator informs our understanding of the suffering we view in photographs. I will argue that our passive and uncritical gaze upon suffering human beings in photographs may reinscribe the role of viewer as spectator and "normalize" the suffering of the humans upon whom we gaze.[7] This divide between spectator and "sufferer," between agent

---

5. Marita Sturken and Lisa Cartwright, *Practices of Looking: An Introduction to Visual Culture* (New York: Oxford University Press, 2001), 88.

6. Anna Szorenyi, "Distanced Suffering: Photographed Suffering and the Construction of White in/vulnerability," *Social Semiotics* 19, no. 2 (June 2009): 94.

7. Here, I will limit my use of the term "spectator" and "spectacle" in this article. To draw upon these ideas points to a body of literature that is beyond the scope of this article. Marita Sturken and Lisa Cartwright define "spectacle" as "a term that generally refers to something that is striking or impressive in its visual display." These scholars point out that a spectacle will "dominate contemporary culture and *all social relations are mediated by and through these images*" (*Practices of Looking*, 366; my emphasis). The term "spectacle" was employed in a specific way in 1967 in

and object, subverts the fundamental claim and responsibility of the dignity and radical sociality of being made in God's image and likeness. To realize dignity and radical sociality, the task of the viewer is to make visible the privilege that masks shared human vulnerability with the suffering human being in the photograph.

The act of gazing involves looking steadily with intention.[8] bell hooks describes how children learn that gazing has power. Children are scolded by parents either because their gaze is defiant or their stare is rude. hooks notes, however, that when being punished the child is told, "Look at me when I talk to you."[9] hooks elaborates on the power of looking by noting that enslaved black people in America could not look at white masters directly; they were punished for gazing upon white people. Who could gaze and who was looked upon constituted

---

Guy Debord's seminal work, *Society of the Spectacle*, trans. Donald Nickolson-Smith (New York: Zone Books, 1994). Stuart Hall's work brilliantly uses this concept to interrogate the dynamics of racist cultural representation. See Stuart Hall, "The Spectacle of the 'Other,'" in *Representation: Cultural Representations and Signifying Practices*, ed. Stuart Hall (Thousand Oaks, CA: Sage, 1997), 223–90. To understand the dynamic of spectacle in relation to visual-cultural studies currently, see W. J. T. Mitchell, *What Do Pictures Want: The Lives and Loves of Images* (Chicago: University of Chicago Press, 2005). For a fascinating introduction to this issue, see Larry Gross, "Privacy and Spectacle: The Reversible Panopticon and Media Saturated Society," in *Image Ethics in the Digital Age*, ed. Larry Gross, John Stuart Katz, and Jay Ruby (Minneapolis: University of Minnesota Press, 2003), 95–113. Spectacle and spectator are referring to social roles and processes of power. My use of this language is limited in this essay to denote the powerful social role the viewer has in gazing upon an image of suffering and not having to act in relationship to this anguish. See also Lillie Chouliaraki, *The Spectatorship of Suffering* (Thousand Oaks, CA: Sage, 2006).

8. "Gaze" is defined as "to look steadily, intently, and with fixed intention" (*The American Heritage College Dictionary* [Boston: Houghton Mifflin, 1993], 565). The term "gaze" within visual-cultural studies is multifaceted and imbedded in a rich and interdisciplinary body of literature, including film theory, feminist theory, literary criticism, and psychoanalytic thought. For the purposes of this essay, I am using the term to connote the power relationship of the one who looks. Here, I am drawing upon Michel Foucault's idea that gaze is not only something a person does but a relationship of power into which one enters through the mechanism of vision in society as a whole. See Michel Foucault, "The Eye of Power," in *Power/Knowledge: Selected Interviews and Other Writings 1972–1977*, ed. C. Gordon (New York: Pantheon, 1980); Michel Foucault, *Discipline and Punish: The Birth of Prison*, trans. Alan Sheridan (New York: Vintage, 1979). For a clear overview of the idea of gaze and power in visual-cultural studies, see Marita Sturken and Lisa Cartwright, "Spectatorship, Power, and Knowledge," in *Practices of Looking*, 72–108.

9. bell hooks, *Black Looks: Race and Representation* (Boston: South End Press, 1992), 115.

relationships of dominance and subordination. Gaze in this social context reinscribed subject and object positions for white masters and black slaves. "The politics of slavery, of racialized power relations, were such that slaves were denied their right to gaze."[10] bell hooks's writing deftly illustrates the core insight of visual-cultural studies with regard to looking at photographs of suffering. The issue of gaze concerns not only the act of looking itself but, more important, how gaze constitutes power relationships.

Scholars of documentary photography argue that the gaze of privilege is imbedded in the unequal power relations that are intrinsic to the structure of documentary photojournalism. Martha Rosler contends that documentary photography is presenting the "powerless" to the group addressed as "powerful."[11] The structure of the relationship of viewer and viewed is that the one who gazes is observing the unfortunate. The photo creates a "perch" from which we can both get up close and be far away at the same time.[12] Those who look do not directly share the experience and are therefore regarded as "lucky."[13]

The roots of documentary photojournalism reveal how power relationships are constitutive of the production and viewing of photographs of human anguish. The work of Walker Evans, James Agee, Margaret Bourke-White, and Dorothea Lange demonstrate this privilege of the viewer in documentary photojournalism.[14] Dorothea Lange's iconic image, "Migrant Mother," illustrates this privileged perspective and how it functions in documenting suffering. Lange's photo of a migrant farm–working mother surrounded by her children in California has become iconic in portraying the poverty of white, working-poor people during the Depression.[15] One function of the photograph was to give a face to a news story that described the reality of the New Deal in

10. Ibid.

11. Martha Rosler, "In, Around and Afterthoughts (On Documentary Photography)," in *The Contest of Meaning: Critical Histories of Photography*, ed. Richard Bolton (Cambridge, MA: MIT Press, 1989), 321.

12. Ibid., 23.

13. Luc Botalski, *Distant Suffering: Morality, Media and Politics*, trans. Graham Burchill (Cambridge: Cambridge University Press, 1999), 3.

14. See, further, William Scott, *Documentary Expression in Thirties America* (Chicago: University of Chicago Press, 1973); James Agee and Walker Evans, *Let Us Now Praise Famous Men* (Boston: Houghton Mifflin, 1941); Margaret Bourke-White, *You Have Seen Their Faces* (New York: Simon and Schuster, 1937).

15. For historical background on this photograph, see Robert Hariman and John Luis Lucaites, *No Caption Required: Iconic Photographs, Public Culture, and Liberal Democracy* (Chicago: University of Chicago Press, 2007), 49–67.

California.[16] The emotionally evocative power of the image crossed geographic and economic barriers, making an appeal to shared humanity among Americans. The photograph invoked compassion, "an impulse to help that crosses social boundaries."[17] The viewer, to whom this photo appeals, does not share the same anguish but is invited from within his or her privilege to be aware of, understand, and help those who are suffering.

The problem is that this mediated knowledge is rooted in what Shawn Copeland calls the "ocular epistemological illusion."[18] This illusion "equates knowing with simply looking at that which is visible."[19] The problem with the visual as a basis for knowledge is that "such a foundation for knowing is easily seduced to support the Eurocentric aesthetic 'normative gaze' with its attendant racist, sexist, imperialist, and pornographic connotations."[20]

In other words, the illusion of this gaze is that the knowledge generated from this viewpoint is reality, not a mediated picture of reality. This gaze is inherently privileged because this gaze assumes a universalizing capacity in knowing the world without accounting for any of the layers of mediation that have created the representation before one's eyes.

This privileged gaze holds a dangerously ironic twist in regard to "knowledge" of suffering human beings. David Theo Goldberg writes that this gaze gives the viewer the illusion of knowing while the person—and the reality of his or her suffering—may actually remain invisible. "Invisibility also happens when one does not see people because one 'knows' them through some fabricated preconception of group

16. "What Does the 'New Deal' Mean to This Mother and Her Child," *San Francisco News* (March 11, 1936), 3.

17. Hariman and Lucaites, *No Caption Required*, 56.

18. I want to thank Margie Pfeil for this insight. See her article, "The Transformative Power of the Periphery: Can a White U.S. Catholic Opt for the Poor?," in *Interrupting White Privilege: Catholic Theologians Break the Silence*, ed. Laurie Cassidy and Alex Mikulich (Maryknoll, NY: Orbis, 2007), 113.

19. Ibid.

20. M. Shawn Copeland, "Foundations for Catholic Theology in an African American Context," in *Black and Catholic: The Challenge and Gift of Black Folk*, ed. Jamie T. Phelps (Milwaukee, WI: Marquette University Press, 1997), 112. Copeland makes this same point in "The Exercise of Black Catholic Theology in the United States," *Journal of Hispanic/Latino Theology* 3, no. 3 (1996): 11. See also Susan Griffin, "Pornography and Silence," in *Made from This Earth: An Anthology of Writings by Susan Griffin* (New York: Harper & Row, 1982), 110–60; Clarence Rufus J. Rivers, "The Oral African American Tradition Versus the Ocular Western Tradition; The Spirit of Worship," in *Taking Down Our Harps, Black Catholics in the United States*, ed. Diana Hayes and Cyprian Davis (Maryknoll, NY: Orbis, 1998), 239.

formation."[21] The photograph becomes a known commodity while the suffering person and the viewer's relatedness to this anguish are obfuscated.

While acknowledging the imbedded politics of photography, the power of such images offers the possibility of destabilizing the viewer as merely a passive spectator because of his or her emotional appeal to the viewer. The viewer is appealed to by the evocative emotional medium of seeing a human face in the photograph. Judith Butler has persuasively argued that photographs of suffering human beings can promote ethical response. She maintains the photograph will promote ethical response to the extent it can provide the privileged viewer to realize the shared vulnerability with the object of his or her gaze. The photographs must be a means to reflect on shared vulnerability.[22] As Szorenyi writes, "Butler is careful to point out that not just any image will provoke this ethical response."[23] According to Butler, if the viewer is presented with a stereotype or an image that is "expected," the image will not create reflection on the reality of shared vulnerability.

So the question for Christians becomes how to engage and be engaged with photographs to shift the viewer from the gaze of unmarked/ invisible privilege to the position of shared vulnerability with those upon whom we gaze. This shift of the viewer to shared humanity and vulnerability is a journey to which I will return in the last section of this essay. This shift begins by questioning. Susan Sontag explains that questioning photographs is necessary because "we understand very little just looking at the photographic witness of some heart breaking arena of indignity, pain and death. Seeing reality in the form of an image cannot be more than an invitation to pay attention, to reflect, to learn, to examine rationalizations for mass suffering offered by established powers."[24] A photograph cannot "do the moral work for us, but it can start us on the way."[25] Sontag states emphatically, "There are questions to be asked."[26] The moral work begins as the viewer questions his or her

21. David Theo Goldberg, *Racial Subjects: Writing on Race in America* (New York: Routledge, 1997), 80. For a profound treatment of how this dynamic of being "known" and invisible impacts the understanding of domestic violence against black women, see Traci West, *Wounds of the Spirit: Black Women, Violence and Resistance Ethics* (New York: New York University Press, 1999), 57–59.

22. Judith Butler, *Precarious Life: The Powers of Mourning and Violence* (London: Verso, 2004), 20.

23. Szorenyi, "Distanced Suffering," 95.

24. Susan Sontag, "Preface," *Don McCullin* (London: Jonathan Cape, 2001), 16.

25. Ibid.

26. Ibid.

power and privilege; questioning one's concrete historical particularity holds the possibility of locating oneself on the same map of humanity as the suffering person.

Photographs as Cultural Representations

"Everyone is a literalist when it comes to photographs."[27] This observation by Susan Sontag brings to awareness the commonly accepted assumption—even in this digital age—that a photograph is a literal depiction of reality. The power of Sontag's work is that she adroitly enables viewers to question the evidentiary claim of photographs while also maintaining a value of the medium for suffering human beings. According to Sontag, the moral authority is not found in the photograph but in the human viewer.

My preoccupation in analyzing photographs of suffering is to explore how these images engage the viewer's agency in relationship to suffering human beings. Three central questions orient my inquiry: *What does this representation imply about causes of this human anguish? How does the representation draw the viewer to the viewed to understand the human ties that bind them? What response does the representation evoke on behalf of the suffering person(s)?*

To explore these questions in relation to the claims of photographs as cultural representations I will analyze Kevin Carter's 1993 photo of a Sudanese child.[28] First, I will explore this image through the lens of Susan Sontag's observation that photographs are a record of the real and a personal testimony—in the case of Carter's photograph, a record of the genocidal famine in Sudan and also an interpretation of that suffering. Second, I will analyze Carter's photograph as an "icon of starvation"

27. Susan Sontag, *Regarding the Pain of Others* (New York: Farrar, Straus and Giroux, 2003), 47.

28. To view this image, please see the following URL: http://www.corbisimages.com/stock-photo/rights-managed/0000295711-001/famine-in-sudan?popup=1. It is problematic that as a white North American social ethicist I will focus on a photograph from Africa to argue that representation inscribes racist power relations. Barbara Andolsen and M. Shawn Copeland have pointed out that North American Christian social ethicists and theologians often use examples in Africa rather than the United States to obfuscate their own involvement in white privilege. I join with this critique and intend my analysis to show how this representation is an expression of this obfuscation. This photo serves as a "spectacle of the other," which reveals the global implications of North American white privilege. See George Frederickson, *The Black Image in the White Mind* (Hanover, NH: Wesleyan University Press, 1987); hooks, *Black Looks*.

that misrepresented the actual material conditions of Sudanese famine but revealed the global power relations that define the subaltern position of suffering black bodies in sub-Saharan Africa.[29]

Looking back at the history of photography Sontag sees photographs as always uniting two contradictory features. "Their credentials of objectivity were inbuilt. Yet they always had, necessarily, a point of view."[30] Sontag explains that the contradictory features of photographs are nowhere more problematic than in photographs of human suffering.

> Those who stress the evidentiary punch of image-making by camera have to finesse the question of the subjectivity of the image-maker. For the photography of atrocity, people want the weight of witnessing without the taint of artistry, which is equated with insincerity or mere contrivance. Pictures of hellish events seem more authentic when they don't have the look that comes from being "properly" lighted and composed.[31]

As Sontag states, photographs are a record of the real, since both a machine was there doing the recording and a human being was present bearing witness to the event.[32] Photographs are always, however, "both an objective record and a personal testimony, both a faithful copy or transcription of an actual moment of reality and an interpretation of that reality."[33]

Sontag's claims about the interpretive element of photography are powerfully demonstrated in Kevin Carter's Pulitzer Prize–winning photograph of a Sudanese girl crawling to a feeding station. Carter's photo depicts a small black female child, barely larger than an infant. The little girl is naked except for a bracelet on her wrist and a necklace around her neck. "She appears bowed over in weakness and sickness, incapable, it would seem, of moving; she is unprotected."[34] Ominously present in the frame is a vulture. No family appears in the photo to

29. Donatella Lorch, "Sudan Is Described as Trying to Placate the West," *The New York Times* (March 26, 1993).

30. Sontag, *Regarding the Pain of Others*, 26.

31. Ibid., 26–27.

32. Ibid., 26.

33. Ibid.

34. Arthur Kleinman and Joan Kleinman, "The Appeal of Experience: The Dismay of Image; Cultural Appropriation of Suffering in Our Times," in *Social Suffering*, ed. Arthur Klienman, Veena Das, and Margaret Lock (Berkeley: University of California Press, 1997), 4.

protect the little girl and "to prevent her from being attacked by the vulture, or succumbing to starvation and then being eaten."[35]

The historical context of the photo and the photojournalism of Kevin Carter demonstrate the ambiguous moral character of photographs as "real and interpretations of reality." Kevin Carter, a white South African, was a photojournalist who worked for the *Johannesburg Star*.[36] In March 1993, Carter and a colleague went north from South Africa to photograph the rebel movement in famine-stricken Sudan.

> Immediately after their plane touched down in the village of Ayod, Carter began snapping photos of famine victims. Seeking relief from the sight of masses of people starving to death, he wandered into the open bush. He heard a soft, high-pitched whimpering and saw a tiny girl trying to make her way to the feeding center. As he crouched to photograph her, a vulture landed in view. Careful not to disturb the bird, he positioned himself for the best possible image. He would later say he waited about 20 minutes, hoping the vulture would spread its wings. It did not, and after he took his photographs, he chased the bird away and watched as the little girl resumed her struggle. Afterward he sat under a tree, lit a cigarette, talked to God and cried. "He was depressed afterward," Silva recalls. "He kept saying he wanted to hug his daughter."[37]

After the photo was bought and printed by the *New York Times* hundreds of people wrote and called to inquire about this Sudanese child.[38] The paper reported that it was not known whether she had reached the feeding center.[39] Papers around the world reproduced the photograph, and the image generated political will to aid Sudan and helped NGOs raise money to stop hunger in Africa.[40] In 1994 the photograph won the Pulitzer Prize and was deemed the "icon of starvation."[41]

35. Ibid.

36. Carter and three other white South Africans (Joao Sliva, Greg Marinovich, and Ken Oosterboek) were on a mission to use photojournalism to expose the brutality of apartheid. The four men became so well-known in the townships for capturing the violence of apartheid that they became known as the "Bang-Bang Club."

37. Scott MacLeod, "The Life and Death of Kevin Carter," *Time* 144, no. 11 (September 12, 1994): 70–73.

38. Ibid.

39. Bill Keller, "Kevin Carter, a Pulitzer Winner for Sudan Photo, Is Dead at 33," *The New York Times* (July 29, 1994), B8.

40. Klienman and Klienman, "The Appeal of Experience," 4.

41. On April 13, 1994, *The New York Times* ran a full-page advertisement in recognition of the three Pulitzer Prizes it won in that year. In describing Carter's

Within a few months of winning the prize Carter committed suicide, leaving a note, saying, "I am haunted by the vivid memories of killings and corpses and anger and pain . . . of starving or wounded children, of trigger-happy madmen, often police or killer executioners."[42]

The notoriety of the photograph and the public nature of Carter's death generated a firestorm of controversy about this photo, about photojournalism, and about how photos of human suffering function in contemporary culture.[43] What did Carter do after he took the photo? Was the photo posed because he waited so long for the vulture to spread its wings? How could Carter allow the vulture to get so close to the little girl without doing something to protect her? "Inasmuch as Kevin Carter chose to take the time, minutes that may have been critical at this point when she is near death, to compose an effective picture rather than to save the child, is he complicit?" It was suggested that Carter was a predator, another vulture on the scene of this little child's anguish.[44] Even Carter's friends wondered aloud why he had not helped the little child.[45]

The implication of Carter's complicity in this Sudanese child's death and the account of his suicide surface the complex ethical and moral world of photographs of human suffering: "Carter becomes a subject in the cultural story his photograph helped write by being transformed, infected more than affected, by what he had to bear."[46]

The photograph of this Sudanese child is problematic because its power is in its compelling capacity to make it appear as though the viewer is close enough to touch her, to hold her, to feed her, and to rescue her. This photograph is a representation that appears not to be.

My purpose here is not to dispute the immense achievement of the photograph; it is because of its power in making a moral appeal that its political and cultural assumptions are instructive to analyze.[47] My point here is to interrogate how this moral appeal was made. My intent is to understand the relations of power that deeply inscribe themselves upon

---

photo it read, "To *The New York Times* for Kevin Carter's photograph of a vulture perching near a little girl in the Sudan who had collapsed from hunger, a picture that became an icon of starvation." Quotation from Klienman and Klienman, "The Appeal of Experience," 5.

42. MacLeod, "The Life and Death of Kevin Carter," 73.

43. Richard Harwood, "Moral Motives," *The Washington Post* (November 21, 1994), A25. Using Carter as an example Harwood explores the positive contribution of photojournalists while also giving a nuanced picture of their ethical dilemmas.

44. MacLeod, "The Life and Death of Kevin Carter," 73.

45. Ibid.

46. Kleinman and Kleinman, "The Appeal to Experience," 7.

47. Ibid., 18.

the representation of this child's suffering. In documenting the anguish of this Sudanese child, what does the photo say about the causes of her suffering? How does this photograph enable the viewer to reflect "on how our privileges are located on the same map as [her] suffering"?[48] And what moral claim does it make upon the agency of the viewer?

First, Carter's photograph first appeared in the *New York Times* in March 1993. Carter's photo accompanied an article by Donatella Lorch titled "Sudan Is Described as Trying to Placate the West."[49] Lorch's article documents food aid that was allowed by the Sudanese government for the starving people in the south. At the time of this aid, more than a million people were suffering from famine and were at risk of starvation in southern Sudan. In her article, Lorch gives an accounting of this nightmare of social suffering.

> Forced to leave their lands and with their cattle herds virtually decimated, hundreds of thousands of mostly nomadic southern Sudanese are either on the brink of starvation or face severe malnutrition, relief officials say. In the area around the town of Kongor, 625 miles from Khartoum, 145,000 displaced people face starvation, and more than 15 are dying each day. About 100,000 more, mostly from the cattle-herding Dinka, have been pushed to camps along the Kenyan border. In some areas there are no children under 5 years of age.[50]

The famine suffered by the southern Sudanese was (and is) the result of political violence and chaos resulting from the civil war in Sudan. The article explains that famine was used as a tool of "ethnic cleansing" by the Sudanese government in Khartoum to subjugate the people in the South.[51] Moreover, in 1993 the United Nations Human Rights Commission had "accused the Sudan of widespread executions, torture, detention and expulsions and had voted to appoint a special investigator."[52]

Lorch's article documented the first convoy of aid, which she judged to be placating the Western governments. This gesture was deemed a response to the threat of the United States government to place Sudan on the list of countries that sponsor terrorism.[53]

48. Sontag, *Regarding the Pain of Others*, 102–3.
49. Lorch, "Sudan Is Described as Trying to Placate the West."
50. Ibid.
51. Ibid.
52. Ibid.
53. Ibid.

The caption of Carter's photo read, "A little girl, weakened from hunger, collapsed recently along the trail to a feeding center in Ayod. Nearby, a vulture waited."[54] For this photograph to accompany Lorch's article about famine as systemic violence is problematic in a number of ways. The article is documenting the systemic causes of the suffering of the people in Southern Sudan. The famine is not a "natural" occurrence but is the result of human intent.[55] The famine is a systemic form of violence, and it is interpreted today as a weapon of genocide in Sudan. The photo, however, situates the suffering of this little girl against the horizon of "nature." The child's nakedness, the presence of the vulture, the dried grass and trees in the background give the impression of her starvation as the result of the crop failure and cycles of nature, absent of any collective human intent. "The vulture embodies danger and evil, but the greater dangers and real forces of evil are not in the 'natural world': they are in the political world, including those nearby in army uniforms or in government offices in Khartoum."[56] The photo represents the causes of suffering in a manner that contradicts the documentation of the article it accompanies.

In addition, the next inference of the viewer to seeing this child alone is to assume that there are no families, no communities, no local institutions or programs to assist her. "The local world is deemed incompetent, or worse."[57] This child is helpless without immediate outside assistance.

> There is, for example, the unstated idea that this group of unnamed Africans (are they Nuer or Dinka?) cannot protect their own. They must be protected, as well as represented, by others. The image of the subaltern conjures up an almost neocolonial ideology of failure, inadequacy, passivity, fatalism, and inevitability. Something must be done, but *from outside* the local setting.[58]

54. Ibid.

55. Jean Dreze and Amartya Sen, *Hunger and Public Action* (New York: Oxford University Press, 1991). Dreze and Sen demonstrate the political causes of famine in sub-Saharan Africa.

56. Kleinman and Kleinman, "The Appeal of Experience," 4.

57. Ibid., 8. For another such example, see the photo by Ruth Fremson of an unnamed Haitian woman, with the caption, "A woman in Fort Dimanche laying out biscuits to dry, biscuits made of butter, salt, water and *dirt*" (*The New York Times* [May 5, 2004], 1; my emphasis). I want to thank Anna Perkins, PhD, who commented that the perspective of the photo and caption's message implies that Caribbean peoples may be thought by Americans as destined to eat dirt.

58. Kleinman and Kleinman, "The Appeal of Experience," 7; emphasis in original.

The authorization for foreign aid and intervention to help this Sudanese child comes from indignation at the absence of her local world; foreign aid is evoked by erasing local voices and acts.[59]

What is most troubling is the "racial knowledge" that this picture reinscibes about suffering in Africa.[60] This child's representation is not without precedence but is rather part of the archive of images of black suffering children in Africa who appear desperate and victimized in the Western media.[61] The image of this little child's suffering body becomes an overcrowded intersection of views of the racialized suffering "Other." Her suffering—her blackness—and her predatory surroundings make her "not us." The photo in one image links together the ideology of the primitive with suffering and blackness in such a way that all these together in one body appear naturalized.[62]

Photographs and the Imperative of *Imago Dei*

Using the insight of visual-cultural studies to analyze the image of this Sudanese child demonstrates that images like this are not morally neutral in regard to the person or persons suffering. This photograph is not simply evidentiary but rather a morally ambiguous representation of this suffering Sudanese child. As a morally ambiguous representation, its function is unclear, unresolved, and incomplete. This ambiguity demands further reflection and analysis of what is at stake in the realization of the dignity of viewer and the viewed as *imago Dei*.[63]

59. Ibid.

60. The term "racial knowledge" is from David Goldberg, *Racist Culture: Philosophy and the Politics of Meaning* (Cambridge: Blackwell, 1993), 148–84.

61. One example is the photograph, titled "Helpless," of a frightened Rwandan child on the cover of *The Economist* (July 23, 1994). For more on this, see Stuart Hall, "The Spectacle of the Other," 225–77.

62. "Those thus rendered Other are sacrificed to the idealization, excluded from the being of personhood, from social benefits, and from political (self-)representation" (Goldberg, *Racist Culture*, 151).

63. I am indebted to Susan Ross for her thought-provoking work on the theological virtue of ambiguity. She writes, "When a situation is marked by ambiguity, its resolution is unclear: there is more than one possible solution, more than one meaning. It is often marked by tension, as competing resolutions are suggested by those involved. In between order and chaos, ambiguity demands further reflection, consideration of new and different outcomes, decisions on what issues are at stake in its resolution. . . . But such a situation means that those involved must be able to tolerate, at least for a time, a certain 'lack' of order. This 'disorder' allows for dimensions of the situation to reveal themselves, or to be uncovered by questioning, opening up issues and concerns that could affect the situation's resolution"

In this section I use the principle of *imago Dei* to offer an alternative practice of gazing on photographs of human suffering. This Christian doctrine is key to the alternative gaze because it claims just relationality as that which makes us like God: "We are like the Trinity: of and for one another."[64] It is the imperatives of dignity and radical sociality that flow from this principle that ground the work of deconstruction and reconstruction in viewing and responding to photographs of human suffering.

The revelatory text of Genesis offers a vision of creation as sacred and interconnected. The first chapter of Genesis reveals creation as coming from God and as reflecting the Creator. This story of creation proclaims that being from God and reflecting the Creator generates a sacred and interrelated character of all of reality. Genesis informs humanity of our origin, our character, and our destiny.

The revelatory vision of Genesis grounds Christian belief in human beings made in God's image and likeness. The doctrine of *imago Dei* functions as a root metaphor disclosing the connection of belief in the trinitarian God as Creator, the vision of radical sociality of the human person, and the call by God to realize this sociality through communion with God and one another.[65] This doctrine is a rich resource that informs moral imagination about what it means to be human and holds out an imperative to realize our sociality in suffering.[66]

Contemporary trinitarian theology breaks open implications of being made in God's image, being human, and the nature of reality. Jürgen Moltmann describes humanity made in God's image as "*Imago trinitas.*"[67] To claim humanity as imaging the Trinity is to articulate more clearly being human as grounded in the deeper mystery of God

---

(Susan Ross, *Extravagant Affections: A Feminist Sacramental Theology* (New York: Continuum, 1998), 69.

64. Vilma Seelaus, *Distraction in Prayer: Blessing or Curse? St. Teresa of Avila's Teachings in the Interior Castle* (Staten Island: Alba House, 2005), 52.

65. Lucien Richard explains that a root metaphor functions by disclosing the connection of different elements of an identity by its relatedness to reality as a whole, specifically to Ultimate Reality. As a root metaphor, the doctrine of *imago Dei* reveals the connection of God as Creator, the dignity and value of the human person, and the communitarian nature of the human vocation. See Lucien Richard, "Toward a Renewed Theology of Creation: Implications for the Questions of Human Rights," *Eglise at Theologie* 19 (1986):149.

66. For more on this point, see David Tracy, "Religion and Human Rights in the Public Realm," *Daedalus* (Fall 1983): 248.

67. Jurgen Moltmann, *God in Creation*, trans. Margaret Kohl (San Francisco: Harper and Row, 1981), 216.

as relation. God as Trinity is a faith proclamation of God's essence as being-in-relation. "At the heart of reality is relationship, personhood, communion."[68] Elizabeth Johnson states that "the Trinity as pure relationality . . . epitomizes the connectedness of all that exists in the universe. Relation encompasses and constitutes the web of reality, when rightly ordered, forms the matrix for the flourishing of all creatures, both human beings and the earth."[69] This theology of the Trinity informs how to imagine human beings in God's image and likeness by its focusing believers' attention on kinship with God and with each other. It is our orientation to communion as persons that makes us like the Creator.

This fundamental principle that all human beings are made in God's image and likeness theologically undergirds all Catholic social teaching.[70] It is essential to the understanding of what it means to be human.[71] The principle of *imago Dei* is the primary category both to interpret personal value and also to understand human relationality.[72] In other words, this principle of *imago Dei* is not only a lens to see, to understand, and to interpret human inherent and inestimable value; it is also the imperative that gives rise to right relations.[73] Mary Catherine Hilkert explains this connection clearly:

> Every human being is endowed with radical dignity, every aspect of humanity as created by God shares in the human potential to imagine the divine. As fundamentally social and relational beings, we image God most profoundly when our human relationships, our families and our communities, and our social, political, economic, and ecclesiastical structures reflect the equality, mutuality, and love that are essential to the trinitarian God revealed in Jesus and in communities living in the power of his Spirit.[74]

68. Mary Catherine Hilkert, "Cry Beloved Image: Rethinking the Image of God," in *In the Embrace of God*, ed. Ann O'Hara Graff (Maryknoll, NY: Orbis, 1995), 200. See also Catherine Mowry LaCugna, *God for Us: The Trinity and Christian Life* (San Francisco: Harper San Francisco, 1991), 243–317; Walter Kasper, *The God of Jesus Christ* (New York: Crossroad, 1984).

69. Elizabeth Johnson, *She Who Is: The Mystery of God in Feminist Theological Discourse* (New York: Crossroad, 1993), 222–23.

70. See *Gaudium et Spes* 3, 12. For an overview of this basis of Catholic social teaching, see Charles Curran, *Catholic Social Teaching: 1891–Present* (Washington, DC: Georgetown University Press, 2002), 136.

71. Hilkert, "Cry Beloved Image," 192.

72. See Lisa Sowle Cahill, "Toward a Christian Theory of Human Rights," *The Journal of Christian Ethics* 8 (1980): 279.

73. Hilkert, "Cry Beloved Image," 195.

74. Ibid., 203.

Contemporary Catholic social teaching demonstrates the inextricable link between the theological principle of *imago Dei* and Christian practice. For example, the bishops of the United States teach that the dignity and sociality of our being *imago Dei* must serve as criterion for measuring our collective life.[75] Human beings are ends, not means, and deserve to be respected "with a reverence that is religious."[76] The bishops suggest that this reverence should inspire awe that arises "in the presence of something holy and sacred."[77] While this teaching arose in relationship to national economic concerns, it also has profound implications in relation to cultural production of images of human beings. Such reverence is particularly fitting in regard to photographs of human suffering. The bishops' teaching may suggest a reverence and awe as we look at photographs of human beings who suffer. Such reverence interrupts Kevin Carter's photograph as "icon of starvation." Such a reverential gaze upon this young Sudanese child creates a relationship in which the viewer and the viewed are persons. From within the gaze of reverence this image can become an icon of God's suffering and objectified black body in the world.

M. Shawn Copeland describes the painfully true reality that recognizing God's image and likeness in human beings who do not "look like us" is the most difficult task in living out the imperative of *imago Dei*. "Nothing has proved harder in the history of civilization than to see God, or good, or human dignity in those whose language is not mine, whose skin is a different color, whose faith is not mine and whose truth is not my truth."[78] This struggle points to the fact that socially constructed messages about "others" obfuscate the reality of our shared humanity.

This indictment of human gaze proves true in regard to the photograph by Kevin Carter that I have examined in this essay. This small, crouched, and starving female child in Sudan is caught up in a photographic genealogy of representing black children as animals. The image of the black child as pickaninny bears an uncanny resemblance to Carter's image of this small Sudanese child in the African countryside being pursued by a vulture. As Emilie Townes writes, "Black children depicted as pickaninnies were small and almost subhuman if not animal

75. See *Economic Justice for All* 28.
76. Ibid.
77. Ibid.
78. M. Shawn Copeland, "Knit Together by the Spirit as Church," in *Prophetic Witness: Catholic Women's Strategies for Reform* (New York: Herder and Herder, 2009), 20. Here she quotes Johnathan Sacks, *The Dignity of Difference: How to Avoid the Clash of Civilizations* (New York: Continuum, 2003), 65.

like. They were often mistaken for animals and were often pursued by hunters and other animals—dogs, chickens and pigs."[79] Emilie Townes explains the (im)moral implication of such representations of black children in white people's imagination. The image of the pickaninny generated a (mis)belief that "black parents were inherently indifferent to their children's welfare."[80] Such a view of black parents and children made it easier for white people not to feel any sense of responsibility for the welfare of black children. Moreover, as Townes so keenly reveals, "The existence and maintenance of these caricatures prevented or made difficult any acknowledgement or examination of how elite White-controlled economic factors might have contributed to the slovenly appearance and substandard education of Black children."[81] This blotting out of the fundamental humanity of black children in representing them as animals is a heinous illustration of the essential connection of dignity and radical sociality in the claim to *imago Dei*.[82] The process of representing a black child that denies dignity is also an obfuscation of how the white viewer is essentially related to this child's suffering.

Questioning as Facing the Suffering Subjects of History

Each day images of suffering human beings are appropriated in visual culture as "infotainment" in the nightly news or in the commercial exploitation of "charitainment."[83] To question photographs of suffering is to refuse to be a voyeur to the spectacle of the suffering victims of human history. In this final section I will demonstrate that questioning is a practice that interrupts the representational process and holds the

79. Emilie Townes, *Womanist Ethics and the Cultural Production of Evil* (New York: Palgrave/McMillan, 2006), 142. On the history and cultural (dis)function of this image, see Marilyn Kern-Foxworth, *Aunt Jemima, Uncle Ben, and Rastus: Blacks in Advertising Yesterday, Today, and Tomorrow* (Westport, CT: Praeger Publishers, 1994); and Patricia Turner, *Ceramic Uncles and Celluloid Mammies: Black Images and Their Influence on Culture* (New York: Anchor Books, 1994).

80. Townes, *Womanist Ethics and the Cultural Production of Evil*, 143.

81. Ibid., 144.

82. "Racism is a sin: a sin that divides the human family, blots out the image of God among specific members of that family, violates the fundamental dignity of those called to be children of the same Father" (*Brothers and Sisters to Us: U.S. Bishops' Pastoral Letter on Racism in Our Day* [Washington, DC: United States Catholic Conference, November 14, 1979], 3).

83. Kleinman and Kleinman, "The Appeal of Experience," 1. For more on this notion of "Charitainment," see James Poniewozik, "The Year of Charitainment," *Time* (December 26, 2005): 93.

possibility for solidaristic response to human suffering. I will offer a constructive theological rationale for the practice of questioning as one element of a stance of a political compassion toward human suffering. I will also suggest a series of specific questions to be used by the viewer that makes up a spirituality and ethic that faces the suffering subjects of history, even as we gaze on their images in photographs.

Visual theorists demonstrate the irony that gaze can actually be an evasion of an authentic vision of reality. Gaze upon photographs of suffering can reinscribe the very power relations the photos propose to contest. The shift from the universalizing gaze begins with becoming conscious of this illusion of this gaze, to become conscious of our limited standpoint in looking at the photograph of a human being. Facing the privilege of our standpoint is one small step toward becoming vulnerable to the lived and shared humanity of the person we view.

To begin acknowledging and unpacking the "invisible knapsack" of privilege,[84] one critical question is, Does this image interrupt or reinscribe the stereotypes of people who look like this or share this social position? This question has a dual function. First, the question makes the viewer stop and examine the images within the mind that determine perception of this person(s) and their situation.[85] This inquiry is the first step in acknowledging shared human vulnerability. To inquire into these stereotypical images in the mind is to acknowledge the human vulnerability to be conditioned and impacted by the communities in which we live. These socially construed internalized images make human beings vulnerable to ignorance and bias and blind us to the reality of being made in God's image.

The second function of this first question is that it shifts the viewer from being a passive receptor of the representation to being an engaged participant in a message of the photograph. To inquire into the nature of how the suffering person is being represented is to begin understanding the photograph as a text and "reading" its message about the causes and possible responses to this anguish.

The stance of questioning holds an energy and engagement that leads to relationship and responsibility rather than theoretical justification or

---

84. This term of "unpacking the invisible knapsack" was coined by Peggy McIntosh in her now classic article, "White Privilege: Unpacking the Invisible Knapsack," *Peace and Freedom* (July–August 1989): 11–12.

85. For more on this idea of the unconscious but very active images that condition perception and judgment, see Shankar Vedantam, *The Hidden Brain: How Our Unconscious Minds Elect Presidents, Control Markets, Wage Wars and Save Our Lives* (New York: Spiegel and Grau, 2010).

legitimation. One such question that holds this dynamic relational quality is, If I or a loved one were in this photograph, how might I want this image to be different? This question is a deeper step in the journey of shared human vulnerability because viewers now begin to imagine themselves and their relations as inhabiting this same social space of suffering. Would it be acceptable for us to be photographed naked and violated? Would it be acceptable for us to be captured at the moment of shattering pain or grief? Would it be acceptable for our loved one to be pictured as tortured or dismembered? Even to consider these images as possible may be painful. This consideration of how we might want the knowledge of our suffering to be communicated has heuristic quality. The question creates a space in the viewer's moral imagination that acts as a bridge between the humanity of the viewer and the humanity of the person who is viewed.

To question in this way can be an act of crying out to God if we claim our vulnerable humanity in the moment of viewing photographs of suffering. This person I see could be me! For the viewer to cry out at the suffering of others is to feel and to face the pain of shared human existence. Such crying out to God with our questions is to lament. Rather than succumbing to the numbness engendered by visual-cultural questioning as a prayer of lament is a practice that implicitly acknowledges shared human existence. To cry to God while looking at a photograph is to claim that the image and the person who suffers matter. Questioning in this way is an act of re-membering our human bonds of connection and discovering how our existence is inextricably related to this suffering human being.

In Kathleen O'Connor's profound work, *Lamentation and the Tears of the World*, she explains the connection of lament to the work of justice for those who suffer: "Laments create room within the individual and the community not only for grief and loss but also for seeing and naming injustice. Laments name the warping and fracturing of relationships—personal, political, domestic, ecclesial, national and global."[86]

The activity of questioning is a practice that enables the viewer to begin to interrogate how her privileges may be located on the same map as the subject's suffering. For example, another question the viewer might ask is, Is this suffering avoidable and how so?[87] To question the image in this way resists any way that the photograph may imply that

---

86. Kathleen M. O'Connor, *Lamentations and the Tears of the World* (Maryknoll, NY: Orbis, 2002), 128.

87. This question is compiled from a series of questions suggested by Sontag, *Regarding the Pain of Others*, 116–17.

Kimberly Vrudny

AIDS, Accountability, and Activism

The Beauty of Sue Williamson's Resistance Art

When someone perpetrates an act of rape, it's about reclaiming a sense of power.
> —*Kelly Hatfield, People Opposing Women Abuse*

In 1973, Adrienne Rich published a collection of poetry called *Diving into the Wreck*, which includes a poem called "Rape." The poem explores how the survivor of rape is traumatized again by the male-dominated criminal justice system. An officer's voyeuristic titillation by her disclosure when she gives an account of the crime implicates him, Rich asserts, in something of a gang that continues to perpetrate violence against her:

> And you see his blue eyes, the blue eyes of all the family
> whom you used to know, grow narrow and glisten,
> his hand types out the details
> and he wants them all
> but the hysteria in your voice pleases him best.[1]

---

1. Adrienne Rich, *Diving into the Wreck: Poems 1971–1972* (New York: W. W. Norton & Company, 1994).

Rich's words denounce both the banality and the brutality of violence inflicted against women. Her poetry functions to resist this kind of dehumanization and unveils how enmeshed it is in a culture that scarcely recognizes misogyny as out of order. Today, forty years since the poem's publication, investigative law enforcement worldwide remains a field dominated by men. The matter has only been complicated by the introduction of a potentially deadly sexually transmitted virus, HIV/ AIDS, into this already charged situation. Nongovernmental organizations have materialized to raise awareness and relieve suffering where violence and high HIV prevalence rates converge to put populations of women particularly at risk. Governmental and academic sectors are also responding to varying degrees.

Among those responding in the academic sector in South Africa, a country where the convergence of rape and HIV/AIDS is particularly evident as both epidemics are attributable in many ways to the disastrous policies of apartheid, is Sue Williamson, a South African artist and intellectual who is also an activist for justice and peace. Sue Williamson's art resists the dual epidemics of rape and HIV/AIDS by calling for public accountability in the face of the multidimensional social, economic, and political challenges now facing South Africa in the postapartheid era. In her series of photographs called *From the Inside*, particularly in her portrait of Busi Maqungo, Williamson confronts the issue of violence against women within the context of the project's larger attempt to speak openly about HIV/AIDS.

While this essay speaks specifically of the situation in South Africa, the patterns witnessed there are, to be sure, detectable elsewhere. Prevalence rates in underprivileged neighborhoods in the United States are approaching levels seen in central Africa. Both democracies, the one in South Africa as well as the one in the United States of America, are struggling against a backdrop of great disparity between black and white, poor and rich, women and men. These situations warrant accountability and activism—a call to which many artists have responded in South Africa and elsewhere but few with the exactitude demonstrated by Sue Williamson. By living creatively and in solidarity with those mistreated by systems as they stand, Williamson embodies how to live beautifully, actively attentive and resistant to powers that seek to damage and destroy human community and human thriving. Her sharp analysis of social oppression, as well as her compassionate ability to work with communities marginalized by oppressive systems as they stand in order to offer a critique of power and its abuses, is a compelling model for how to be human in our globalized world increasingly enmeshed in cycles of violence.

Indeed, by creating this kind of artistic political and social commentary, Williamson is an influential example for me—a white female academic, photographer, and activist for justice and peace who resides in a country implementing its own destructive policies in relation to segregation, education, and militarization, policies that have deep repercussions in relation to health and human thriving. Williamson's way of being human in the world as both intellectual and artist is one inspiration behind my efforts to live in service to the common good, resisting the powers that threaten to destroy the bonds that make human community possible.[2] Without romanticizing her work or her lifestyle, aware as I am that there have been wounds, sacrifices, and compromises along the way, Williamson's artistic and political witness models for me ways in which I can live my life with greater integrity. By studying the work that Sue Williamson has created in South Africa, the implication as well as the hope is that the impact of an artist like Williamson can be replicated elsewhere, motivating response in like-minded artists and activists throughout the world who are confronting apartheids in their own contexts.

Although overturned in 1994, apartheid's impact continues to be experienced in the distrust and friction that persists between communities delineated in South Africa on the basis of ethnicity and distinguished by class. Among the challenges facing contemporary South Africa today is violence against women. South Africa has the highest ratio of reported rape cases per capita (per one hundred thousand people) in the world.[3] *Time* magazine recently reported that more than a quarter of men in South Africa admitted to having committed rape: "46% of those said

2. While on sabbatical in South Africa during academic year 2009–2010, I photographed thirty people impacted by the HIV/AIDS pandemic, whether through an infection directly or indirectly through care for a loved one or engagement in humanitarian response. The resulting exhibit, called *30 Years / 30 Lives*, is traveling around the country. See http://30years30lives.org. Sue Williamson's series was one inspiration behind the work, as was the exhibit and accompanying catalog edited by Mark Reinhardt, Holly Edwards, and Erina Duganne, *Beautiful Suffering: Photography and the Traffic in Pain* (Williamstown, MA: Williams College Museum of Art and University of Chicago Press, 2007). The theological construction operating behind the work is forthcoming in Kimberly Vrudny, *Beauty's Vineyard: An Aesthetic of Anguish and Anticipation*.

3. F. M. Orkin, "Quantitative Research Findings on Rape in South Africa" (Pretoria, 2000), http://www.statssa.gov.za/publications/Rape/Rape.pdf (accessed August 30, 2011).

that they had raped more than once."[4] Gangs are implicated in as many as 75 percent of the rapes committed in South Africa.[5] Estimates suggest that a woman is raped every twenty-six to thirty-six seconds in South Africa, where a child is raped every fifteen minutes.[6] South Africa also has a high number of incidents of infant rape or "baby rape," as it is more commonly called. Indeed, 41 percent of those raped in the country are under the age of twelve, according to South African police reports. "A nine-year study by Cape Town's Red Cross Children's Hospital, published in the *South Africa Medical Journal* in December 2002, found that the average age of children raped was three."[7] In a country where at one time as many as one in every five people were HIV-positive, "[r]esearch has shown that 40 percent of those raped in South Africa are at risk of becoming HIV-positive if they do not receive PEP [post-exposure prophylaxis]."[8]

In an effort to understand the underlying causes of this epidemic of violence against women in South Africa, scholars have pointed to relationships between structural injustices and individual acts of direct violence. Correlation does not necessarily signify causation, but identification of a relationship between structural injustices and individual acts of rape suggests that, when certain situations are in place and are left unchallenged, individual acts of aggression, while horrifying, are nevertheless to be expected. Researchers have identified at least six factors that reliably predict sexual violence directed against women. These theories go beyond the obvious conclusion that individual men have made violent choices. The truth probably lies in an interweaving of explanations, both individual and structural. That is to say, the individual choice to commit sexual assault against a woman, a choice that is not excused on account of factors influencing it, is correlated to endemic poverty, circulation of myth, persistence of cultural norms related to the subordination of women, male disempowerment, broken familial structures, and lack of legal deterrents.[9] This means that where these

4. Megan Lindow, "South Africa's Rape Crisis: 1 in 4 Men Say They've Done It," *Time* (June 20, 2009); http://www.time.com/time/world/article/0,8599,1906000,00 .html (accessed August 30, 2011).

5. Ibid.

6. "Every 26 Seconds" (February 11, 2009); http://www.cbsnews.com/stories /2000/02/01/60II/main155627.shtml (accessed September 1, 2011).

7. Charlene Smith, "Rape Has Become a Sickening Way of Life in Our Land," *Sunday Independent* (accessed September 26, 2011).

8. Ibid.

9. For a discussion of these factors, see my summary about "violence against women" at http://30years30lives.org/2010/08/11/violence-against-women/.

phenomena converge, risk is high for incidents of rape and sexual violence to be committed against women. Where there are high incidents of rape and sexual violence committed against women, there is a high risk of HIV/AIDS infection. In fact, women account for 51 percent of all people infected with HIV worldwide; in sub-Saharan Africa, rates are even higher. Sixty percent of those testing seropositive are women.[10]

The renowned early twentieth-century South Africa novelist Alan Paton was prescient by observing the relationship between structural oppression and direct violence in his novel *Cry, the Beloved Country*. Through the characters of Rev. Stephen Kumalo, a black preacher in Ixopo, a town in what today is the province of KwaZulu-Natal, and James Jarvis, a white farmer who lives just a short distance from the reverend's church, Paton explores the dynamic between structural oppression and isolated criminal acts by following the lives of these two neighbors in the already segregated South Africa of the 1940s. Absalom, the son of the black preacher, has left his rural village to find a better life in Johannesburg, only to turn to a life of petty crime when he cannot find meaningful work. One ill-fated day, Absalom is caught off-guard when a resident is unexpectedly home during a theft. Startled, Absalom shoots and kills him and then flees the scene of the crime. The victim turns out to be Jarvis's son, Arthur, who, despite his white European ancestry, has immersed himself in the black community as an act of solidarity with the African population already suffering before apartheid. In his search for his missing son, Rev. Kumalo travels with dread to Johannesburg and visits his brother, in whose mouth the author puts a treatise on European engagement and exploitation in South Africa. It is because of the injustices inflicted upon the indigenous peoples of Africa, John Kumalo explains to his brother, that there is unrest, crime, and violence in the African community:

> Here in Johannesburg it is the mines, he said, everything is the mines. These high buildings, this wonderful City Hall, this beautiful Parktown with its beautiful houses, all this is built with the gold from the mines. This wonderful hospital for Europeans, the biggest hospital south of the Equator, it is built with the gold from the mines.
>
> There was a change in his voice, it became louder like the voice of a bull or a lion. Go to our hospital, he said, and see our people lying on the floors. They lie so close you cannot step over them. But it is they who dig the gold. For three shillings a day. . . . We live in the compounds, we must leave our wives and families behind. And when

10. http://www.who.int/gender/hiv_aids/en/ (accessed August 31, 2011).

> the new gold is found, it is not we who will get more for our labor. It is
> the white man's shares that will rise, you will read it in all the papers.
> They go mad when new gold is found. They bring more of us to live
> in the compounds, to dig under the ground for three shillings a day.
> They do not think, here is a chance to pay more for our labor. They
> think only, here is a chance to build a bigger house and buy a bigger
> car. . . . [But] it is built on our backs, on our sweat, on our labor. Every
> factory, every theatre, every beautiful house, they are all built by us.[11]

The character of John Kumalo in his conversation with his brother articulates poignantly economic injustices that pervaded South Africa at the time of Paton's writing, injustices that tragically foreshadowed the destructive legalization of the practice of apartheid, the mandatory segregation according to degree of skin pigmentation, in South Africa in 1948, the year of the book's publication. The multiple wounds alluded to in this passage, wounds inflicted at the hands of white Europeans, were based on perverted understandings of ethnic difference or "race." The system resulted in creating three generations and more of men, women, and children whose immersion in a cycle of exploitation, oppression, and obscene poverty has left no one unharmed.

Bridging South Africa under apartheid to the new democratic South Africa is artist and scholar Sue Williamson. Born in England in 1941 and relocating with her family to South Africa in 1948, Williamson studied art in New York from 1963 to 1965, staying there until returning to South Africa in 1969. She received an advanced degree in art from the Michaelis School of Fine Art at the University of Cape Town in 1983. In her work, Williamson imagines art as a means of resistance to the "powers that be":[12]

> My work is about people, rather than about myself. It's about stories of
> people in the community. At the same time, I feel allowed to use these
> stories to make my work so I like to put something back in again. . . .
> I try to make things that are popular and will be understood by most
> people who look at it. I don't just want to talk to other artists, many
> of whom make work for their peers.[13]

Williamson imagines the common good and participates in its creation by installing art calling for accountability when what is beneficial for

---

11. Alan Paton, *Cry, the Beloved Country* (New York: Scribner, 1948, 1987), 67–68.
12. Walter Wink, *The Powers That Be: Theology for a New Millennium* (New York: Three Rivers Press, 1999).
13. http://www.artthrob.co.za/03nov/artbio.html (accessed August 28, 2011).

the collective has been betrayed by the self-interested desires of the few. She accesses the power of art to express the will of the people and enlists communities marginalized by the powerful and privileged to articulate the underrepresented views of the largely silenced majority in public works, both political and influential.

As a white woman immigrating to South Africa during the very year of the institutionalization of apartheid and coming to maturity during the height of its regime, Williamson has wrestled with her own quietism and complicity in the face of apartheid's horrors. Her awakening came with many of her fellow citizens when Soweto's children stirred their nation to action in 1976. At that moment, her personal history became intertwined with aspirations newly arising for her nation. About this experience, Williamson has written:

> A jagged faultline cuts through recent South African history. It is a year, 1976, the year the children of Soweto decided to resist their oppression. Peaceful protest was met with police gunfire, and soon Soweto was aflame. The furious sparks set the rest of the country alight; hundreds died, thousands fled. In the space of a few months, things in South Africa had been changed forever.
>
> The flames melted the oppressive ice which had frozen South Africans, black and white, into apathy for so long. Slowly the glacier began to move. It was a time for counting the cost, for accepting responsibility, for asking the question, "What could I have done, what can I do now, to work for freedom?" New organizations mushroomed in opposition to the state, new possibilities for action came into focus.
>
> I was one of those jolted out of lethargy by Soweto.[14]

A second moment of awakening occurred a year later, when a section of Cape Town was being razed under the demands of the Group Areas Act. About her experience of bearing witness to the destruction of a squatter settlement, Williamson has said:

> In August 1977, I spent seven days watching the total demolition by state employees in bulldozers backed up by police of the 2000 houses of Modderdam, a settled squatter community just outside Cape Town. Witnessing the cold brutality of this operation had a profound effect on my life. I became involved in community action, an involvement which spilled over into my work in the studio.[15]

14. Sue Williamson, "Introduction," in *Resistance Art in South Africa* (New York: St. Martin's Press, 1989), 8.

15. Ibid., 74.

Williamson's artwork is a testament to her social engagement in South Africa's unfolding history. In three works commemorating District Six, for example, once a vibrant, mixed-race community situated on the slopes of Table Mountain in Cape Town, then declared a "white area" by the state in the 1960s and subsequently leveled in the 1970s, she bears witness to the violence committed against the neighborhood and its people. In 1981, with rubble she collected from the demolition site piled on the white tiled floor of the Gowlett Gallery, Cape Town, she created an installation called *The Last Supper*. Chairs from the Muslim home of Naz Ebrahim, once a resident of District Six, were covered in white cloth and were situated around and facing the mound. An audio projected into the space "angry outbursts, nostalgic reminiscences, sounds of bulldozers, [and] calls from the mosque."[16] The religious overtones of the exhibit implicate the Christian rationales provided by theologians during the crafting of apartheid law, including the belief shared by some Afrikaaner and English theologians that God willed the separation of the races, pointing to the Tower of Babel incident as proof text (Gen 11).[17]

Ten years later, Williamson took scraps she collected from the demolished community and encapsulated them in clear resin blocks that she set on a glass table with the underside painted black but leaving spaces unpainted to light the blocks from below. Williamson installed the table at the Irma Stern Museum in Cape Town in 1993 and called it *The Last Supper Revisited*, where she played the same tape made for the installation in 1981. Again, she raises religious questions by the reference of the title to the famous scene of Jesus dining with his disciples prior to his crucifixion. Among them: What cruelty has been served consequently in Christ's name? What other "last suppers" are holy and sacred before acts of terror and violence destroy the communal breaking of bread? Likewise, in an installation, called *Mementoes of District Six*, for the Venice Biennial of 1993, Williamson created a house frame out of steel. She made walls out of resin blocks encapsulating more treasures from the demolished site of District Six. "The rows of small clear bricks containing linoleum scraps, curtains, flakes of paint and china chips could be closely examined, locating the piece somewhere

16. Sue Williamson, *Sue Williamson: Selected Work* (Cape Town: Double Storey Books, 2003), 78.

17. Richard Elphick and Rodney Davenport, eds., *Christianity in South Africa: A Political, Social, and Cultural History* (Berkeley: University of California Press, 1997), 376. See also John de Gruchy, *The Church Struggle in South Africa* (Grand Rapids, MI: Eerdmans, 1986).

between museum display and commemorative chapel."[18] Again, religious allusion emanates from her work, sacralizing objects of everyday life otherwise overlooked and left behind. By creating such installations, she has helped her country to process and thereby heal memories of its tortured past.[19]

The Truth and Reconciliation Commission (TRC), officially charged with helping the country to address crimes of the state against its people, has also captured Williamson's eye and attention. In a series from 1998 called *Truth Games*, Williamson enlarged photographs from the TRC hearings of an accuser, a defender, and an image representing the alleged violation. These were affixed on a board. Phrases from the hearings were overlaid in movable slats, inviting viewers to interact with the piece by sliding the words from defender to accuser and back again, evoking questions about intent, bias, and the possibility of redemption. Williamson has shared how the idea for the series came into being:

> When the TRC started proceedings, I knew I wanted to make work about it: some cases I had followed or even been peripherally involved in for years. I had known the police were lying about their non-involvement in the deaths and disappearances of activists, but not the truth and the precise details behind the lies. I understood that ideological motives had caused five young men from the Azanian People's Liberation Army to burst into a church in a quiet suburb of Cape Town in July 1993, mowing down the congregation with AK-47s, until 11 lay dead on the floor, but not why they had chosen a church as a target. I began cutting and clipping the newspaper stories and photographs about each new case, building up fat files. I was interested in the exact words people used to present their case. I wanted to use those phrases. And even in low-quality newspaper photographs, the body language of the speakers came through, the gaze either direct or averted. A scene in a 1950s film of an incident in a room seen from the outside when the venetian blinds are suddenly opened gave me one part of the idea. Another came when I was standing in an office and watched someone while leaving slide a name panel across an IN/OUT board for staff members. . . . At no time is the whole picture visible. Viewers are invited to engage with the work by sliding the slats across the images, revealing a glance, a hidden detail, underlining the complex and shifting nature of the evidence.[20]

18. Williamson, *Selected Work*, 78.

19. See the work of the Institute for Healing of Memories, founded by Fr. Michael Lapsley, http://www.healing-memories.org.

20. Williamson, *Selected Work*, 44.

In 2000, Williamson's social consciousness began to address her country's struggle with HIV/AIDS. Indeed, just down the road from Williamson's studio in the Observatory section of Cape Town is Manenberg, a township established outside of Cape Town during apartheid, known today for its high rates of unemployment and attendant gang activity, drug abuse, and violent crime. Rusted signs direct traffic along Manenberg's thoroughfares to the "trauma center," or the G. F. Jooste Hospital, one of the few hospitals serving the million-plus residents living in the squatter camps surrounding it. In Jonny Steinberg's 2008 book *Sizwe's Test*, which struggles to understand the mentality of those South African men who are reluctant to be tested for HIV/AIDS, Steinberg describes the hospital through a conversation between himself and Hermann Reuter, a doctor working with Médicines Sans Frontières (Doctors without Borders) in Khayelitsha, the largest but youngest township outside of Cape Town:

> "I would send people there and they would start crying," Hermann recalls.
>
> "They would say, 'Send me anywhere except there.'"
>
> "I [Steinberg] say: 'Why?'"
>
> "They say, 'People die there.'"
>
> "That hospital was overcrowded. It was mainly geared toward surgical patients because of that area. You know, knives and guns and lots of blood. You go to that hospital and you have to go through the security guards. On a Friday night that place smells of alcohol and blood and you need to bleed to be let in there."
>
> "Sometimes I went there on weekends with Treatment Action Campaign people who fell sick, and the guards outside looked at us and said, 'This one is not sick: she can't come in.'"
>
> "I [Hermann] said, 'No, she is very sick; she has meningitis.'"
>
> "They said, 'What is that? I can see she has HIV. Go home.'"
>
> "That was the security guards. I'd tell them I'm a doctor, and that would get me past security. The next line was the nurses. They would say, 'No, this is a chronic patient, take her home.'"
>
> "That was the attitude throughout South Africa: we cannot deal with HIV, especially not on a Friday night."[21]

Meandering through the seemingly endless hallways of the Jooste Hospital, one will eventually encounter the Thuthuzela Care Center. Occupying its own small wing of the hospital, the Manenberg location is

---

21. Jonny Steinberg, *Sizwe's Test: A Young Man's Journey Through Africa's AIDS Epidemic* (New York: Simon and Schuster, 2008), 95–96.

one of forty-five centers operating under the same name and established in South Africa by UNICEF, with additional centers now established as well in Asia and Latin America. These centers, named with the Xhosa word for "comfort," are rapidly becoming a model globally for comprehensive rape care management, offering survivors of rape medical, psychological, and legal services under one roof. These centers exist because, as Carolyn Demptser of the BBC once commented so bluntly, "It is a fact that a woman born in South Africa has a greater chance of being raped, than learning how to read."[22]

In addition to efforts undertaken by nongovernmental organizations like the Thuthuzela Center in responding to the crisis of violence against women, now further complicated by the epidemic raging in the communities most ravaged by apartheid, academic, intellectual, and artistic communities have a vital role to play. Intersecting all three, and recognizing the problem of the stigmatizing and silencing effects of an HIV/AIDS infection in South Africa, Williamson began collaborating with people testing positive in 2000, interviewing them about how an infection had changed their lives. She then painted selected quotes from these interviews on public walls in graffiti-like style, often to be painted over again hours later. Williamson took photographs of the wall while participants' quotes were still visible and combined them with portraits of their authors to create diptychs for a series called *From the Inside*. Her series demonstrates how violence against women is contributing to the epidemiological data revealing that more than half of those living with HIV worldwide today are female. Of the series, Williamson has written:

> How does one make work that reaches people not only . . . in the gallery [but also on the street]? Starting in 2000, a collaborative project with people living with HIV/AIDS attempted to address this problem. Conversations around how the infection had changed their lives identified the most important thing each person felt he or she had learnt from the experience. This "message" was put up on a public wall, with the name of the speaker underneath, together with their HIV status, thus presenting it as an attributed quote and moving it beyond the anonymity of graffiti. The willingness to be named is important in a society where shame and silence over the illness prevail. A photograph of the wall would then be paired with a portrait of the person, to become part of the *From the Inside* series.[23]

22. Carolyn Dempster, "Rape: Silent War on South African Women," British Broadcasting Corporation (April 9, 2002); http://news.bbc.co.uk/2/hi/1909220 .stm (accessed August 30, 2011).

23. Williamson, *Selected Work*, 28.

"It should be taken as a crime if someone doesn't wear a condom and he makes you go to bed."—Busi, HIV-Positive. Sue Williamson, *From the Inside: Busi Maqungo*, 2000. Digital print, Perspex, wood. Edition of 3, 90 cm x 200 cm

Busi is featured in one of the works for *From the Inside*. Seated in a stately way, with her hands folded and resting gently on her lap, Busi looks with poise and confidence directly into the camera. Her silhouette casts a light shadow against an otherwise blank white wall. In an interview with Williamson, Busi said, "It should be taken as a crime if someone doesn't wear a condom and he makes you go to bed." This line was selected by the pair for the graffiti work to accompany Busi's photograph. In addition to sharing her statement, rendered in yellow paint and in a calligraphic font on a cement slab lining a roadway and covering messages left earlier by gangs and pranksters, Busi granted permission for Williamson to use her name and to disclose her status, thereby challenging the stigmatizing and silencing patterns that sometimes accompany an HIV infection in South Africa. Busi's statement is a double indictment. She condemns rape but also the refusal of men to protect women from HIV/AIDS by wearing protection. By confronting the lens, Busi claims her voice and her power and insists on a reckoning from those who peer at her. Williamson demands this as well.

In commenting on the series, Nicholas Dawes attempts to demonstrate how, despite its focus on social issues and "self-evident polemic," Williamson's work is not merely about raising consciousness or documenting tragedy:

The photographs of people with HIV/AIDS are portraits in the proper sense, but the specific humanity of these images is complicated by their juxtaposition with pictures of graffiti, halting slogans and homilies drawn from interviews with the subjects and painted in highly public areas around Cape Town and Johannesburg. The strange relationship between the portrait and the text—reproduced first as transcript, then as public protest, and finally as paired photographs inside a gallery— sketches the ineluctably fractured public and private subjectivity of people living with HIV and AIDS in South Africa, where the disease has introduced to the ideology of the ruling party a fracture so damaging that it can barely speak coherently on the subject, much less act. And what is one to make of the private and public ends of these subjects who will surely die before their time and yet who are fixed here in a state of fragile repose? It is in this register that Williamson's work begins to unwork the limits of a debate about the relationship of African artists to social concerns.[24]

To say that Sue Williamson's work is challenging is an understatement. She is astutely observant and unflinchingly honest. She has a unique ability to translate sociopolitical commentary into graphic visual representations, acceptable to the most discriminating of art galleries in the world as well as to the communities most vulnerable to the inequities, injustices, and indecencies her works expose. Unafraid to confront the viewer with stark images about the intensely disturbing capacity of human beings to harm one another and themselves by the ideologies to which they become wedded, Williamson's work avoids proclamation, preferring instead to dwell in a liminal space between self-assurance and insecurity, where difficult questions are raised without a rush to easy or righteous resolution, even when her political orientation is evident. Williamson rarely provides closure, subjecting herself to the same scrutiny with which she has examined her topic. She demands, in the interest of the common good, for her audiences to do the same.

Although Williamson's framework is not a theological one, for she rejected the institutional church long ago and is as critical of it as she has been of the institution of apartheid, her secular humanism aligns in many ways with the imagination driving many political theologians and Christian humanists, including South Africa's own John de Gruchy, who served as Robert Selby Taylor Professor of Christian Studies at the University of Cape Town and who is now professor emeritus from

24. Nicholas Dawes, "Sue Williamson and the Trauma of History," in *Selected Work*, 7.

the same institution. He writes of the intersections among aesthetics, politics, and theology in many of his books, including *Christianity, Art and Transformation: Theological Aesthetics in the Struggle for Justice*,[25] and *Confessions of a Christian Humanist*.[26] In the latter, he writes a preliminary manifesto for his version of Christian humanism, which he defines as "a critical humanism that arises out of the Christian gospel, challenging the dehumanizing powers of the world, whether secular or religious, in the interests of human well-being."[27]

In his manifesto, de Gruchy lifts up five major points that William-son would share without their attachment to Christianity, including the rootedness of human life on the earth, the shared humanity of people of diverse ethnicities and traditions, and the importance of protecting human rights, celebrating plurality, and unlocking the potential and creativity in all people. Of his Christian humanism, de Gruchy writes, "Christian humanists affirm the integrity of creation, recognizing that human life is rooted in and dependent on the earth. . . . Christian humanists recognize that all of life is bound together in an amazingly complex evolutionary web that evokes humility and awe."[28] Moreover, he writes about a shared humanity among persons of diverse ethnicities and religions. "Christian humanists believe that we share a common humanity with all other human beings." In order to honor our common humanity, de Gruchy emphasizes that we must learn to respect difference and to celebrate plurality.[29] Also, he stresses how people need to come together to protect basic human rights. "Christian humanists believe that we should join with secular humanists and people of other faiths in the struggle for human rights, freedom, dignity, justice and peace, and sustainable policies for the environment."[30] He also addresses the importance of art, creativity, and beauty in unlocking human potential: "Christian humanists today, like those of the past, have a love of learning in search of practical wisdom; a respect for difference yet a commitment to truth; a passion for justice and peace that transcends

---

25. John de Gruchy, *Christianity, Art and Transformation: Theological Aesthetics in the Struggle for Justice* (Cambridge: Cambridge University Press, 2008).

26. John de Gruchy, *Confessions of a Christian Humanist* (Minneapolis: Fortress Press, 2006).

27. Ibid., 18.

28. Ibid., 30.

29. Ibid.

30. Ibid.

the confines of national loyalties; and a sensibility to the aesthetic that espouses beauty and encourages creativity."[31]

Such a theology is one that is fitting to lift up in a book titled *She Who Imagines*, in honor of Elizabeth Johnson's book, *She Who Is*, for it constitutes a reimagined way of being in the world, a way that is lived out in the person of Sue Williamson. The lives of both Williamson and de Gruchy have been informed by their resistance to the policies of apartheid, and by their commitment to the creation of a more peaceful and more equitable South Africa. Their desire to work for the common good overcomes the theological rift between them.

Likewise, Alan Paton was committed to the common good. Although he died before apartheid was overthrown (1903–88), in *Cry, the Beloved Country* he anticipated the turn to violence that would wreak havoc in his country, a violence that was turned against women in particular. Of this violence, he lamented:

> Have no doubt it is fear in the land. For what can [human beings] do when so many have grown lawless? Who can enjoy the lovely land, who can enjoy the seventy years, and the sun that pours down on the earth, when there is fear in the heart? Who can walk quietly in the shadow of the jacarandas, when their beauty is grown to danger? Who can lie peacefully abed, while the darkness holds some secret? What lovers can lie sweetly under the stars, when menace grows with the measure of their seclusion?
>
> There are voices crying what must be done, a hundred, a thousand voices. But what do they help if one seeks for counsel, for one cries this, and one cries that, and another cries something that is neither this nor that.[32]

Paton recognized the destructive power that was overtaking his country. Moreover, he recognized that the danger was maximized both by collective endorsement and tolerance of it and by complacent indifference and ambivalence to it. But he pointed in his novel to its resolution as well. Alan Paton pointed to the power of love, the only power creative enough to undo the devastating trends he was witnessing from his prophetic stance on the eve of the institutionalization of apartheid.

> [T]here is only one thing that has power completely, and that is love. Because when a man loves, he seeks no power, and therefore he has power. I see only one hope for our country, and that is when white

31. Ibid.
32. Paton, *Cry, the Beloved Country*, 107.

men and black men, desiring neither power nor money, but desiring only the good of their country, come together to work for it.

He [Rev. Msimangu] was grave and silent, and then he said somberly, I have one great fear in my heart, that one day when they are turned to loving, they will find we are turned to hating.[33]

Williamson models Paton's proposal, for Paton's novel is about a love demonstrated through a responsibility for the establishment and protection of the common good. He imagined that such a structure could exist for creative ends, just as structures were under construction with devastating consequences. For him, it was clearly not only Absalom, Kumalo's son, who was responsible for the murder of Arthur. The powerful ones in the collective community who pitted white against black, rich against poor, men against women were, to some degree, responsible for those harmed, raped, and murdered by individuals in a society that continued to tolerate appalling levels of inequity. Segregation that would become institutionalized created desperation when meaningful work came to be out of reach for the majority of the people in Paton's country, particularly when a quality education was denied the African majority. Exploitation of the labor force created understandable resentment too, when a gulf developed between the wealthy classes whose luxuries came at the expense of the laborers who received only a pittance of the profits acquired at their hands. Without denying the unique experience of those impacted by the circumstances of apartheid and its prequel in South Africa, these patterns are not limited to the African continent with its former Dutch, English, and French colonies. They have been implemented in Argentina and in Yugoslavia. They have been replicated in El Salvador, Guatemala, and Nicaragua. They have been exercised in Australia and in the United States of America.

But the destructive potency of apartheids, institutionalized and informal, is undone when the collective no longer tolerates segregation and radical inequity as acceptable and actively, peacefully, and nonviolently resists the status quo. Historically rooted but timely and unfortunately perhaps timeless, Paton's novel exposes how xenophobia, or fear of the other, scapegoated a particular people when resources were considered scarce and when greed and desire for security of luxury overcame the desire to ensure the security of the masses. It was a pattern that plagued South Africa in Paton's day, and it continues to plague many others in our own. Paton's analysis is that the epidemic of violent crime taking place in his own day and continuing into the

33. Ibid., 71.

modern day in South Africa can be traced in part to the violent crimes inflicted by white people against black people and to the quietism that enabled it to persist for decades. The role of racial violence resulted, in some cases, in turning black men against women, and against black women in particular, who by a triple degree of jeopardy have been impacted most of all.

The violence about which Paton wrote, that Williamson addresses in her work, and that Busi has experienced continues to perpetuate and prevents us from realizing the *ubuntu* about which Archbishop Desmond Tutu has written so profoundly. It prevents us from realizing that our individual humanity is inextricably interwoven with the humanity of the other, such that what diminishes one diminishes all and what nourishes one nourishes all. The work of artists like Sue Williamson has the capacity to enlarge our common vision and our moral imagination and to open new ways of thinking about what it means to be human and how it is we want to live our lives on this planet that we share for such a very short time. Williamson's work calls us to accountability and action in the creation of a world where we redouble our commitment to nourish rather than to diminish our sisters and brothers to whom the welfare of all is intricately bound.

Just as Elizabeth Johnson invited a reimagining of God's nature and activity in the world by publishing *She Who Is*, so by producing images that ignite revolutionary potential does Sue Williamson provide insight into *She Who Imagines*. Her works of art empower us to dismantle structures that dehumanize and to create systems that acknowledge the dignity of all life in order to break the cycles of violence that threaten to alienate us all. By her socially engaged art of resistance and political activism, Sue Williamson presents viewers with a vision of wholeness by juxtaposing intolerable realities against the violent philosophies that enable them to emerge and persist. Healing of memory and restoration of community radiate from an activism that calls for accountability in working for the common good, an activism that can only arise when people who are unlike one another encounter one another in meaningful ways. Such an artistic engagement of integrity, courage, and imagination as that embodied by Sue Williamson is, indeed, a way of beauty—a way of being to which each of us is called to participate in whatever ways we are able.

Part 3

She Who *Imagines*

Rebecca Berru Davis

Picturing Paradise

Imagination, Beauty, and Women's Lives in a Peruvian Shantytown

La vida en Pamplona Alta es muy dura. Life in Pamplona Alta is very difficult. That is what Antonia told me as she stitched her *cuadro* with her three-year-old wiggling by her side (fig. 1). Antonia is one of many displaced Peruvian women who make and sell appliquéd and embroidered fabric pictures called *cuadros* to help support their families. She does this in Pamplona Alta, one of the poorest shantytowns located on the perimeter of Lima, the capital city of Peru. A shantytown might seem an unlikely place to encounter beauty, yet each day women like Antonia are creating imaginative and ingenious works of art. With bits of brightly colored fabric, they meticulously stitch by hand pictures reflecting distilled memories, present realities, and images of a world they would choose to shape.

Shantytowns, abundant in densely populated urban centers around the globe, are inhabited by the forgotten poor, and it is often women, like Antonia, who "get lost" and forgotten in this universe.[1] Many of those

---

1. This reference is taken from Jon Sobrino, "The Kingdom of God and the Theological Dimension of the Poor," in *Who Do You Say I Am?*, ed. J. Cavadini and L. Holt (Notre Dame, IN: Notre Dame Press, 2004), 131. Sobrino states, "The poor continue to be a concrete reality that the Church and theology cannot seem to figure out how to handle adequately. To put it thus, they are understood as a part of the human universe, but they 'get lost' in this universe."

Figure 1. Antonia Quispe Carapi creating a *cuadro*. Photo courtesy of Dr. Rebecca Berru Davis.

145

who live in Pamplona Alta were initially dislocated from their homes in the interior during the terrorism beginning in the 1980s.[2] Caught between the militia of the right-wing government and the guerilla tactics of the left-wing Shining Path, these *desplazados* or displaced people were often witnesses to brutal violence or targets of terrorist aggression. Seeking a safe haven and in search of better economic opportunities, they made their way to Lima. Claiming small parcels of land as squatters, they created makeshift communities known as *pueblos jóvenes* (young towns). They are what Jon Sobrino names as the "victims" of economic and political instability and oppression.[3] Today they are typical of the poor majorities that continue to exist throughout Latin America, constructing temporary shelters from reed matting, plywood, or whatever materials they can find, with the hope of rebuilding their homes, *ladrillo por ladrillo* (brick-by-brick), one story at a time, with more permanent materials.

My first visit to Pamplona Alta was in 2006 as an art historian. My initial intention was to carry out a systematic study of the *cuadros*: document the process, consider the work within a tradition of textile and fabric art, and interview the women artists. Overwhelmed by the austerity of life in the *pueblos jóvenes*, particularly in contrast to the brilliant colors and picturesque scenes depicted in the women's art, the focus of my research began to take a different shape. New questions emerged. What are the sources of these images? What internal and spiritual resources are the women drawing from in order to create this work? How is it that beauty persists in such challenging conditions? With subsequent opportunities to return to Pamplona Alta, I continue to grapple with these and other questions. Motivated by a fundamental interest in exploring the role art and artistic activity plays in the lives of ordinary women I began to consider how art created by women living on the margins of society reveals religious and theological understandings. Rooted in the women's

2. The extent of the effects of this period of terrorism is still being determined. Among sources that document this period: Olga González-Casañeda, "Unveiling Secrets of War in the Peruvian Andes" (PhD diss., Teacher's College, Columbia University, 2006); Robin Kirk, *The Monkey's Paw: New Chronicles from Peru* (Amherst: University of Massachusetts Press, 1997); David Scott Palmer, ed., *Shining Path of Peru* (New York: St. Martin's Press, 1994); and Deborah Poole and Gerardo Rénique, *Peru: Time of Fear* (London: Latin American Bureau, 1992).

3. Jon Sobrino, *Jesus the Liberator: A Historical-Theological Reading of Jesus of Nazareth* (Maryknoll, NY: Orbis, 2006), 80–81. Sobrino identifies both the economic poor as "those who live bent (*anawim*) under the weight of a burden" and the sociological poor as those marginalized and denied the minimum of dignity.

theological imagination and made explicit in their art is their vision of a just and hopeful world.

This essay draws attention to the creative work of women like Antonia, who live on the periphery of society. I introduce you, the reader, to the women and the *cuadros* they create. I consider their images as personal and collective narratives of displacement and survival but also as expressions of resilience and hope. Finally, I explore spaces where women, like Antonia, often deemed silent and invisible, are able to tell their stories and assert their visions of a paradise they envision. I present the art of these women as evidence of liberation theologian Jon Sobrino's contention that if the kingdom of God is Good News, its recipients, the poor, will fundamentally help in clarifying its content.[4]

In this essay, I employ ethnography, a methodology that serves to keep me both alert and humble as I explore questions related to art and theology in a Peruvian shantytown. I turn to ethnography because I am inspired by Ada Maria Isasi-Díaz's call for a theological method that seeks to understand the lived experiences of Latina women.[5] This method positions me as one who accompanies the women throughout their daily tasks. It keeps me attentive to generative themes that emerge in conversation and in art.[6] And in the process I become not merely observer but also "witness" in a theological sense to their struggles and joys, their wisdom and eloquence.[7] At the same time, as outsider, I am always conscious of the thorny issues related to power, subjectivity, relationship, and voice. Although ethnography is disposed to the

4. Sobrino, *Jesus the Liberator*, 79.

5. Ada Maria Isasi-Díaz, *En La Lucha: Elaborating a Mujerista Theology* (Minneapolis: Fortress Press, 1993). In chapter 3, Isasi-Díaz outlines "ethnomethodology," a strategy for understanding and the procedures she employs in shaping a *mujerista* theology. Other books by Isasi-Díaz that address this methodology include *Mujerista Theology: A Theology for the Twenty-First Century* (Maryknoll, NY: Orbis, 1996), and *La Lucha Continues: Mujerista Theology* (Maryknoll, NY: Orbis, 2004).

6. Isasi-Díaz, *En La Lucha*, 70. Isasi-Díaz explains, "The purpose in doing 'translations' for *mujerista* theology is to discover the themes that are important to the women, the ones about which they feel the strongest, which move them, which motivate them. In *mujerista* theology we refer to these themes as generative words. They emerge for the world of Hispanic Women and express the situations they have to grapple with as well as their understanding of themselves in those situations. These generative words or themes are not only those 'with existential meaning, and, therefore, with greatest emotional content, but they are also typical of the people.'"

7. I thank Dr. Joanne Doi for this insight. Doi develops this notion of "witness" in a theological sense as opposed to participant/observer in her dissertation "Bridge to Compassion: Theological Pilgrimage to Tule Lake and Manzanar" (PhD diss., Graduate Theological Union, Berkeley, CA, 2007), 23–27.

complexities, confusions, and unexpected turns of human relationships, creating at times what James Clifford calls "lucid uncertainty,"[8]
I find it useful in that it begins with the lived realities of these women.
Through shared experiences and dialogical processes it attempts to get
at meaning and bring to light the women's sensibilities, understandings, and perceptions. It assumes that their experiences and wisdom
warrant attention and that knowledge is not limited solely to experts
in the academy.

This project also places emphasis on art as visual language, as it
attempts to expand the notion of discourse to include visual text. It
honors what some might dismiss as tourist art or popular art.[9] As an
artist familiar with art making, I am attentive to the women's creative
use of materials and skillful techniques, evidence of their fluency with
a visual language they have masterfully devised. Like many resource-
ful women, they give new life to recycled remnants in inventive and
effectual ways. As an art historian, I have an interest in how their art
is situated within a cultural and historical trajectory. Indeed, women
throughout the world who experience trauma, often turn to cloth to
tell their stories, as evidenced by Hmong refugees. Their *pan dau* or
"Flower Cloth" became story cloth, recording the war and resettlement
experiences of the Hmong people.[10] Or as in the "Memory Cloth" that
documents what South African women witnessed during apartheid.[11]
It was the Chilean *arpilleras*, created by women with the intention of
conveying their realities and at the same time critiquing the oppres-

8. James Clifford, *Routes: Travel and Translation in the Late Twentieth Century*
(Cambridge, MA: Harvard University Press, 1997), 13.

9. Sources that explore the value and significance of tourist art and popular
art include Ruth B. Phillips and Christopher B. Steiner, eds., *Unpacking Culture: Art
and Commodity in Colonial and Postcolonial Worlds* (Berkeley: University of California
Press, 1999); H. H. Nelson Graburn, ed., *Ethnic and Tourist Arts: Cultural Expressions
from the Fourth World* (Berkeley and Los Angeles: University of California Press,
1976); Walter Morris, *Handmade Money: Latin American Artisans in the Marketplace*
(Washington, DC: Organization of American States, 1996); William Rowe and Vivian
Schelling, *Memory and Modernity: Popular Culture in Latin America* (London and New
York: Verso, 1993).

10. See *Hmong Art: Tradition and Change* (Sheboygan, WI: John Michael Kohler
Arts Center, 1986); and Guy Brett, *Through Our Own Eyes: Popular Art and Modern
History* (Philadelphia, PA: New Society Publishers, 1987).

11. See Carol Becker, "Amazwi Abesifazone (Voices of Women)" *Art Journal*
63, no. 4 (2004): 117–34; or "Create Africa South" (CAS) http://www.cas.org.za
/projects/voices.htm for more information on South African Memory Cloth.

sive Pinochet regime during the 1970s, that became the inspiration for the *cuadros*.[12]

For Latin American women, textiles are a traditional form of creative activity, and the making and embellishing of cloth is an avenue for demonstrating skill and communicating information.[13] Art historian Janet Catherine Berlo, in her essay "Beyond Bricolage: Women and Aesthetic Strategies in Latin American Textiles," explains that "[t]extiles are eloquent texts, encoding history, change, appropriation, oppression and endurance, as well as personal and cultural creative visions. For indigenous Latin Americans, especially women, cloth has been an alternative discourse."[14]

As a theologian, I also attend to art as artifacts or objects that can, like textual material, reveal a community's belief system or an individual's personal understanding of faith and hope. Indeed, art is the manifestation of our visual imagination at work in the world. It is the direct expression of the gift of creation we share with the divine. Thus, art's capacity to enlighten is not solely the work of the art historian to discover. For the theologian, the work of art holds potential for disclosing and discerning new understandings about God, about our relationship with God, and about each other. With this in mind, an appreciation for art understood in its broadest scope, both noted and nameless works, warrants attention.

12. Key sources for the history of the Chilean *arpilleras* include Marjorie Agosín's books: *Scraps of Life: Chilean Arpilleras, Chilean Women and Pinochet Dictatorship* (Trenton, NJ: The Red Sea Press, 1987), and *Tapestries of Hope, Threads of Life: The Arpillera Movement in Chile*, 2nd ed. (New York: Rowman and Littlefield, 2008). Chapter 1, "All This We Have Seen," in Brett, *Through Our Own Eyes* documents the story of the Chilean *arpilleras*.

Barbara Cervenka, *Cuadros: Textile Pictures from the Pamplona Alta* (exhibit brochure), and Gaby Franger, *Arpilleras, cuadros que hablan: vida cotidaiano y organización de mujeres* (Lima, Peru: Movimiento Manuela Ramos, 1988), discuss the introduction of Chilean *arpilleras* into the shantytown of Pamplona Alta by a German schoolteacher, Roswitha Lopez, and their subsequent transformation by the Peruvian women.

13. Andrea M. Heckman, *Woven Stories: Andean Textiles and Rituals* (Albuquerque: University of New Mexico Press, 2003); Betty La Duke, *Compañera: Women, Art, and Social Change in Latin America* (San Francisco: City Lights Books, 1985); Rebecca Stone-Miller, *To Weave for the Sun: Ancient Andean Textiles in the Boston Museum of Fine Arts* (New York: Thames and Hudson, 1992); Annette B. Weiner and Jane Schneider, eds., *Cloth and Human Experience* (Washington, DC, and London: Smithsonian Institution Press, 1989).

14. Janet Catherine Berlo, "Beyond Bricolage: Women and Aesthetic Strategies in Latin American Textiles," in *Textile Traditions of MesoAmerica and the Andes: An Anthology*, ed. Margot Blum Schevill, Janet Catherine Berlo, and Edward B. Dwyer (New York and London: Garland Publishing, 1991), 439.

Pamplona Alta

In shantytowns like Pamplona Alta, women like Antonia often turn to other women for support and to "make do." Common kitchens are formed and art cooperatives are organized as collaborative efforts to do so make survival feasible. The two cooperatives I became acquainted with, *Compacto Humano* ("Human Compact" established in the 1980s) and the more recently formed *Manos Ancashinas* (Hands from Ancash),[15] provide steady work and dependable income to about thirty women from ages sixteen to sixty-six. The women gather together daily to stitch *cuadros* that are then sold in tourist markets either locally or abroad.

Driven by subsistence, their art is also a means of self-expression: the stitching together of meaningful narratives.[16] The *cuadros* are visual stories about the quotidian rhythms of life these women once knew. Lush landscapes include exquisite details such as specific flowers, animals, and birds that are essential features of an Andean world.[17] *Lo cotidiano* (daily life) in the marketplace and in the countryside are common themes (fig. 2). Religious events and festivals depict regional dress, dance, and food preparation and record the continuity of traditions that are still celebrated today in their home villages. Their *cuadros* also tell stories of significant events that occurred, such as the phenomenon of El Niño, the border dispute between Ecuador and Peru, and the violence and terrorism that occurred in Ayacucho.[18]

15. Ancash is a province in northern Peru where the women in this group originally came from.

16. Philip Sheldrake, *Spaces for the Sacred: Place, Memory and Identity* (London: SCM Press, 2001), 19. Sheldrake, a theologian, writes that "without stories we are trapped in the immediacy of the present" (19). Jeanette Rodriguez, *Stories We Live, Cuentos Que Vivimos: Hispanic Women's Spirituality* (New York: Paulist Press, 1996), 6. Rodriguez, a Latina theologian, speaks about the power of stories to connect us with the past, help us to understand the present, and offer hope for the future.

17. Latin American art historian Teresa Gisbert explores pre-Hispanic Andean imagery in her book *Iconografía y mitos indigenas en el arte*, 4th ed. (La Paz, Bolivia: Editorial Gisbert y CIA, 2008), 17–73. Also see Teresa Gisbert, *El paraiso de los pájaros parrlantes: la imagen del otro en la cultura andina* (La Paz, Bolivia: Universidad Nuestra Señora de La Paz, 1999).

18. Among the estimated sixty-nine thousand victims of the terrorist activities between 1980 and 2000, twenty-three thousand are known to be from Ayacucho. Sources for these statistics were recorded from a presentation by Cecilia Tovar, staff member at the Instituto Bartolome de las Casas, in a lecture titled "Los años de violencia y sus secuelas," on June 3, 2009, Lima, Peru. For further information on the results of terrorist activity in Peru between 1980 and 2000, see *Informe Final de*

Figure 2. Betty Rojas, *Cosecha (Harvest)*, n.d., 17" x 19". Photo courtesy of Dr. Rebecca Berru Davis.

In all of these images the women depict themselves as active agents, whether leading a campaign for milk for their children, a teachers' strike, or a march for peace. Their fabric canvases assert a version of the story not always included in the "official record." In the *cuadros*, like *Violence in the Pueblo*, the whimsical quality of the little figures and the bright, cheerful palette juxtaposed against the disconcerting depictions of protest and strife create an unexpected dissonance. Indeed, the subtle strength of the *cuadros* lies in the images and themes with multivalent meanings that create complexity and gravity under the guise of simplicity and charm.[19]

Spiral of Life is an extraordinarily large *cuadro*, measuring seventy-six inches by seventy-eight inches. It was created by Noris Vásquez

---

la Comisión de la Verdad y Reconciliación (Lima: Instituto de Decocracia y Derechos Humanos de la Pontificia Universidad Católica del Perú, 2008), 3.

19. An examination of the notion of "hidden transcripts" employed by subordinate groups and the "arts of public disguise" can be found in James C. Scott, *Domination and the Arts of Resistance: Hidden Transcripts* (New Haven, CT, and London: Yale University Press, 1990). In the introduction of *The Subversive Stitch: Embroidery and the Making of the Feminine* (London: Women's Press, 1996), author Rozika Parker argues for a reexamination of the multiple meanings of women's textile traditions.

Liñares and is her story but is also representative of the stories of the many women who have migrated from the countryside to the city (fig. 3). In the center is a little house in which, seen through the window, a baby girl is born. As the young girl grows, she is depicted helping the family with household and outdoor tasks. Life in her village centers around religious festivals and growing cycles until an avalanche of rocks destroys their home and the family decides to move to Lima. Unable to find a place to live, the family constructs a makeshift hut of straw mats on claimed land. The family sells vegetables at a market and the young girl works as a maid in the house of a well-to-do family in order to make ends meet. She becomes pregnant by the son of the family and is left to look for work elsewhere. She finally finds support among women,

Figure 3. Noris Vásquez Liñares, *Spiral of Life*, 76'' x 78''. (Collection: Con Vida: Popular Arts of America).

working in a cooperative located in the *pueblos jóvenes*. The spiral ends with the young woman making *cuadros* together with other women.[20] The narrative told in this *cuadro* is epic in that it represents both calamities and challenges endured by many women in the shantytown.

Whether the work is large or small, individually or collaboratively carried out, the physical act of stitching these stories becomes important memory work whereby the women artists make sense of events inwardly and outwardly.[21] Thus, the making of *cuadros* provides a means for the women to stay linked to a vanished past and to help process the realities of the present.

Stitching Theology

As I witnessed this, the idea for a special project emerged. With funds from a grant I received set aside to commission some work from them, I proposed a task that I knew could be completed within a short time without disrupting the pattern of their daily operation. I asked the women to each create a small *cuadro* (ten inches by ten inches) illustrating their hopes and dreams. I purposely framed the task to be as open-ended as possible and left it to the women to visually express their ideas. The resulting *cuadros* revealed very personal wishes as well as universal aspirations.

There were dreams of permanent homes with roofs, employment opportunities for themselves or their family members. They envisioned living in a garden or traveling with their families to places they had never been before. They created sanctuaries where their children could play without fear of violence or environmental contamination.

For some women their dreams were as uniquely defined as anticipating the birth of another child. Emma explained:

> In this garden of many flowers, my husband and I are embracing as we await the arrival of our second baby. Here you can see my little

20. This description is drawn from Noris Vásquez Liñares's explanation of her work and documented in the exhibition brochure by Barbara Cervenka, *Cuadros: Textile Pictures from the Pamplona Alta*.

21. James Young, "Living with the Fabric Arts of Memory," in *The Weavings of War: The Story of War Textiles*, September 6–October 5, 1997 (New York: The Puffin Foundation, 2005), 31. See also Lewis P. Hinchman and Sandra K. Hinchman, eds., *Memory, Identity, and Community: The Idea of Narrative in the Human Sciences* (New York: State University of New York Press, 1997), for a discussion of the significance of narrative (and, in this case, visual story) in preserving memory, shaping identity, and forming community.

daughter playing with a ball. My brother Javier, who I love like a son, because I have known him since he was a baby, is swimming in the river with an inner tube. Notice the butterflies fluttering about and my well-built two-story house. This is my dream.

Mirtha's hope was for the creation of a world where all life is protected (fig. 4):

In this *cuadro* I depict a dream that I have always hoped for. . . . In order to make the world better, we must preserve sea life so that the whales, dolphins, sea wolfs, and fish do not become extinct. We must protect and care for all the animals and plants that are running the danger of extinction.

Lucy's concern was for a place where all persons, regardless of race or social status, live together in peace:

This *cuadro* depicts a dream that may only come true if there is a world without wars. This would be a world like Paradise. My dream is to have people of different classes and different races live together. In this *cuadro* there are people of all colors and animals of all kinds. If there weren't wars, racism, and violence we could live together with people from different countries. We would be able to live together with our animals, because animals represent everything that is beautiful in the world. The tree that I have made here represents heaven on earth. We are all together and sharing.

Julia described her dream:

My dream is to travel—to leave my house with my husband and to help people in need. Here we are passing through Puna and entering the jungle when we encounter a group of natives. Our journey continues in a boat throughout the world.

Thank you, she said, for the opportunity to share my dream even though it may seem impossible. I had never thought of sharing my dreams with anyone, because no one ever asked us about our dreams.

Always self-conscious of my position as benevolent outsider with resources to leave the shantytowns at will, Julia's unexpected words of appreciation served to allay my hesitations about intruding in the women's lives. Moreover, I realized that, for Julia, the project provided her and the others an opportunity to make manifest their hopeful visions—dreams that would otherwise remain imperceptible to others.

Figure 4. Mirtha Aliaga, *Hopes and Dreams*, 2006, 10'' x 10''. Photo courtesy of Hernán L. Navarette.

The women's *cuadros* were evidence of what Sobrino claims as the graced insights of the poor. They were, in fact, "focused expressions of a utopian vision where there can be life, justice, fraternity and dignity in a world in which history seems to render them impossible": a world that is good, that is both imminent and eschatological—*here* and *not yet*.[22]

In January 2007, I returned to Pamplona Alta. Again I involved the women in a project, but not without first spending time with them at their sewing tables. The idea for a new theme emerged as I learned more about their daily lives. Each day they leave their makeshift homes and make their way down to the workshop. Some of the women arrive with babies wrapped tightly onto their backs in blankets or with toddlers in tow. All of them appear with plastic sacks stuffed with partially completed *cuadros*; projects that were worked on in their spare time at home. This was their daily routine. I wondered how they persevered, so I asked them to draw from a past event or their present reality to illustrate what inspired or motivated them to carry on each day.

They *created* narratives called *La Vida Diaria* (Daily Life) or *Mi Caminar* (My Path). Their images reflected that inspiration, and motivation was found in the *compañerismo* (companionship) they experienced with their families, their friends, and the other women in the workshop. They stressed the meaning of their work as something that directly benefits their children. In this project, the women's art reflects what Latin American theologian Ivonne Gebara names as vital centers and quotidian rhythms of human existence, those places where women's theological expression always starts: family and community.[23]

Their notion of *convivencia* (social living together), highlighted in Julia's *cuadro*, includes expressing gratitude for blessings received, an imperative and generative cycle in their lives (fig. 5). Julia explains:

> In this *cuadro* I tell a very beautiful story that took place in December in my hometown village in Ancash. I prepared a *chocolatada*. The car is arriving at the village. You can see that everyone is receiving gifts. In front of the house I am making the *chocolatada*. There is a fig tree, flowers, and animals and cows. There is also a horse carrying a load to my village. My mother and brother are helping.

22. Sobrino, "The Kingdom of God and the Theological Dimension of the Poor," 120–21.

23. Ivone Gebara "Women Doing Theology in Latin America," in *Through Her Eyes: Women's Theology from Latin America*, ed. Elsa Tamez (Maryknoll, NY: Orbis, 1989), 45.

Figure 5. Juliana Liñan Retuerto, *La Chocolatada*, 2007, 10'' x 18''.
Photo courtesy of Hernán L. Navarette.

In Julia's *cuadro*, titled *La Chocolatada*, she tells a "beautiful story" of returning to her village, and she does this annually during the Christmas season, to distribute hot chocolate and gifts to family members and friends—never forgetting her home and always seeking some way to give back to her community. In this account of her annual return to her village, a bold image of a fig tree dominates in the lower register. While I was eager to ascribe some iconographic, even biblical, interpretation to the motif, I held back and asked Julia to tell me about the tree. She explained that, as her mother told her, the fig tree is one of the few trees that survive, even under the harsh Peruvian conditions, and represents *la mujer luchando* (the fighting woman). Julia's interpretation was like visual poetry where, as Gebara asserts, one finds the deepest meaning and mystery expressed.[24]

In July 2008 I returned to Peru once more and after time spent with the women at their sewing tables, in their homes, and among parishioners at the neighborhood church, a theme emerged for their commissioned work: *"Quién soy yo?"* (*Who Am I?*). While the first project elicited the women's hopes and dreams, the second called forth their inspirations and motivations; this third project was intended to encourage them to think about themselves as individuals. The themes that surfaced challenged the paradigm of identity I was familiar with, one that highly values self-reliance, independence, and individualism. Instead, the women's *cuadros* reflect their understanding of themselves in relationship to and interconnected with one another.

Sixty-six-year-old Rosa, who depicted herself working in a *comedor* (soup kitchen), explained:

> I am a person who always saw what was needed in my home. I have also always been concerned about the needs of those persons with few economic resources. For this reason, I promised to work in a community kitchen so that I would be able to help many families. I have never regretted doing this even as I age.

Cuadros like Rosa's confirm that the women's identities are reciprocally and meaningfully linked with identities and the concerns of others (fig. 6).

For me, the art created by the women reveals the deeper meaning of joy and abundance and makes me aware of our shared utopian dreams. Their art recalls for me that our journey toward God is not as isolated individuals but as an entire community. Despite the severity of their

24. Ibid., 45.

grey and barren surroundings, these women bring forth images of the
world as garden. Clearly, they are picturing paradise.

The women's experiences of displacement and survival are depicted
in their *cuadros* as narratives that serve to document the past and present
while their visions of a just world reveal their resilience and hope. The
integrity and persistence they demonstrate in carrying out this creative
activity despite the experiences they endure lends credence to their
struggles for full humanity, healing, wholeness, and liberation.[25]

The content of their art and its aesthetic sensibility is informed by
their understanding and experience of creation. What gives them life

25. Elizabeth Tapia as cited in Chung Hyun Kung, *Struggle to Be the Sun Again:
Introducing Asian Women's Theology* (Maryknoll, NY: Orbis, 1990), 100.

Figure 6. Rosa Fernandez, *¿Quien soy yo?*, 2008. 10" x 10". Photo courtesy of Dr. Rebecca
Berru Davis.

and energy is apparent. Their creative work sustains them and gives them power to cope with adversity. Alejandro García-Rivera says, "Art's theological dimension has its origin in God's own art, the natural beauty of Creation. Indeed, the human participates in that natural beauty by virtue of being one of God's creatures."[26] A feminist aesthetic informed by the intimate experience of creation and creating keeps us connected with God's creative activity in the world. The women artists of Pamplona Alta invite us to look and see again. Those of us who live comfortable lives can become inured to really looking and then can fail to truly see and comprehend. The women remind us that in our capacity to imagine worlds of human flourishing, we take an important step toward justice. To conceive of such worlds, the women recognize and visually name the necessary components. We are reminded through their art that a world bound together in right relationship is a just world when we care for creation, attend to each other, choose life, and express gratitude. Indeed, their images, appreciated as visual theology, reflect their conviction that God continues to act graciously in the world and in grace-filled ways through us.

Despite the challenges they have endured, a profound optimism is evident among the women of Pamplona Alta who stitch together images of paradise in an environment that is far from idyllic. Their *cuadros* underscore the deeper meanings of joy and abundance and make us attentive to our shared utopian dreams. They remind us that we make the journey toward God not as isolated individuals but as an entire community reveling in camaraderie, creation, and color.[27]

La vida es muy dura en Pamplona Alta, but the women's articulate voices are testimony, and their creativity is evidence of the paradise they so clearly envision—and, we with them, strive for.

26. Alejandro García-Rivera, *A Wounded Innocence: Sketches for a Theology of Art* (Collegeville, MN: Liturgical Press, 2003), 5.

27. Gustavo Gutierrez, *We Drink from Our Own Wells: The Spiritual Journey of a People* (Maryknoll, NY: Orbis, 1985), 72.

Maureen H. O'Connell

A Harsh and Dreadful Beauty

The Aesthetic Dimension
of Dorothy Day's Ethics

"The world will be saved by beauty," Dorothy Day would often say, quoting the wisdom of Dostoyevsky's Prince Myshkin in *The Idiot*. As a possible indicator of the aesthetic foundation of Day's social ministry, Dostoyevsky's tomes were second only to the Bible in helping her to discern the demands of justice. She also regularly invoked his description of a "harsh and dreadful love," articulated by Father Zosima in *The Brothers Karamazov*, to explain the ethos of the Catholic Worker Movement she founded with Peter Maurin in 1933: "active love is labor and fortitude, and for some people too, perhaps a complete science."[1] In other words, Day sought after a love that didn't shield her from the ugliness of the human condition but rather a love that pulled her to the brink of despair and loneliness so familiar to so many while at the same time warning her against sins of pride and righteousness latent in any attempt to care for the less fortunate neighbor. "What does the modern world know of love?" she wrote in her column in *The Catholic Worker*, "On Pilgrimage," in 1946. "It has never reached down into the depths, to the misery and pain and glory of love which endures to death and beyond it. We have not yet begun to learn about love. Now is the time to begin, to start afresh, to use this divine weapon."[2]

1. William Miller, *Dorothy Day: A Biography* (San Francisco: HarperCollins, 1984), 24–25.
2. Dorothy Day, "Love Is the Measure," *The Catholic Worker* (June 1946), 2. See http://www.catholicworker.org/dorothyday/Reprint2.cfm?TextID=425.

Day's personal and public writing reveals that beauty is no stranger to this harsh and dreadful approach to love. In fact, what I call a "harsh and dreadful beauty" is fundamental to Day's spirituality and an essential facet of the distinctive Personalism that animated the ethos of the Catholic Worker Movement. By this I mean Day's paradoxical sense that "our life is charged with drama about which we can do nothing"[3] and an awareness that creative self-expression and encounters with beauty can "break us out of our lives, and find . . . God, the meaning of things, a purpose, faith."[4] Her approach to beauty makes Day a valuable resource for contemporary feminist aesthetics. Through it she implicitly underscores the moral agency of women as creators, as well as the power of beauty to pull us into the ugliness of social injustice and to sustain us to love the neighbor in radical ways. Day's sense of beauty, often revealed through her vivid descriptions of the ugliness of poverty, heightens our awareness of what justice looks and feels like when we seek it in the faces of others.

It is important to note from the outset of this essay that Day is the *subject* of beauty here, one who creates and comments on the beautiful, and not the object of it. The latter would also be possible because she was, indeed, a strikingly beautiful woman. Those who knew her use a variety of words to describe her: "immensely beautiful and gorgeous," recalled close friend Ned O'Gorman;[5] one of her biographers, Jim Forest, who met Day when he joined the movement in the late 1950s, describes her as "arresting, fresh-scrubbed with a statuesque physique" and "a mobile expression, eyes that were teasing one moment, laughing the next, grey the next."[6] "You felt she could see into your depths, and maybe she could. Dorothy was a magnet," recalls another Catholic Worker, Pat Rusk.[7] And another acquaintance notes that "in her old age she had a beauty beyond the physical, a beauty that come through her."[8]

Engaging Day as a subject of beauty, however, as one who created beauty, further illuminates the inherent feminist dimensions of her work:

3. Mark and Louise Zwick, *The Catholic Worker Movement: Intellectual and Spiritual Origins* (New York: Paulist Press, 2005), 280.

4. Robert Coles, *Dorothy Day: A Radical Devotion* (Reading, MA: Addison-Wesley Publishing Company, 1987), 158–59.

5. Rosalie G. Riegele, *Dorothy Day: Portraits by Those Who Knew Her* (Maryknoll, NY: Orbis, 2003), 123.

6. Jim Forest, "All Is Grace," Clarification of Thought, Maryhouse Catholic Worker, October 28, 2011, New York City, in conjunction with publication of *All Is Grace: A Biography of Dorothy Day* (Maryknoll, NY: Orbis, 2011).

7. Riegele, *Dorothy Day*, 132.

8. Ibid., 160.

her insistence on addressing social injustice through her intentional relationships with poor persons she knew by name and not simply through abstract intellectualism; the hermeneutic of suspicion she brought to all of her dealings with institutions, whether governmental or ecclesial, that made her watchful of the abuse of power; an awareness of a matrix of systems of oppression and their impact on women and persons of color; and an insistence on moving from particular experiences of suffering to more universally applicable moral claims about human dignity, the rights of workers, and the wrongs of war.[9]

Moreover, as a subject of beauty, Day expands our notions of it, particularly in terms of the connections she makes between the beautiful and the just that I attempt to outline here. Forest notes that Day's spirituality was nourished by an "aesthetic discipline" best understood in terms of her self-proclaimed "duty to see beauty" or a "determination not to be blind to the beauty around [her]."[10] What she delighted in, as recorded in her various written works, reveals a notion of beauty that is deeply relational and oriented toward loving union with God and, perhaps more important, with persons she made it her duty to know and love.

After preliminary remarks about her affinity for beauty in the arts and the natural world, I examine four elements of Day's notion of beauty that illuminate important connections between beauty and love of neighbor that attends to the demands of justice in our contemporary context: creative, enlarging, harsh and dreadful, and dutiful.

Prelude: Day, the Lover of the Arts and Natural Beauty

Dorothy Day, who some have called the most significant American Catholic of the twentieth century, was no stranger to beauty or the arts. For one, she had an affinity for artists. In her anarchist days as a young adult, she was a regular among the Greenwich Village artistic elite—playwright Eugene O'Neil, poet Francis Thompson, and a host of columnists and writers like herself who honed their craft amid the angst of industrialization and socialism. Those who knew her also recall her love of opera. "You did not knock on her door on Saturday afternoons because she was listening to the weekly broadcast of the Metropolitan Operation," recalls Forest.[11] She joked with one of her compatriots that

---

9. For more on a feminist appropriation of Day, see June O'Connor, *The Moral Vision of Dorothy Day* (New York: Crossroad, 1991).

10. Forest, "All Is Grace."

11. Ibid.

she'd like to come back in the next life as a "Wagnerian soprano."[12] Ade Bethune, who created the iconic woodcut images on the masthead of *The Catholic Worker*, recalls Day encouraging her to adorn the pages of *The Catholic Worker* with images of "good things," "beautiful things, vines and grapes, and mothers and children, and works of mercy" to counter the "troubleness and bitterness of the world."[13] She insisted that a book of Käthe Kollwitz's paintings, a cherished gift from a friend, be available to all in the library of the Maryhouse community on the Lower East Side in New York City so that all could "feast on beauty."[14]

Moreover, books often rivaled Day's fellow Workers and guests in Catholic Worker houses of hospitality when it came to sustaining her spiritual life and social ministry. Forest remembers her lamenting that the "loss of books is the hardest thing about living in community."[15] After all, she unapologetically credits novelists—Dostoyevsky, Tolstoy, Dickens, James, Norris—as the first to introduce her to the forgotten people that she would spend the entirety of her life living with and loving. "The very fact that *The Jungle* was about Chicago, where I lived, whose streets I walked," she writes in her 1952 autobiography, *The Long Loneliness*, "made me feel that from then on my life was to be linked to ['the destitute'], their interests were to be mine: I had received a call, a vocation, a direction in my life."[16]

Peter Elie, another biographer, notes that fiction "comforted her better than religion could, for even as novels gave solace, they cried out against injustice."[17] She was compelled by authors since, in many ways, as a novelist and columnist, she too understood only too well that "in the heat of searching the words take on life."[18] Like other authors, she wrote in order to "break out" of her life, to find and then share a sense of purpose rooted in God but constantly affirmed by the people "on the line": the homeless, the mentally ill, the incarcerated, the substance abusers, the chronically unemployed.

12. Riegele, *Dorothy Day*, 159.

13. Ibid., 78.

14. Dorothy Day, "On Pilgrimage—February 1976," *The Catholic Worker* (February 1976), 2, 4. See http://www.catholicworker.org/dorothyday/Reprint2.cfm?TextID=567.

15. Forest, "All Is Grace."

16. Dorothy Day, *The Long Loneliness* (New York: HarperOne, 1997), 38.

17. Paul Elie, *The Life You Save May Be Your Own* (New York: Farrar, Straus and Giroux, 2004), 15.

18. Ibid., 153, quoting *The Long Loneliness*.

Day also acknowledges the role of beauty in sparking her long-suffering conversion experience. "The beauty of nature which includes the sound of waves, the sound of insects, the cicadas in the trees—all were part of my joy in nature that brought me to the Church," she reflectively writes during a period of convalescence in the late 1970s.[19] Biographer William Miller notes it was no coincidence that Day's first sense of peace—an emotional space that allowed a deep desire for love to blossom—occurred during the five years she lived in her fisherman's shack on the shores of Staten Island: a love for Forster Batterham, for her child, and for God. The beauty of the place "spoke to my soul" she recalled.[20] "I had been passing through some years of fret and strife, beauty and ugliness, even some weeks of sadness and despair," she writes of this time. "There had been periods of intense joy but seldom had there been the quiet beauty and happiness I had now."[21]

Creative Beauty: Writing and Mothering

Perhaps nowhere is Dorothy Day more a subject of beauty than in her creative labors of writing and mothering (and later grandmothering) her biological family as well as the ever-growing Catholic Worker family. Through both of these expressive endeavors—writing and mothering—she literally brought new things into being and in so doing found deep contentment and purposefulness. Each afforded her the ability to enter more fully into the inherent contradictions of the human experience in order to encounter God: joy and suffering, accompaniment and loneliness, limitlessness and finitude, tastes of heaven and hell. Each of these navigations was a creative form of love, bringing into existence something from nothing, whether conceiving, delivering, and raising a child; putting out a monthly newspaper; or forming intentional communities whose vision of social relationships offered an arresting alternative to conventional attitudes and structures. In these creative endeavors she

---

19. Dorothy Day, "On Pilgrimage—October/November 1976," *The Catholic Worker* (October–November 1976), 1, 4, 7. See http://www.catholicworker.org/dorothy day/Reprint2.cfm?TextID=574.

20. Miller, *Dorothy Day*, 177. He goes on to note that Day attributed "the awakening of her consciousness to little things as well as to nature's grandeur" to her "common-law husband," Forster Batterham, further noting that "throughout her life it was nature that produced in her the most direct sense of goodness and peace" (171).

21. Day, *The Long Loneliness*, 135.

reveals beauty as that which integrates deeply personal experiences with pressing social questions and heightens social consciousness.

She took up writing as a young woman, reporting on labor issues for a variety of New York papers and magazines, even writing a novel in 1924, *The Eleventh Virgin*, whose autobiographical content she reluctantly claimed later in life. She would write two memoirs, nearly fifteen hundred columns, and five books by the time of her death in late November 1980, "all grounded," in the words of Elie, "in her conviction that firsthand experience and the art of recording it in prose are vital to religious insight."[22] That many of those who have joined the Catholic Worker Movement recall being attracted to Day through her writing underscores Elie's point as well as the inherent beauty in her craft. "To read *The Long Loneliness*," explains Jim Forest, who first met Day after reading her 1952 memoir, "is to meet her in the flesh. There were not two Dorothys." Notes Jane Sammon, a member of the Maryhouse community on the Lower East Side since the 1970s, "You open up Dorothy's books and that's she."[23]

Although several have noted the distinctiveness of Day's writing style, what Elie describes as a blend of documentary and homiletic, it is *what* she wrote about and *why* that reveals the role of beauty in her creative gift.[24] "We write in response to what we care about, what we believe to be important, what we want to share with others," she explained. "I have never stopped wanting to do so. I have been reached so many times by certain writers. What is this distinction between writing and doing that some people make? Each is an act. Both can be part of a person's response, an ethical response to the world."[25]

What did Day write about? Her journals, memoirs, and columns call our attention to the ways in which God can be encountered and justice and injustice meted out in the ordinary lives and circumstances of people "on the line" in the Catholic Worker houses of hospitality, people whose names she knew and whose stories she made it a priority to learn. In a 1955 column titled "The Insulted and Injured," she explains how her rationale for writing arose when reading an exchange between two characters in the book with the same title by Dostoyevsky. The protagonist reads a story he has written out loud to his father who responds by saying, "It's simply a little story, but it wrings your heart,

22. Elie, *The Life You Save*, 39.
23. Jane Sammon, comment during Clarification of Thought, Maryhouse Catholic Worker, October 28, 2011, New York City.
24. Elie, *The Life You Save*, 245.
25. Coles, *Dorothy Day*, 33.

and what's happening all around one grows easier to understand and to remember, and one learns that the most down-trodden, humblest man is a man, too, and a brother." Day continues in her column: "And I thought as I read these words,—'That is why I write, and that is the purpose of the story I am going to tell now, the story of Felicia."[26]

Folks like Felicia were Day's muses, and she shares the insights she learned from them in conversations over meals, confessions over cups of coffee, or disputes over the rules of the house—the day-to-day activities in the Worker—in a style that was more than reportorial. Her writing pulls her readers into her encounters, potentially concretizing the demands of that harsh and dreadful love of the neighbor. In one instance, she likens her writing to Kollwitz's paintings, which concretized the suffering of war in arresting and deeply personal visual images. "An ordinary journalistic device is to paint a picture with contrasts. It is an emotional way of making a point," she writes in *On Pilgrimage*, her journal from 1948. "Our aim is to move the heart, stir the will to action; to arouse pity, compassion; to awaken the conscience. We want to do such work as Käthe Kollwitz."[27] In another column, she situates her craft in the tradition of novelists who take up the plight of the poor and yet fail, in her estimation, to bridge the experiential gap between themselves and their subject. Many novelists bring the reader "very close to [the poor]," she said, but don't "help you get inside them the way I'd like, the way a novelist who has never been with such people might. I mean, inside their hearts, not their minds."[28]

She wrote because she understood the power of her words to share the news that God is indeed at work in the mundane and that through participating in that mystery a more just social order is possible.[29] The beauty of this mystery lay in the ordinariness and practicality that a life loving the poor entails, details that she refused to dismiss as inconsequential—the physicality of the guests and Workers, the emotions associated with day-to-day life in the houses of hospitality, the senses in which the mundane work and mystery occurred. She names her

26. Dorothy Day, "The Insulted and Injured," *The Catholic Worker* (April 1955), 1, 6. See http://www.catholicworker.org/dorothyday/Reprint2.cfm?TextID=684.

27. Dorothy Day, *On Pilgrimage* (Grand Rapids, MI: William B. Eerdmans Publishing Company, 1999), 223–24. Day was struck by Kollwitz's engagement with war through her personal encounters with it. See Jayme Hennessy's essay on this very subject in this collection.

28. Coles, *Dorothy Day*, 144.

29. O'Connor, *The Moral Vision*, 30–33.

writing as a Work of Mercy—a way of attending to Christ in his various manifestations in the people "on the line."

Her second creative labor began shortly before she turned thirty when she gave birth to her daughter Tamar Teresa in 1926, although not before she had read the "childbirth scenes by the great writers" in preparation for the event, recalling in the midst of labor that they were all men. "'What do they know about it, the idiots,' I thought."[30] Jim Forest notes that "she regarded her daughter as a miracle. It was not just the usual miracle that all pregnancies are. It was a miracle with a capital 'M,' since she thought she was barren because of her abortion. A healing miracle. And then to have nine grandchildren? This was the mercy of God."[31]

Her maternal labor was equally monumental: "If I had written the greatest book, composed the greatest symphony, painted the most beautiful painting or carved the most exquisite figure," she wrote, "I could not have felt the more exalted creator than I did when they placed my child in my arms."[32] Her two creative endeavors were fused shortly after Tamar's birth when Day wrote about the experience for *The New Masses*, "in order to share [her] joy with the world." It is the first of many accounts that situate what was going on in her personal life in the context of the beautifully gritty world around her, or that bridge the private and public spheres in a way that was unprecedented for a woman in her generation:

> Sitting up in bed, I glance alternately at my beautiful flat stomach and out the window at tug boats and barges and the wide path of the early morning sun on the East River. Whistles are blowing cheerily, and there are some men singing on the wharf below. The restless water is colored lavender and gold and the enchanting sky is a sentimental blue and pink. And gulls wheeling, warm grey and white against the magic of the water and the sky. Sparrows chirp on the windowsill, the baby sputters as she gets too big a mouthful, and pauses, then, a moment to look around her with satisfaction. Everybody is complacent, everybody is satisfied and everybody is happy.[33]

---

30. Dorothy Day, "Having a Baby—A Christmas Story," *The Catholic Worker* (December 1977), 8, 7. See http://www.catholicworker.org/dorothyday/Reprint2.cfm?TextID=583.

31. Forest, "All Is Grace."

32. Elie, *The Life You Save*, 53.

33. Dorothy Day, "Having a Baby—A Christmas Story."

Her personal and public writing on her experiences of mothering reflect an attempt to integrate the larger reality of the world into the intimate context and relationships of her family life. That she was a mother does not necessarily make her a feminist; that she refused to fashion her life according to the dichotomous expectations of the public and private spheres that continue to shape the lives of women, however, does. For Day, the personal—whether personal relationships or her private spirituality—was inherently political, and beauty reminded her of this connection. Paying attention to it empowered her to blend the two since beauty illuminated the common denominator between seemingly disparate activities such as raising Tamar and running a Catholic Worker household or writing about mothering and commenting on the demands of pacifism. That common thread was the call to love more fully the neighbor whose needs transcended both the private and public spheres. The beauty she notices in children provided a touchstone for this difficult and balancing act. "I'll cut this short and take the children up the hill to hunt for salamanders in the spring. In spite of strikes and brutality, controversy and war, this world is filled with joy and beauty and the children bring it to us anew and help us to enjoy it through their eyes."[34]

Her unsentimental descriptions of the duties of motherhood, concretely captured in sensorial language, also reflect the harsh and dreadful love so foundational to her ministry in the Catholic Worker, the third creative project she labored to birth and nourish along with Peter Maurin when her daughter was only seven. She was the uncontested matriarch of the movement, at least from the perspective of her fellow Workers. She often writes with a maternal perspective about the demands of fellow Workers and the work itself—cleaning dirty bodies, continual laundering of bedding, preparing endless meals, stretching limited resources—often to counter misunderstandings of their mission from within the community and from outsiders. She describes the women's work within the Worker to remind the community of the concrete demands of its intellectual roots in Catholic Personalism. A harsh and dreadful love of the neighbor requires a daily regime of exhausting work, known only too well by women, as well as the intellectual motivations often articulated by men. The latter were useless without the former. "We have said these things many times in the pages of *The Catholic Worker*," she writes in a column mapping out the aims and

34. Dorothy Day, *House of Hospitality*, chapter 12, 205–24. See http://www .catholicworker.org/dorothyday/Reprint2.cfm?TextID=447.

goals of the worker, "but it is to reassure these dear friends that I write this again. Perhaps it is easier for a woman to understand than a man. Because no matter what catastrophe has occurred or hangs overhead, she has to go on with the business of living. She does the physical things and so keeps a balance."[35]

She conjures the embodied experiences of this work to challenge those who dismissed the Catholic Worker as little more than a "sentimental" response to poverty and, in so doing, also challenged those who would sentimentalize and dismiss the moral agency and political significance of mothers. "Her eyes are affronted by disorder, confusion, the sight of human ailments, and human functions," she writes of women's work. "Her nose also; her ears tormented with discordant cries, her appetite failing often; her sense of touch in agony from fatigue and weakness."[36]

The Catholic Worker Movement depended on both Day's creative writing and her mothering skills. As Catholic Workers attest, her writing introduced the movement and its ideas to a wide audience and seduced many to take up the work in their own local contexts. Royalties from her books helped to pay the bills. Creative tasks of writing, mothering, and Workering would remain entwined for the remainder of Day's life, as she relied on experiences of purposefulness as a writer and mother to navigate the tensions that fueled a loneliness she felt even in the midst of her spiritual calling: between her creative gift and family as an escape from the ugliness of the world or as a means to better enter into it; between the needs of her biological family, which grew to include nine grandchildren and four great-grandchildren in her lifetime, and the needs of Catholic Worker family, which spanned the country by the 1960s; and between the demanding expectations she had for herself to "live in such a way that one's life would not make sense if God did not exist"[37] and the expectations placed on her by the countercultural movement that she started.

Enlarging Beauty: Personalism

Although not explicitly mentioned in Day's writings or in the day-to-day life in houses of hospitality, beauty and creative self-expression

---

35. Dorothy Day, "On Pilgrimage—December 1969," *The Catholic Worker* (December 1969), 1, 2, 5. See http://www.catholicworker.org/dorothyday/Reprint2.cfm?TextID=905.

36. Day, *On Pilgrimage*, 76.

37. Coles, *Dorothy Day*, 160.

were essential to Day's own appropriation of Personalism, the human-ist philosophy that provided the intellectual foundation and spiritual charism of the movement, via what June O'Connor describes as a com-mitment to "receive the other into the self."[38] Day relied on both beauty and creativity to answer her prayer about the kind of love she sought in her conversion experience and that later animated the Catholic Worker: "We confess to being fools and wish that we were more so. . . . [T]here is nothing that we can do but love, and dear God—please enlarge our hearts to love each other, to love our neighbor, to love our enemy as well as our friend."[39] Attention to beauty in her writing reveals a Personal-ism that was grounded in an embodied humanism and not simply an intellectual one.

The Catholic Worker Movement was nothing if not an attempt to incarnate the principles of Personalism that animated Catholic social thought in the early twentieth century in the bleak context of New York City's slums. Peter Maurin, itinerant French intellectual and cofounder of the movement, indoctrinated Day with the central tenets of Person-alism from their first meeting on December 9, 1938, until his death in 1949. Maurin insisted that a mysterious dynamism within each person provides the source of human dignity and the catalyst for reaching beyond the limits of the self in ongoing acts of cocreating with God. Human beings are inherently social and can only fully flourish in the context of community, and the goods persons need to live distinctively human lives are both material and spiritual. Maurin believed that inten-tional and localized communities provide the ideal way to protect the person from being subsumed by either the individualism of democratic capitalism or the collectivism of Marxism.

In one of his "easy essays" on the topic, Maurin implicitly notes the inherent creativity in their undertaking: "In Houses of Hospitality social workers can acquire that art of human contact and that social-mindedness or understanding of social forces which will make them critical of the existing environment and the free creative agents of a new environment."[40] Day described Maurin in terms of a "heavenly fire" toward which she was drawn for many reasons, but most notably for the role that visioning played in Maurin's practical philosophy. Miller explains that this "very long view made the work of the day, what we did here and now so important that each thought, each decision, each

38. O'Connor, *The Moral Vision*, 65.
39. Dorothy Day, "On Pilgrimage," *The Catholic Worker* (1946).
40. Zwick, *The Catholic Worker Movement*, 39.

step we took determined the future, not only for ourselves, but for the world."[41]

Later, another French Personalist and fellow convert to Catholicism, Jacques Maritain, would nurture those seminal ideas through a friendship with Day. His own ideas about Personalism incorporated beauty via what he called "creative intuition."[42] Creativity, according to Maritain, is an outward expression of the dynamism of persons and generates "communicable goods" that persons need to flourish. In other words, creative self-expression that puts people in touch with the mysterious depths of themselves and others generates the spiritual goods that foster life in community—empathy, mutuality, solidarity. These, in turn, increase the individual person's capability for fulfillment.

Day's writings reflect the bodily demands of this philosophy and the role of beauty in restoring capabilities for relationship, not only for Workers like herself, but also for those whose lack of access to beauty was a marker of destitution that so alarmed her. Beauty extended Day's conversion process beyond those initial years on Staten Island and sustained her in the arduous labor of the movement, which she admitted embroiled women in the day-to-day tasks to such an extent that the long view of which Maurin spoke became easily obscured. She made regular trips to the community farms on Staten Island and Newburgh, as well as frequent retreats outside of the city, in order to recharge and regroup. "One afternoon on a walk I stood there and listened to the crows and starlings and the chatter of the little brook over iced stones and grasses and had my fill of beauty for an hour before I had to go back to the city again."[43] And in another place: "It is a terrible thing to see the ugliness and poverty of the cities, to see what man has made of man. I needed those few days at Newburgh to brace myself for work."[44] She notes that a deprivation of beauty is a contributing factor of poverty precisely because it denies the poor of this restorative energy that leads to the creative moral agency of which Maurin often spoke: "But the poor, it seems, have no right to beauty, to order. Poverty must be

41. Miller, *Dorothy Day*, 243.

42. Jacques Maritain, *Creative Intuition in Art and Poetry* (New York: New American Library, 1953). See my examination of these ideas in *If These Walls Could Talk: Community Muralism and the Beauty of Justice* (Collegeville, MN: Liturgical Press, 2012), 206–9.

43. Dorothy Day, "On Pilgrimage," *The Catholic Worker* (February 1951), 1, 6. See http://www.catholicworker.org/dorothyday/Reprint2.cfm?TextID=910.

44. Dorothy Day, "On Pilgrimage, January," *The Catholic Worker* (n.d.), 3–26. See http://www.catholicworker.org/dorothyday/Reprint2.cfm?TextID=476.

squalor, filth, ugliness, to be esteemed as poverty. But this is destitution, and it was usually from such destitution that our family had come 'up in the world.' "[45]

Beauty also afforded Day the physical, emotional, and spiritual space for clarification of thought and the formation of conscience, two activities at the root of Maurin's Personalism. She saw both as increasingly central to the ministry of the Catholic Worker as she grew older. "I have been asking why [we are all here in the first place] all my life; when you ask why, you're alone, because you don't ask answers from other people of questions that are not answerable—by other people."[46] She walked miles of Staten Island's shorelines to allow the ocean to quiet the gymnastics of her mind, initially tumbling in the undertow of an immanent conversion experience and later in the changing tides of American Catholicism during the fifty years that followed her baptism. "The ocean is especially helpful: the sight of and the sound of it give me great reassurance, make me feel strangely at peace. . . . When I look at the sea I know that we are meant to stop our intellect dead in its tracks every once in a while or we'll torture ourselves to death with it."[47]

Perhaps most arresting for her were the flashes of beauty she noticed in intimate human interactions, moments that brought her to a reflective standstill with the wonders of the human being. "There is so much beauty in this world. Why do I single out books?" she asked herself in her journal after watching a mother and baby on a city bus who emitted "as much beauty and grace there as in any book."[48] In her column in 1973 she highlights "the beauty of a human being who had been through war and the humiliation of beatings in a prison camp and who sat by the bedside of a dying woman, Peggy Baird, my old friend, and drank with her and talked literature with her and when she said she wanted to die a Catholic brought out that beautiful old Baltimore Catechism and 'brought her into the Church.' "[49]

An eye for this kind of beauty made Day attuned to the creative intuition of those "on the line" that was so essential to loving them as

45. Dorothy Day, "Reflections during Advent, Part Two" and "The Meaning of Poverty," *Ave Maria* (December 3, 1966), 21–22, 29. See http://www.catholicworker .org/dorothyday/Reprint2.cfm?TextID=560.

46. Coles, *Dorothy Day*, 62–63.

47. Ibid., 70.

48. Ibid., 158–59.

49. Dorothy Day, "On Pilgrimage—January 1973," *The Catholic Worker* (January 1973), 2, 6. See http://www.catholicworker.org/dorothyday/Reprint2 .cfm?TextID=527.

brothers and sisters and empowering them to become contributing members of houses of hospitality or the movement more broadly construed.

Harsh and Dreadful Beauty: Realism

"The ugliness of life in a world which professed itself to be Christian appalled me," Day recalls of the years of struggle against her conversion.[50] And yet one might wonder whether it was beauty or its antithesis that evoked the deepest response from her, since she refused to shield herself from the ugliness of poverty precisely because of the sharp contrasts it brought into focus for her: the inherent dignity of persons assaulted by these conditions and the God to be encountered and loved in those people. "If we long for beauty," she wrote in *On Pilgrimage*, "the more our faith is tried, as though by fire, by ugliness."[51]

Day refused to sidestep the dark underbelly of poverty—what Catholic poet and activist Daniel Berrigan recalls her describing as a "'filthy, rotten system' producing misery in every direction"[52]—or the role of the ugliness in orienting us toward justice and acting justly. Day's descriptive attention to beauty's antithesis reminds us of the "harsh and dreadful love" that she identified as the main ingredient of any approach to justice: a love that dared to acknowledge the dreadful realities of the dehumanizing power of poverty and to accept the harsh criticism that such poverty is fueled by our individual and collective participation in that dehumanizing power. The realism in her aesthetic—captured in her descriptions of the dreadful harshness of poverty—invites increased social responsibility rather than moral scapegoating and, as such, becomes a catalyst for beautiful acts of neighbor love that risk entering more fully into the suffering experiences of others rather than romanticizing them. "We get used to ugliness so quickly," she says in her memoir about the Catholic Worker Movement. "What we avert our eyes from today can be borne tomorrow when we have learned a little more about love."[53]

Day's quest for beauty paradoxically brought her face-to-face with destitution that she found repugnant. And she minced no words in viscerally describing it—smells, sounds, tastes—and its devastating impact on actual persons, their bodies and their spirits. She did so in part to counter accusations that Worker responses to destitution were merely "sentimental." "Let their flesh be mortified by cold, by dirt, by

50. Elie, *The Life You Save*, 16.
51. Day, *On Pilgrimage*, 227.
52. Riegele, *Dorothy Day*, 77.
53. Dorothy Day, *Loaves and Fishes* (Maryknoll, NY: Orbis, 1983), 84.

vermin," she wrote in *The Catholic Worker*, articulating the community's pacifism shortly after Pearl Harbor. "Let their eyes be mortified by the sight of bodily excretions, diseased limbs, eyes, noses, mouths. Let their noses be mortified by the smells of sewage, decay and rotten flesh."[54]

But, in large part, her attention to the ugliness of poverty intended to concretize it in order to evoke personal responsibility for actual people rather than to put forward yet another intellectual argument about face-less social problems. Describing the sensorial dimensions of poverty was her attempt to help her readers understand on an intuitive level the social systems and structures that fueled this reality—lack of mean-ingful work, the military industrial complex, the prison system. Beauty seems fleeting compared with these seemingly permanent conditions. "The stink of the world's injustice and the world's indifference is all around us," she explains in an account of visiting a house of hospitality in Harrisburg in 1948. "The smell of the dead rat, the smell of acrid oil from engines of the Pennsylvania railroad, the smell of boiled bones from Swifts. The smell of dying human beings."[55]

An attention to ugliness resisted abstracting poverty as well as abstract responses to it. Poverty is real, it is tangible, and it can be ex-perienced in the senses by those who are not poor and in the physical bodies of those who are; it will only be redressed by an approach to justice that is equally real, tangible, experienced in the senses and bod-ies of persons through a harsh and dreadful love.

The ugliness of poverty and poor persons sparked a harsh self-criticism Day used to interrogate herself—her intentions, the mean-ingfulness of her writing, her participation in relationships rooted in domination and subordination. "We run the risk of thinking we're God's gift to humanity, those of us who struggle in our soup kitchens and hospitality houses to be loyal to him."[56] Ultimately, she believed that attention to the ugliness and brokenness within the self would create the kind of humility needed to avoid replicating in neighbor love the social values and systems that sustain dreadful poverty. "There are some days when I feel as though we have made a big mistake always writing what we think, for others to read, always telling the world what we want to see happen," she told Robert Coles in an extensive inter-view in 1970 while reflecting on the wisdom of one of the characters of the twentieth-century Italian novelist and activist Ignazio Silone, who

54. Miller, *Dorothy Day*, 343–44.
55. Day, *On Pilgrimage*, 222–23.
56. Coles, *Dorothy Day*, 116.

knew "the silence of long-suffering humanity that ought to humble us as talkers and writers."[57]

Dutiful Beauty: Hospitality

Hospitality was fundamental to Day's political mysticism, or the deeply personal relationship with God that guided her relationships in more public arenas, and it too coincided with her notion of beauty. "Her best prose was about hospitality. Not just opening the door but opening your face and your heart to that person," recalls Jim Forest.[58] This spirituality of hospitality was nourished by what he describes as an "aesthetic discipline" best understood in terms of Dorothy's self-proclaimed "duty to see beauty" or a "determination not to be blind to the beauty around [her]."[59] This aesthetic discipline was at once welcoming and resilient. Whether in the dining room at one of the Catholic Worker communities, on the farms, or on front lines of protests against war, Day insisted that the face of the human being was a doorway to transcendence, either to heaven in the decision to love or to hell in the choice to turn away. The ability to perceive beauty was critical for making the moral choice that presented itself in each face-to-face encounter.

Paying attention to the ordinary places beauty burst forth in her daily routine—in "the smell of garlic or cabbage soup, in marigolds, in grass bursting through the cracks in the sidewalk outside of Maryhouse, in the activity of light on leaves"[60]—increased Day's capability to be present to others in a way that seduced countless people to the Catholic Worker, both as Workers and guests.

Her aesthetic discipline was also shaped by an appreciation for simple and sustainable living, since both heighten our attention to the abundance of the present moment and free the moral imagination from distractions and entrapments that keep us from envisioning countercultural alternatives. In a more practical way, this simple living also freed the Worker movement from dependence on institutions and systems that perpetuated dehumanizing poverty. Her journals and columns are filled with accounts of butter, fresh vegetables, clean shirts, handmade sweaters, blankets, and soaps whose beauty lie in the hands that created them and in the works they sustained. "Since the two towels I use are

---

57. Ibid., 150.

58. Forest, "All Is Grace."

59. Ibid.

60. Tom Cornell, Clarification of Thought, Maryhouse Catholic Worker, October 28, 2011, New York City.

also handwoven and hand-spun by my daughter, I have those samples of beauty in the midst of a city slum."[61] And the point of this simplicity is to keep us attuned to the neighbor, captured in the parenthetical statement in the following note from her column in 1979: "We had hard, baked potatoes for supper, and cabbage over-spiced. I'm in favor of becoming a vegetarian only if the vegetables are cooked right. (What a hard job cooking is here! But the human warmth in the dining room covers up a multitude of sins.)"[62]

Day frequently invoked the "duty of delight," another phrase of one of Dostoyevsky's characters, to remind herself and others of the resilient power of hope, both in overcoming personal mistakes and shortcomings and in buoying the collective spirit of the movement against the reality of systemic injustice they faced. "Irene pointed out a phrase to me recently of Ruskin's which appealed to us both. It was 'the duty of delight,'" she writes to her readers in her column in 1951. "To reverence and be thankful for life itself, in a time when the world holds human life so lightly there is again joy."[63] And just as she insisted there was no shortage of people in need or injustices to protest, there was also no lack of things in which to delight. "Who can say there is no delight, even in a city slum, especially in an Italian neighborhood where there is a pot of basil on the window sill and the smell of good cooking in the air, and pigeons wheeling over the roof tops and the tiny feathers found occasionally on the sidewalk, the fresh smell of the sea from the dock of the Staten Island ferry boat (five cents a ride)."[64]

Postlude: A Catholic Feminist Aesthetic

"To make the kind of society in which it is easier to be good," Day opines in her column in 1951, "one needs to be happy in order to be good, and one needs to be good in order to be happy."[65] Dorothy Day implicitly believed that beauty stood at the intersection of morality and

61. Dorothy Day, "On Pilgrimage—May 1969," *The Catholic Worker* (May 1969), 2, 8. See http://www.catholicworker.org/dorothyday/Reprint2.cfm?TextID=898.

62. Dorothy Day, "On Pilgrimage—February 1979," *The Catholic Worker* (February 1979), 7, 8. See http://www.catholicworker.org/dorothyday/Reprint2.cfm?TextID=596.

63. Dorothy Day, "On Pilgrimage," *The Catholic Worker* (February 1951), 1, 6. See http://www.catholicworker.org/dorothyday/Reprint2.cfm?TextID=910.

64. Dorothy Day, "On Pilgrimage—May 1969," *The Catholic Worker* (May 1969), 2, 8. See http://www.catholicworker.org/dorothyday/Reprint2.cfm?TextID=898.

65. Dorothy Day, "On Pilgrimage," *The Catholic Worker* (February 1951), 1, 6. See http://www.catholicworker.org/dorothyday/Reprint2.cfm?TextID=910.

flourishing. Attention to it orients us to those around us. Participating in it restores our capacity for living in right relationships with other people. Offering it to others can move them from destitution to dignity and us from paternalism to neighborliness. Creating it contributes to the ongoing work of the reign of God. In these ways, Day offers a distinctively Catholic feminist aesthetic. Sixty years later, as the institutional Catholic Church struggles to assert the relevance of its social teaching in the wake of a crisis of credibility and as social movements in cities around the country call our attention to the disparity in wealth, situations with which Day was so familiar, her aesthetic can guide us to deeper understandings of the demands of justice.

First, Day always paired social criticism with creativity. Although bitingly critical of systems of social injustice and perversions of Christian values that sustained them, she dutifully followed the advice of her mentor, Peter Maurin, in not simply speaking of alternatives but embodying them. She was an "announcer" of the good and the just and not simply a "denouncer" of that which she sought to resist. She exercised moral creativity in her solutions to problems on the micro and macro levels—from the distribution of butter in the Catholic Worker to proposals for redistribution of the military budget. Like any form of beauty, her creativity was powerfully seductive and still attracts others to the creative work of imagining different possibilities and working together to bring them to fruition. Her aesthetic sensibility reminds us that we have a duty not only to protest injustice but to delight when we experience justice, no matter how small or fleeting.

In addition, she recognized the relationship between beauty and restorative justice or the power of beauty to resist the ugliness of dehumanizing poverty. She insisted on making beauty—no matter how simple—an essential part of the hospitality she and others in the Catholic Worker family extended to their neighbors. Glimpses of the beautiful healed the wounds inflicted by destitute poverty: despair, the monotony of invisibility, the permanence of ugliness, the eternity of lack of work or hard labor. In this way, her aesthetic reminds us that justice is more than a moral calculus for distributing goods or meeting needs, more than a covenant that binds people in a common vision. Rather, justice must also incorporate a deep sense of well-being, a tactile experience of gratuitous abundance, an embodied participation in something that is far bigger than the self and attractive enough to galvanize us to risk something different.

Finally, her resilient claim that beauty will save the world, and the ways in which that belief animated her relationships with so many different kinds of people, reflects the power of beauty to overcome fear: fear of ugliness, fear of "the other," fear of failing, fear of allowing oneself to be loved by God. Day believed that it is fear that creates the conditions of hell on earth, since it causes us to turn our faces away from our brothers and sisters and thus perpetuate dehumanizing poverty. Beauty, on the other hand, empowers us to turn and face the various "others" in our lives—the poor, those who oppose our positions or ideas. Attending to the inherent beauty in the other emboldens us to meet their gaze and perhaps risk something new together. That newness, that possibility of something different, will save the world in the end. Day's sense of the inherent goodness and contentment of this choice to seek the beauty in the other, offered to us each day, is captured here:

> I have seen sunrises at the foot of a New York street, coming up over the East River. I have always found a strange beauty in the suffering faces which surround us in the city. Black, brown and grey heads bent over those bowls of food, that so necessary food which is always there at St. Joseph's House on First St., prepared each morning. . . . We all enter into the act of hospitality, one way or another. So many of those who come in to eat return to serve, to become part of the "family."[66]

66. Dorothy Day, "On Pilgrimage—September 1974," *The Catholic Worker* (September 1974), 2, 8. See http://www.catholicworker.org/dorothyday/Reprint2.cfm?TextID=543.

Little Garden of Paradise (*Das Paradiesgärtlein*), Upper Rhenisch Master, ca. 1415, Städel
Museum, Frankfurt am Main, © Städel Museum – ARTOTHEK.

Mary Ann Zimmer

Being Immaculate
Images of Oppression and Emancipation

What have you done to me? What have you made of me?
I cannot find myself in the woman you want me to be
Haloed, alone . . . marble and stone:
Safe, Gentle, Holy Mary.

Anon.[1]

"Did Mary have a placenta?" This question was put to me urgently and without preamble by a woman in the audience after a lecture on Mary, the Mother of Jesus. When I asked her the origin of her question, the woman said, "Women want to know." She elaborated that she was an obstetrical nurse in a Catholic hospital, and she had been asked this question by numerous women. It seemed that women in labor had a strong sense of accompaniment with Mary's shared experience. The nature of that sharing was of urgent concern: Was she a real woman like them?[2] What image were they carrying that made this inquiry necessary and of such import?

---

1. Excerpted from an anonymous poem titled "Mary Song," in "Mariology: A Pakena Perspective," Consultation on Asian Women's Theology (unpublished paper, 1989). Reprinted in Chung Hyun Kyung, *Struggle to Be the Sun Again: Introducing Asian Women's Theology* (Maryknoll, NY: Orbis Books, 1990), 74.

2. A medieval discussion of this precise point can be found in the accounts of St. Bridget of Sweden in Sarah Jane Boss, *Empress and Handmaid: On Nature and Gender in the Cult of the Virgin Mary* (London: Cassell, 2002), 192–94.

While I say "image" here in both its literal sense of picture and in the sense of the emotional, mental, and spiritual relationship to Mary constructed in dialogue with discourse about her, in this essay I focus on the former, particularly the fate of Marian images depicting the immaculate conception as these traversed from medieval to contemporary times. Marian images are important, as my questioner insisted, for many women's religious self-understandings. I examine problematic images of the immaculate conception in current use and propose an alternative: the enclosed garden. This image can be reconstructed in ways that deepen understanding of the doctrine and offer women a more religiously whole identification with Mary.

While it is impossible to separate image from discourse, social practices, and the full panoply of surrounding cultural production, it is clear from the ongoing responses of feminist artists to traditional Marian images that these evoke a strong aesthetic reconstructive reaction from them. What is the significance of Alma López's photo collage "Our Lady," showing a woman with many of the familiar accouterments of Our Lady of Guadalupe—clothed, however, in roses arranged in a very modest, as one reviewer said, "bathing suit from the 30s"?[3] What is at the root of the reactions that raised enough disturbance to fill an entire book?[4] What was the inspiration behind Ester Hernández's karate-kicking *"La Virgen de Guadalupe Defendiendo los Derechos de los Xichanos"*? Why does Julie Vivas's book *The Nativity*, with its seriously playful watercolors of a very pregnant Mary and her anatomically correct son, reap both delight and horror from its online reviewers?[5] How did the powerful gaze of Mary, the enthroned empress with her imperial son, of the Byzantine mosaics evolve into the featureless Mary planters of the 1950s or the lone, barely pubescent girl with bowed head, downcast eyes, and folded hands who has come to occupy many of the Marian altars in contemporary US churches? What effects do these depictions have—even if they are not part of an overt discourse defining the identity of women? As the questioner after my lecture reminds us, images of women, religious or not, are of vital concern to feminists because of

3. Although only one image could be included in this essay, all the images mentioned in this essay are available online.

4. Alicia Gaspar de Alba and Alma López, eds., *Our Lady of Controversy: Alma López's "Irreverent Apparition"* (Austin: University of Texas Press, 2011). See also http://www.almalopez.net/.

5. Julie Vivas, ill., *The Nativity* (Orlando, FL: Harcourt, Inc., 2006). It is important to note that Vivas's images are not part of an articulate, explicit project of resistance. They simply exist in the context of a children's picture book.

the role images play in the oppression and emancipation of women.[6] *Women want to know.*

Images of Mary matter for Christian women worldwide because of the degree to which she has been idealized and, often, contrasted to other women. The traits attributed to her also serve to create a scaffold on which to map the ideal woman who will form a standard for all. Even if a person repudiates devotion to her or membership in the cult that honors her, the image can continue to operate with a life of its own. As feminist political philosopher Iris Marion Young argues, images continue to create their effects even after the reform of the discursive formulations that surround them.[7] For this reason, merely critiquing oppressive representations is not an adequate response; the creation of new images—a counterfiguration of Mary—is essential.

This counterfiguration, I argue, is also essential for the development of doctrines currently captive to inadequate images of Mary. Here, I focus on the doctrine of the immaculate conception of Mary, a doctrine with a long-forgotten range of images and that, I will show, is currently held captive by seventeenth-century Spanish understandings of the restrictions imposed on religious art by the Council of Trent. If, as Paul Ricoeur has famously argued, the symbol gives rise to thought, depictions of the immaculate conception today lend themselves to anemic understandings of this rich doctrine.[8] I show that new images can fund an understanding of the doctrine that responds more helpfully to the realities of sin and grace as women and other Christians understand them today.

I develop this thesis by drawing on the work of philosopher Diana Tietjens Meyers and her analysis of the role of images in the cultural

---

6. I use an adaptation of bell hooks's definition of feminism. She calls it a "struggle to end sexist oppression." She points out that sexist oppression does not operate alone but is closely linked to race and class. See *Feminist Theory: From Margin to Center*, 2nd ed. (Cambridge, MA: South End Press, 2000), 33–36. Because of my privileged social location and that most people who will read what I write, I adapt this to read: the *self-critical* struggle to end sexist oppression. This signals the necessity of accounting for one's privilege as part of the issue—especially in the ways sexism differs for women according to race, class, sexual orientation, immigration status, ability, age, etc.

7. Iris Marion Young, *Justice and the Politics of Difference* (Princeton, NJ: Princeton University Press, 1990), 131–33.

8. On Paul Ricoeur, see Elizabeth A. Johnson, "The Symbolic Character of Theological Statements about Mary," *Journal of Ecumenical Studies* 22 (1985): 313–35; and *Truly Our Sister: A Theology of Mary in the Communion of Saints* (New York: Continuum, 2003), 98–99.

construction of women's identities and agency.[9] I will also draw on a second feminist theorist, Iris Marion Young, who emphasizes the workings of images to keep social oppression in place.[10] Both create the foundation for examining the concrete case: the Christian representation of Mary's sinlessness. I will consider the sixteenth-century painting *The Little Garden of Paradise*, through the lens provided by ethicist Traci West, in order to illuminate the considerations that a reconstructed image would need to address.[11] The *Little Garden* pictures Mary at the center of an idealized world—a walled garden of friendship, beauty, and natural abundance. I propose a reconstructed image in this lineage as a more adequate representation of Mary in a state of original grace. Nevertheless, when gazed upon through the lens of contemporary structures of sin, this less familiar image of the immaculate conception displays a "matrix of domination" that needs to be interrogated.[12]

This is not entirely unchartered territory. In particular, Sarah Jane Boss gives a detailed analysis of the major shifts in Marian iconography that took place between the medieval and modern periods, particularly in the aftermath of the Council of Trent (1545–63).[13] What is missing from Boss's discussion, however, is the need for reconstructed images that address Mary's sinlessness and provide the imagination with effective resources for facing structural sin. I argue that such a reconstruction is possible beginning from the resources of pre-Tridentine depictions of the immaculate conception. This counterfiguration has two ethical implications. Reconstructed imagery can increase the degree to which women

9. Diana Tietjens Meyers, *Gender in the Mirror: Cultural Imagery and Women's Agency* (New York: Oxford University Press, 2002). For an overview of the use of agency in a broad range of fields, see Laura M. Ahearn, "Language and Agency," *Annual Review of Anthropology* 30 (2001): 109–37; http://www.jstor.org/stable/3069211 (accessed July 26, 2011).

10. Young, *Justice and the Politics of Difference.*

11. I was introduced to this image through Tina Bettie's "Garden of the New Eve," *The Tablet* (December 19, 2009): 18–19.

12. The term "matrix of domination" comes from the work of Patricia Hill Collins, *Black Feminist Thought: Knowledge, Consciousness, and the Politics of Empowerment* (Boston: UnwinHyman, 1990).

13. On historical changes in the view of Mary in European culture, see Donna Spivey Ellington, *From Sacred Body to Angelic Soul: Understanding Mary in Late Medieval and Early Modern Europe* (Washington, DC: The Catholic University of America Press, 2001); and Gary Waller, *The Virgin Mary in Late Medieval and Early Modern English Literature and Popular Culture* (New York: Cambridge University Press, 2011). For a critical theory perspective that includes attention to gender and to structural oppression, see Sarah Jane Boss, *Empress and Handmaid.*

are able to develop autonomy and can broaden the resources available to motivate Christians to recognize and act against structural sin.

Image and Feminism

My argument casts images and imagination in a potentially emancipatory role. Luce Irigaray, for example, unexpectedly found an emancipatory opportunity for reimaging the roles of mother and daughter in an unfamiliar image in an Italian museum on the Island of Torcello. Emilie Bergmann reports on Irigaray's first encounter with a depiction of the Virgin Mary's mother, Anne, teaching Mary to read: "She [Irigaray] describes the moment of celebration of the mother-daughter bond which she had mistaken for the canonical dyad of the Virgin and her son: 'I was admiring this beautiful sculpture when I noticed that Jesus was a girl! This had a very significant effect on me, one of jubilation—mental and physical.'"[14]

The power Irigaray describes is evident in the urgency of women's questions about Mary's complete or limited womanhood. A similar power resides in the ways women artists have reappropriated Mary outside her traditional limitations. There is also a notable intensity to reactions to these images. These wells of response can partly be explained by attending, as Diana Meyers does, to the issue of how ideal images raise questions of consequence for the concrete lives of women today.

Meyers is concerned with how a patriarchal culture shapes women's identities in a manner that limits their ability to exercise genuine agency and makes these limits seem natural and advantageous for women. In arguing for greater agency for women, Meyers does not see agency and its resulting autonomy as creating selfish individualists. Rather, she sees self-determination as a prerequisite for a just society, arguing that "when a society discourages self-exploration and self-expression, it discourages attention to symptoms of discontent and shields social ideologies and institutions from probing examination and oppositional activism. A society that encourages autonomy exposes itself to criticism and equips people to pursue social change. By thwarting (or trying to thwart) dissent, societies that suppress autonomy perpetuate unjust social structures."[15]

---

14. Luce Irigaray, "Religious and Civil Myths," in *je, tu, nous: Toward a Culture of Difference* (London: Routledge, 1993), 25, quoted in Emilie L. Bergmann, "A Maternal Genealogy of Wisdom: The Education of the Virgin in Early Modern Spanish Iconography," *Confluencia* 24, no. 1 (Fall 2008): 154–61.

15. Meyers, *Gender in the Mirror*, 12.

Meyers is careful to outline the parameters of her theory and her location among other feminist theorists. She does not side with those who deny women any agency under the influence of culture. Women are not programmed automatons; at the same time, however, she does not see them as completely free in the face of their culture's influence. Rather, she takes the line that cultural influence affects everyone, but each woman receives culture's persuasions through the filter of her own temperament, context, and experiences.

To bring out the emancipatory potential of Meyers's argument, two of its characteristics should be highlighted. First, while gender is her focus, she acknowledges, usually parenthetically, other dimensions of identity that are locations for oppression, including race, ethnicity, sexual orientation, age, and class. This acknowledgment is essential to avoid ignoring the concrete conditions of actual women, who experience the effects of Marian images in particular social, cultural, and economic locations. Second, Meyers is clearly constructing her argument from and for Western culture using the theoretical equipment of Western philosophy, art, and psychoanalysis. At the same time, because her account of agency is described as a set of skills, these could be further specified in a number of directions. In this way, her theory might be usefully translated across cultures.

According to Meyers, images and imagination figure heavily in the cultural process of developing gendered identity. In a process that seems "natural," a culture offers women particular pictures of a womanly self and of the possible life trajectories or scripts that are considered "normal." Images and imagination also have a vital role in emancipation from cultural deformation. One can trace their emancipatory necessity through Meyers's description of self-determination. In describing agency, Meyers concretizes her description by laying out ten "agentic skills" that comprise autonomy. These skills are available for anyone in the culture, but certain of them are awarded to women and others for men. They include "introspection skills that sensitize individuals to their own feelings and desires, that enable them to interpret their subjective experience, and that help them judge how good a likeness a self-portrait is." She further names "imagination skills that enable individuals to envisage feasible options—to audition a range of self-images they might adopt and to preview a variety of plot lines their lives might follow."[16]

I wish to return our attention to Irigaray's response to the image of Anne teaching Mary. Bergmann notes, "Irigaray reconstituted this reli-

16. Meyers, *Gender in the Mirror*, 20.

gious image as an aesthetic and ethical figure necessary for her to 'live without contempt for my incarnation, for that of my mother and other women.' "[17] Thus, images can both create and resist social norms—enact normative power, shape desire, and empower escape through alternative visions.

Political philosopher Iris Marion Young offers a helpful reading of the power of images that bridges their effect on the identity development of the individual and their effect on the social order.[18] According to Young, the process of maintaining an oppressive social order goes on at three levels of subjectivity: discursive consciousness, practical consciousness, and the basic security system.[19] What is important for my argument is the way that discourse and image are separated, perhaps even isolated, in these three levels of subjectivity.

Young, describing the threefold structure of the human subject, labels "discursive consciousness" the person's capacity for dealing with those features of actions or situations that most easily lend themselves to being managed through language. One's espoused ideals or formulated convictions would reside in the discursive consciousness. At this level, Young points out, much of contemporary society is committed to the language of equality and tolerance.[20] The second level of subjectivity, practical consciousness, does not require direct awareness but does require "often complex reflexive monitoring of the relation of the subject's body to those of other subjects and the surrounding environment, but which are on the fringe of consciousness, rather than the focus of discursive attention."[21] Young gives the example of driving a car.

Finally, subjectivity includes the basic security system, which Young summarizes as the person's "ontological integrity," that provides "identity, security, and a sense of autonomy."[22] It is at this level, she argues, where the unconscious resides, that deeply embedded prejudices about superior and inferior groups, genders, races, and ethnicities continue to operate.[23]

17. Bergmann, "A Maternal Genealogy of Wisdom," 154.

18. Young's argument here follows Anthony Giddens. See *A Contemporary Critique of Historical Materialism*, 2nd ed. (Stanford, CA: Stanford University Press, 1995), 27.

19. Young, *Justice and the Politics of Difference*, 131.

20. Ibid., 130.

21. Ibid., 131.

22. Ibid.

23. Ibid., 132–33.

Young asserts that even in situations where the stereotyping of the Other has been deemed inappropriate at the level of discursive consciousness, the need to maintain one's identity through the objectification of an Other may still operate at the levels of practical consciousness and the basic security system. In settings where a Norm and an Other have been constituted, habit, bodily reactions, and the unconscious all come into play to reproduce patterns of social relations that one may have repudiated at a conscious level.

Precisely because they are not consciously constituted through discourse, habits located at the levels of practical consciousness and the basic security system can appear to be natural. According to Young, images are located in the basic security system, which means that they can exercise influence over the person's thoughts, feelings, and actions that may not be in line with what the person consciously affirms in speech. For this reason, feminists seeking change in social relations will confront a need for changed images.[24] It is also clear that abandoning oppressive images in the interests of expanding women's imagination and thus their agency will not have the same effect as replacing them. Meyers calls this replacement the necessary work of "counterfiguration."[25]

Images of Mary

A number of feminist scholars have variously argued that the religious and cultural influence of Mary, the mother of Jesus, has been oppressive or liberating for women.[26] Marina Werner contends that the uniqueness attributed to Mary makes all other women diminished in contrast.[27] Sally Cunneen argues that Mary's declining influence after the 1960s was a loss for women.[28] These contrasting views illustrate the polyvalent figure of Mary whose historically multiple interpreta-

---

24. Wioleta Polinska analyzes the work of several woman artists who she argues have created alternative images of the female in art. See "Dangerous Bodies: Women's Nakedness and Theology," *Journal of Feminist Studies in Religion* 16, no. 1 (March 1, 2000): 45–62.

25. Meyers, *Gender in the Mirror*, 97.

26. For a summary of deficiencies of several past major approaches, see section 2 of Johnson, *Truly Our Sister*.

27. Marina Werner, *Alone of All Her Sex: The Myth and the Cult of the Virgin Mary* (New York: Random House, 1976).

28. Sally Cunneen, *In Search of Mary: The Woman and the Symbol* (New York: Ballantine Books, 1996).

tions have no single consistent effect.[29] To this evolving conversation I want to add an aspect of Marian imagery that has particular ongoing relevance for the flourishing of women—the counterfiguration of the sinlessness of Mary.

The Immaculate Conception

The ways in which images of this doctrine have evolved creates significant tension with the best understanding of the doctrine. The narrow range of images in current use limit the symbolization of this doctrine to a passive, lone figure isolated from humanity and the rest of creation. This figuration of salvation contradicts the belief that redemption from sin is a restoration of right relationships. In addition to this concern, Mary's sinlessness has often been interpreted in a way that precludes her having a real human identity that other women might share. This isolates women from her and leaves them with the kinds of questions I received from the obstetrical nurse at my lecture.

Some doctrinal details are necessary to illuminate the choice of symbols that have been used in portraying the doctrine of Mary's immaculate conception.[30] The belief that Mary did not personally commit sins was widespread and virtually unproblematic for early Christians. The immaculate conception, the belief that Mary was conceived without inheriting original sin, was only declared a definitive Catholic Church dogma in 1854, but the belief was a subject of localized devotion and of tremendous theological debate much earlier. Theological questions about such an honor originally arose from the celebration

29. For a different approach to new readings of Marian images and theology, see the work of Tina Beattie, developed in dialogue with the writings of Luce Irigaray, to resituate women in Catholic theology and practice. See especially *God's Mother, Eve's Advocate* (London: Continuum, 2002). For an empirical investigation into the self-reported effect, much of it positive, of Our Lady of Guadalupe on Mexican American women, see Jeanette Rodriguez, *Our Lady of Guadalupe: Faith and Empowerment among Mexican-American Women* (Austin: University of Texas Press, 1994).

30. It is beyond the scope of this project to trace the theological complexities of the historical discussion, but the sources in the footnotes give a good overview. Political issues also colored the debate at certain periods. For a concise discussion of this aspect, see Trevor Johnson, "Mary in Early Modern Europe," in *Mary: The Complete Resource*, ed. Sarah Jane Boss (New York: Oxford, 2007), 373–80. The role of art in Spanish religious and intensely political pressures in favor of the doctrine is detailed in Suzanne L. Stratton, *The Immaculate Conception in Spanish Art* (New York: Cambridge University Press, 1994). An additional theo-political perspective from the US point of view is found in James E. Hennessey, "A Prelude to Vatican I: American Bishops and the Definition of the Immaculate Conception," *Theological Studies* 25, no. 3 (September 1, 1964): 409–19.

of Mary's birth—rather than her death, the usual custom—as her feast day. Such a feast would make no sense to believers if she had been born with original sin.[31] Did this mean that she was *not* born in sin? And at what point had she been saved from sin? Was it conception or some moment of sanctification before birth? Regardless of many theologians' misgivings, a feast of her immaculate conception was a local celebration in many places even before it was placed on the church calendar in 1696.[32]

Nevertheless, disagreements about the doctrine's theological justification were sometimes quite fierce. One major theological stumbling block was the early Christian assumption that original sin was passed from one generation to the next through the "lust" that accompanies procreation.[33] This idea had two consequences. It seemed to tie Mary inevitably to original sin and it attached an elusive but persistent atmosphere of sexual purity/impurity to the idea of the immaculate conception.[34] Franciscan theologian Duns Scotus (1266–1308) addressed this difficulty using an earlier idea from Anselm. Scotus argued that it was the will rather than the body that transmitted original sin. Furthermore, God would surely want the "most excellent thing" for Mary and certainly *could* do it. By doing this "excellent thing," preserving Mary from sin, God performed for Mary, in Scotus's words, "Christ's most perfectly redemptive action."[35]

Despite progress on the issue, those who found it problematic argued that because Mary was human she would have shared the human lot—the need to be redeemed from sin by Christ. This was basically Thomas Aquinas's position. If she was never exposed to sin, what did her redemption consist in?[36] The disagreement continued even while the church was trying to show a united front to Reformation opponents. In 1570, the pope forbade further debates on it—putting the direct theo-

31. Boss, "The Development of the Doctrine of Mary's Immaculate Conception," in *Mary*, 210.

32. Trevor Johnson, "Mary in Early Modern Europe," 377.

33. On Augustine's complex view, see Hilda Graef, *Mary: A History of Christian Doctrine and Devotion* (London: Sheed and Ward, 1985), 97–99.

34. Numerous Catholics as well as others assume to this day that the immaculate conception refers to Jesus' conception because there was no sexual intercourse involved.

35. Boss, "The Development of the Doctrine of Mary's Immaculate Conception," in *Mary*, 213–14.

36. Boss, *Empress and Handmaid*, 129.

logical discussion in abeyance for decades while a silent but intense debate continued through the arts.[37]

Twentieth-century theologians have drawn attention to elements of Christian belief that put Mary's privileged position in perspective. Karl Rahner built his theology around the central Christian theological category of "grace," understood as the free, unearned gift of God's love and offer of relationship. He emphasized that, according to Christian belief, Mary was redeemed in the same way that any person is—by the grace of God. At the same time, although her privileges were not her own doing, her choice to participate in the events of Christian redemption was a matter of freely given consent—also supported by grace.[38] In this way Mary is both privileged and one with the rest of humanity in being redeemed by the grace of Christ—in her case, an anticipated redemption.

Elizabeth Johnson in her comprehensive construction of a contemporary Roman Catholic feminist Mariology emphasizes the way in which privilege can undermine attempts to become realistic about Mary's "socioeconomic, religious, and cultural difference from ourselves."[39] This gap can only

37. Trevor Johnson, "Mary in Early Modern Europe," 373. On the continuing pressure through the visual arts for an official dogmatic declaration, see Stratton, *The Immaculate Conception*.

38. Karl Rahner, "The Immaculate Conception," in *Theological Studies* 1 (New York: Herder and Herder, 1961), 206.

39. Johnson, *Truly Our Sister*, 105.

Details from *Little Garden of Paradise* (*Das Paradiesgärtlein*), Upper Rhenisch Master, ca. 1415, Städel Museum, Frankfurt am Main, © Städel Museum – ARTOTHEK.

be bridged, she says, by "'solidarity in difference,' developed in political and feminist theology to describe the optimum relationship between persons in situations that differ." This solidarity is an active, shared commitment arising out of common humanity. It is a commitment that acts against what dehumanizes others without re-creating them in anyone else's image.[40]

Johnson turns to Rahner to give voice to the importance of holding together Mary's actual human life with whatever privileges she might have received since the sinlessness of Mary has sometimes been described in a way that emphasizes Mary's privileges at the expense of her human connection with other women: "The fact is, we often think holiness and absence of sin incompatible with ordinary life on this solid earth, where people laugh and cry, are born and die."[41] This attitude, though, is a misunderstanding of the doctrine of grace.

Grace does not withdraw people from earthly life but immerses them more deeply in it. From this point of view, Mary knew grief, joy, confusion, pain, and pleasure as part of day-to-day life—just as other human persons do. When her sinlessness has been mistakenly idealized according to the spiritual ideals of each century, ordinary human emotions and ordinary human reactions to events have been misidentified with sin, rendering Mary a marginally human person, which is not Christian doctrine. Rahner and Johnson make us aware that Mary's was a life ordinary in every way. This constitutes a reminder of the central Christian teaching on the incarnation of Christ as a fully human person: holiness is not found outside of humanity but within it. As a consequence, the range of ways to imagine holiness is expanded, as is the range of positive life scripts imagined as possible for women.

A neglected aspect of the doctrine of the immaculate conception is the fact that Mary's freedom from original sin should enable one to locate her in deep union with original creation in its original goodness and interdependence. Although her privilege is believed to be unique, its import has consequences for how all Christians picture the salvation to which they believe grace invites and brings them. Rather than being seen as an individual privilege that might isolate Mary from the rest of humanity, this doctrine could be framed to give all humanity new impetus to see resistance to sin as a reunion with original creation in its human and other life forms. The implications of this doctrine relate

---

40. Ibid., 105–7.
41. Karl Rahner, *Mary, Mother of the Lord* (New York: Herder and Herder, 1963), 78, quoted in Elizabeth A. Johnson, *Truly Our Sister*, 110.

directly to the question of Marian images. In line with the arguments Meyers and Young have raised, new images and imagination will be an integral part of shifting the focus of this doctrine from isolation to community.

Historical Development in Images
of the Immaculate Conception[42]

The tender picture *Kiss at the Golden Gate* depicts the moment that Mary's parents, Joachim and Anne, each rushing to meet the other after separate visitations by an angel, meet in a loving embrace at the Golden Gate of the Jerusalem temple. They have just learned that their long-delayed hope to bear a child will be fulfilled, and their mutual joy is reflected in their faces, posture, and loving gestures.[43] This warm human scene is only one of many attempts by Christian artists to do justice to the highly abstract notion of the immaculate conception. By examining a sampling of these depictions in their historical trajectory, I will show that the tradition narrows in the seventeenth century and begins portraying Mary as increasingly standardized, isolated, submissive, and young. This narrowing symbolizes the doctrine in a way that skews the observer's assumptions about sin, grace, and the nature of human flourishing. In addition, it offers women a very limited range of images for what salvation can signify. Following this historical investigation, I will propose the imaginative reconstruction of a medieval image as a positive way forward.

Catholics today are most familiar with images of the immaculate conception that can be traced back to the reforms of the Council of Trent. Most Catholics would probably find it difficult to interpret the rich range of pre-Tridentine traditions; it has been so long since they were in regular use.[44] As Mirella D'Ancona points out, the earliest depictions of Mary's freedom from original sin are the expression of an

---

42. For a review of the variety of ways this belief has been pictured, see Boss, *Empress and Handmaid*, plates 2 and 6–9; Stratton, *The Immaculate Conception*; and Mirella Levi D'Ancona, *The Iconography of the Immaculate Conception in the Middle Ages and Early Renaissance* (College Art Association of America, 1957). D'Ancona provides the most detailed and complete range of images and correlation with the very gradual development of the doctrine.

43. Examples in several media can be seen in each of the resources listed above. They are found as early as the fourteenth-century breviary illumination cited by D'Ancona, *The Iconography*, 87, fig. 29.

44. For sources, see note 42.

embryonic spiritual instinct that this privilege was appropriate rather than the manifestation of a well-developed theology.[45] D'Ancona quotes the eighth-century deacon Paul Winfrid, who called Mary "the Tree of Jesse which is totally exempt from the knots of sin."[46] There are twelfth-century images that picture her as the apex of a multibranched tree bearing figures from Jesus' genealogy, including Jesse, in the branches.[47] Other images show her as a small figure visible in Anne's womb or a figure who is holding Jesus while she is visible within Anne.[48] A twelfth-century British psalter shows Mary seated on a throne with the child Jesus in her lap while she holds a lily, the symbol of purity, in her hand.[49] The *tota pulcra* image showing Mary as a young woman with folded hands (but an unbowed head) derives from the Song of Solomon of the Hebrew Bible, "You are altogether beautiful, my love, and there is no flaw in you" (4:7). The quote is often spelled out on a banner floating below God in heaven. Many images of this type show Mary in a garden-like setting surrounded by symbols and banners that add other Marian titles from a variety of litanies honoring her. These titles include "a garden enclosed" (Song 4:12), an image to which we will be returning.[50]

In the sixteenth and seventeenth centuries, after the Council of Trent, there was a gradual but definitive shift away from Marian images such as those we have been considering. Although there had as yet been no official definition of the immaculate conception as a dogma, ongoing theological reflection had begun to consider certain explanations inadequate. As this occurred, the images that represented them fell out of favor. The images of Mary in Anne's womb, for example, were judged inadequate for failing to make it clear that Mary's proleptic redemption happened at conception and not at quickening or birth, as some had understood it. The narrow range of images that have survived became taken for granted as "the" immaculate conception.

In the face of varying degrees of theoretical and actual iconoclasm among their Reformation opponents, the bishops reaffirmed the accept-

---

45. D'Ancona, *The Iconography*, 7.
46. Quoted in ibid., 7.
47. Ibid., figs. 35–37.
48. Ibid., figs. 23–25.
49. Ibid., fig. 42.
50. For details of the content and sources of these titles and symbols with illustrations of this type, see Stratton, *The Immaculate Conception*, 40–47.

ability and importance of images in places of worship.[51] Such images, they argued, were not idols but reminded believers of the persons who were pictured and enabled the devout to ponder the mysteries of their faith. This was considered especially pertinent to the ignorant; Pope Gregory I (d. 604) described art as "scripture for the illiterate."[52]

As much as they opposed the iconoclastic views of their Reformation critics, the bishops of Trent clearly had their own objections to a number of existing traditions used for depicting some religious themes. They mandated particular directives for what should and should not be shown in religious iconography: "no images, (suggestive) of false doctrine, and furnishing occasion of dangerous error to the uneducated, [shall] be set up. . . . [A]ll lasciviousness is to be avoided; in such wise that figures shall not be painted or adorned with a beauty exciting to lust. . . . [L]et there be nothing seen that is disorderly, or that is unbecomingly or confusedly arranged, nothing that is profane, nothing indecorous."[53]

These directives were aimed at bishops and others who were likely to commission works for public display in churches. To implement them, individual bishops issued manuals specifying how certain images should be depicted. Some bishops appointed artists to pass judgment on the fittingness of post-Tridentine images.[54] Certain images were specifically discouraged, for example, St. Anne, Mary, and Jesus as a three-generational, female-centered "trinity" was deemed confusing to the people.[55] Images of Mary as a nursing mother, though once quite prized for grounding the belief that Mary gave full humanity to Jesus, had also come to be considered out of step with proper decorum.[56]

51. On the iconoclasm of the English reformers that targeted images of Mary for particularly violent destruction, see Waller, *The Virgin Mary*. On a contemporary theory of iconoclasm, see W. J. Thomas Mitchell, "Offending Images," in *What Do Pictures Want? The Lives and Loves of Images* (Chicago: University of Chicago Press, 2005), 125–44.

52. Carolyn H. Wood and Peter Iver Kaufman, "*Tacito Predicatore*: The Annunciation Chapel at the Madonna Dei Monti in Rome," *Catholic Historical Review* 90, no. 4 (October 2004): 634.

53. *The Canons and Decrees of the Sacred and Oecumenical Council of Trent*, ed. and trans. James Waterworth (London: Dolman, 1848), 235–36; http://history.hanover.edu/texts/trent/ct25.html (accessed August 1, 2011).

54. Bergmann, "A Maternal Genealogy of Wisdom," 158.

55. Ibid., 156. A web search for "Anna Selbdritt" and "Santa Ana Triple" will turn up German and Spanish examples, respectively.

56. For a discussion of the theological and cultural background to this move, see Boss, *Empress and Handmaid*, 33–39.

Some medieval ways of imaging the immaculate conception were deemed theologically confusing, ambiguous, or not representative of a scriptural account and therefore unsuitable for continuing artistic production. Among the medieval images that fell out of use was *Kiss at the Golden Gate*. One issue was the fact that some among the common people believed that the kiss actually *was* the moment of Mary's conception. In addition, the image was one of the traditions about Mary that was not found in the Scriptures. Instead, it developed out of noncanonical writings that were popularly attributed to apostles or other early teachers. The *Protoevangelium of James*, the source for traditions like the names of Mary's parents and the details of her conception, birth, early life, education, and marriage, was particularly influential. Teachers, preachers, and artists did not always distinguish between the stories from it and those in the canonical gospels. Scenes from the *Protoevangelium* were widely used in art.[57]

The images of the immaculate conception that were approved eventually consolidate into a broad common understanding of how Mary should be depicted. This is particularly true of the widely influential Spanish works that people today take for granted as standard expressions of the dogma. The most exacting expression of guidelines for proper iconography comes from the writings of the seventeenth-century Spanish painter and writer, Francisco Pacheco. He comments that earlier paintings include the Christ Child but recommends showing Mary alone, though he acknowledges that her privilege is directly dependent on her being the Mother of God.[58] The essentials of his positive recommendations are these:

> Our Lady should be painted as a beautiful young girl, twelve or thirteen years old, in the flower of her youth. She should have pretty but serious eyes with perfect features and rosy cheeks, and the most beautiful, long golden locks. . . . She should be painted wearing a white tunic and a blue mantel. She is surrounded by the sun, an oval sun of white and ochre. . . . Rays of light emanate from her head, around which is a ring of twelve stars. An imperial crown adorns her head. . . . Under her feet is the moon.[59]

57. For the text, see *The Protoevangelium of James* in *The Apocryphal New Testament: A Collection of Apocryphal Christian Literature in an English Translation*, ed. James Keith Elliott (New York: Oxford University Press, 1993).

58. Francisco Pacheco, *Arte de la pintura* (Seville, 1649). Translated from the edition of F. J. Sánchez Cantón, II (Madrid, 1956), 208–12, quoted in Robert Enggass and Jonathan Brown, *Art, 1600–1750, Sources and Documents* (Evanston, IL: Northwestern University Press, 1970), 165.

59. Ibid., 166.

Pacheco comments that one really ought to have a dragon (Satan) under her feet "whose head she broke when she triumphed over original sin," but he is reluctant to "embarrass" his paintings in this way so he prefers to leave it out.[60] Pacheco gives weight to his recommendations by referring to "the mysterious woman" of the book of Revelation as her inspiration (12:1-4). Depicting Mary using the characteristics of this woman, he claims, "is closest to the holy revelation of the Evangelist and approved by the Catholic Church on the authority of the sacred and holy interpreters."[61]

Pacheco did not entirely invent this version of the immaculate conception, and his contemporaries did not follow his recommendations slavishly. Even so, the immaculate conception images currently in use in Catholic circles are most frequently reproductions or imitations of this Spanish genre.[62] In them a young Mary stands alone or accompanied by cherubs against a background of sky or other nonspecific space. She usually wears a halo of stars and stands on a crescent moon and/or a snake representing Satan—images from the books of Revelation and Genesis.[63] Her eyes may be downcast or turned toward the sky but, in either case, her appearance is submissive. Both the long, tangled theological history connecting original sin with lust and Mary's idealized youth also give an aura to the image that suggests that her state of being uniquely redeemed is somehow related to virginity.[64]

60. Ibid., 167.

61. Ibid., 166.

62. Besides Pacheco, these artists are among those who are well known as painters of the immaculate conception: Francisco de Zurbarán, Barthomé Esteban Murillo, and Diego Velázquez. For analysis of the significance of this image of humility in comparison to earlier images of a powerful Mary, see Boss, *Empress and Handmaid*, 140–51.

63. Revelation 12:1 refers to a woman with a crown of twelve stars, standing on the moon. The text originally referred to the people of God giving birth to Christ and then to the church under persecution. Use of the text for Marian feasts and its reference to the birth of Christ led to it being adopted as a reference to Mary. The dragon or serpent comes from Genesis 3:15. The Latin Vulgate translation actually mistranslated the original Hebrew. In the Vulgate, God says to the snake, "[S]he shall bruise your head." The original Hebrew has the masculine pronoun here. Use of the Vulgate gave this text Marian overtones and the serpent passed into Marian iconography.

64. Our Lady of Lourdes is also considered the immaculate conception, but her connection to the Lourdes shrine is the stronger identity. Our Lady of Grace depicted on the miraculous medal, another image with its source in a French apparition, is also labeled the immaculate conception, but the promises connected to that apparition are also her strongest identity. For discussion of these nineteenth-

Left with this compliant, solitary virgin, the tradition of the immaculate conception becomes limited to images of Mary that are dis-
empowering to women and to the Christian commitment to salvation
as inclusive of social justice. These images have implications for the
self-image of women; the breadth or narrowness of the roles of women
in church, family, and society; optimism or pessimism about the full
humanity of women and the possibility of their salvation; and a fully
developed theology of social sin and social salvation.

Retrieving the Enclosed Garden

Tina Beattie draws attention to one pre-Tridentine tradition as a
more holistic image for a positive role of women and reversing what
can be an undervaluing of creation in favor of the realm of the spirit.[65]
This image is the *hortus conclusus* or enclosed garden, which features
Mary with the infant Jesus seated in a walled garden. Beattie points out
that the image refers to one among the many Old Testament images
that Christians have applied to Mary: "A garden locked is my sister,
my bride, a garden locked, a fountain sealed" (Song 4:12).[66] Although
they are not directly theologically related, Christians, in a complex
interweaving of references, connected Mary's immaculate conception
with purity and purity with virginity—"the garden locked." The garden
also evokes paradise of the Genesis account. Thus, the enclosed garden
can be Mary's virginity, her being impervious to sin, and her role in
redemption that restored creation through her motherhood of Jesus.
Although she may be too optimistic in this particular factor, Beattie also
sees Mary in the garden as a restoration of Eve to paradise—overcoming
the position of blame for women.

The image of the enclosed garden, taken from the text of the Song
of Solomon, has been used to illustrate Mary's virginity, to represent
her function as a foil to Eve, and to refer to her as giving no entrance
for sin. Because it shows relationships between humanity and nature, it
offers some positive possibilities for a new imagination of the immaculate conception. Beattie makes this point but does not pursue it to the
point of the required counterfiguration: "Thus this painting evokes a
vision of redemption that encompasses the whole story of salvation and

---

century images, see Boss, "The Development of the Doctrine of Mary's Immaculate
Conception," 228–29.

65. Beattie, "Garden of the New Eve," *The Tablet* (December 19, 2009): 18–19.
66. Ibid., 18.

includes the entire natural world within its sacramental gaze, that sees the vibrant life of divine grace pulsing within the beauty of Creation."[67]

Examples of the enclosed garden vary widely in what else they include. The elaborateness of the *Little Garden of Paradise* painted by the Master of the Upper Rhine about 1515 makes it one of the most varied and detailed. This is true of its plants, birds, and symbols as well as its collection of persons.[68]

Beattie's analysis, however, can be pushed further to lay out an understanding of salvation that incorporates community and the healing of structural sin.

Counterfiguration of the Paradise Garden

The *Little Garden of Paradise* is a colorful walled enclosure peopled by Mary and her court. The child Jesus plays on the grass and the landscape is brightened by detailed images of birds and flowers. It is an ideal place in many ways. It expresses one view of "paradise" for its own time period.[69] Mary is the ideal woman in beauty, class, learning/holiness,[70] companionship, and motherhood. There are further indications of the ideal life gathered around her: the presence of Christ, a wall of protection, cleanliness, a water source, colorful clothing (including crowns), food, saintly companionship, literacy, prayer, music, freedom from warfare, freedom from the devil (small monkey) and original sin (dead dragon/serpent), and presence of angelic and human protectors. The garden is fertile and beautiful.

The garden image, as Beattie claims, enriches women's sense of inclusion in the mystery of salvation and unity with creation. From Meyers's point of view, an expanded imagination of women's possible religious roles would be a rich alternative to the lone, childlike image of Mary that promotes only humility and acquiescence. The women in the garden are the active figures. They provide water and fruit, coax

---

67. Ibid., 18–19.

68. For a detailed discussion of the work, see Rose-Marie Hagen and Rainer Hagen, *15th Century Paintings* (New York: Taschen, 2001), 8–17.

69. Ibid.

70. Mary with a book is a polyvalent image that, according to some understandings of her origins, is symbolic of the wisdom she received from God when she was eternally chosen to be Christ's mother. This detail of her iconography arises from the text of the Old Testament book of Wisdom that has long been read on the feast of the immaculate conception. The book can also be a prayer book or Bible, and the assumption would be that she is praying. In either case, there would be class overtones since the rare women who were literate would be upper-class women and nuns in monasteries.

music from the Christ Child, and exemplify holiness and learning. They redeem the image of woman as the troublemaker in the original garden. In all of these ways they provide a starting place for greater, more positive, and active religious images of women.[71] This is an image that could convey an understanding of salvation as relational and complex.

In the present day one would need to take into account the evidence of privilege in the original painting to provide a critical counterfiguration of the immaculate conception doctrine. Aside from the one fruit tree, there are no food crops in the garden. Thus, the occupants are not concerned about subsistence. Racist idealization is also present since all the human figures are white while the darkest being in the garden represents evil. Such an image would provide options for women's agency by extending the imagining of a holistic, active, and relational salvation into our time. The image of Mary as privileged underlines Ivone Gebara and Maria Bingemer's claim that the fact that this woman whom many people think of as spiritually privileged was in her own time a poor woman of no importance.[72] This is an especially vital reminder when considering Marian images for three reasons. First, the vast majority of the depictions of Mary express admiration for her by idealizing her in terms of the artist's historical period and the standards of beauty of that time and place, which often include accoutrements of wealth or privilege. This denies her historical situation, including her poverty and colonial oppression. Second, devotees of Mary from privileged situations can identify with her images without having any of their assumptions about her reality or their own challenged. Finally, her identification with and concern for the oppressed, as expressed in her *Magnificat* (Luke 2:47-55), goes unexpressed.

Whether one thinks of freedom from sin as an individual privilege or a resource for the enhancement of social justice and communal right relations matters to women's agency. If the paradigmatic image of perfection is individual, even if that individual privilege is formally defined as "for others," lack of perfection is also solely an individual dilemma. This minimizes leverage for social critique. It cannot be denied that salvation for a Christian is individual. At the same time, because it is salvation in Christ, it is salvation through incorporation into the Body of Christ. This corporate dimension extends still further as we acknowledge that salvation mends the disunity that has ruptured the

---

71. For an extended analysis of this point, see Beattie, *God's Mother, Eve's Advocate*.

72. Ivone Gebara and Maria Clara Bingemer, *Mary: Mother of God, Mother of the Poor* (Maryknoll, NY: Orbis Books, 1989), 113.

bonds among all those who have been created in the image of God. For this reason, images of Mary that idealize the salvation she has received proleptically through Christ but are capable of speaking only to individual purity do not adequately image Christian grace.

Mary's identification with and concern for the oppressed would need to be specifically displayed in a contemporary reconfiguration of the garden. Traci West provides an entrance point with her description of the link between Mary, the unwed teen, and contemporary young, black, single mothers under political regimes like the "Contract with America" that assign "responsibility for violent crime to poor black single mothers."[73] West acknowledges that Mary, with her holiness linked to motherhood and virginity, has been used to denigrate sexually active women. At the same time, she argues for the power of resistance in Mary's story, particularly in her *Magnificat*. In the *Magnificat* one encounters "[b]lessing the particular."[74] No one wants to hear about the real lives of poor women who, West says, are described by everyone but themselves. Mary, West points out, names her lowly circumstances and claims God's attention. The *Magnificat* is also a reversal of and resistance to the humiliation deeply familiar to poor mothers. It also provides what West calls "a key ingredient for struggle: imagination."[75] Finally, in addition to God's redemption of her own particular humiliation, Mary portrays God as establishing a broader just society by reversing unjust structures and situations.[76]

A concrete picture of a Mary-centered "little paradise garden" developed in their own voice by and for poor mothers could be the beginning of new images of a state of salvation. The safety, respect, and adequate resources for a dignified life that they are now denied would need to be symbolized in a way meaningful to them. Perhaps Mary joins with neighbors of every race, nationality, and walk of life in cultivating a community garden of food and flowers. Children play safely under the watchful eyes of the community. Everyone—official and private citizen—has disarmed. Nutritious food is served at a communal table. Elected officials sit down to listen respectfully to their constituents. It is possible that things only they could know would be central to the vision.

---

73. Traci C. West, *Disruptive Christian Ethics: When Racism and Women's Lives Matter* (Louisville, KY: Westminster John Knox Press, 2006), 83.

74. Ibid., 106.

75. Ibid., 107.

76. Ibid.

Conclusion: Women Want to Know

Since West is clear about the churches' responsibility to create these conditions of just reversal, maybe a copy of poor women's counter-figuration of paradise should reside in the local church. Reconstructed imagery can increase the degree to which women are able to develop autonomy and can broaden the resources available to motivate Christians to recognize and act against structural sin. Images that emphasize isolation reinforce the damaging notion that individual responsibility is all that is needed for the lives of the marginalized to be improved. This social myth is reinforced by theological constructs in which individual sinfulness takes priority over social sin as a matter of urgent concern.

Undertaking counterfiguration also has the benefit of clarifying the fact that the construction of images of Mary is just that—a construction—a process that is often missed when images of Mary are used habitually. Griselda Pollack argues that early feminist critiques of "images of women" were inadequate because they assumed some existing population of women who were then imaged in a problematic way. In actuality, she says, women's identities are partially constituted by the images that surround them and "represent" them. In other words, "[r]epresentations articulate/produce meanings as well as re-representing a world already meaningful."[77]

This argument has interesting implications for the creation of Marian images since the identity that is created is created not by her but entirely for her. She is at the mercy of the process of image production. Images of her sponsored by the church are always constructed from current cultural ideals of beauty and propriety. Who, then, is this image? Is it Mary or a construct by and for the purpose of social conformity? In questioning images of Mary, one recognizes that these images are part of the cultural practices of representation that construct women—and continue to construct Mary.

With this in mind, one can see that Mary, as imaged over the centuries, has not existed solely in some independent historical form but has been constituted by her representations. These representations, at any given time, attribute shifting religious idealizations to her using prevailing ideals of feminine perfection, including physical perfection as a representation of spiritual perfection or virtue. At the same time, because she is the religiously ideal woman, her representation "acts back" on

---

77. Griselda Pollack, "Missing Women: Rethinking Early Thoughts on Images of Women," in *The Critical Image: Essays on Contemporary Photography*, ed. Carol Squiers (Seattle, WA: Bay Press, 1990), 206.

other women as a standard and a critique. The power of her religious idealization acts to reinforce selected standards for womanhood.

Women, however, have not been entirely passive but have created counterfigurations expressing their sense of Mary as a companion of their real lives and a champion of their struggles. This is why the questions reported by the nurse at my lecture; the voices that West wants to have heard; and the images of Alma López, Ester Hernández, and Julie Vivas have such intensity. Through dedication to their questions and their imaginations these women, as Meyers says, "envision feasible options" of human flourishing for themselves and for Mary.[78]

The theological importance of this process can only be indicated here. Because images at least partially constitute our understanding of Mary, the interpretation of doctrinal formulations about her are not necessarily controlling the meaning of the images but rather the reverse. This reality should make Christians look around at the iconography of our local churches and ask what they teach and what counterfigurations are necessary.

78. Meyers, *Gender in the Mirror*, 20.

A self-portrait by a participant in the Guadalupe Art Program. Photo courtesy of Rev. Mary Moreno-Richardson.

Susie Paulik Babka

The Feminine Face of God Is My Face

On the Empowerment of Female Self-Portraiture

Am I not here, your Mother? Are you not under my shadow and
protection? Am I not your foundation of life? Are you not in the
folds of my mantle, in the crossing of my arms?
—Nuestra Señora de Guadalupe,
according to the Nican Mopohua[1]

Salma[2] was seventeen and pregnant when her gang coerced her into
shooting a rival gang member, which paralyzed her victim for life. While
incarcerated in Central Juvenile Hall in East Los Angeles, she met Rev.
Mary Moreno-Richardson, who was serving as an Episcopalian chaplain
volunteer. They formed a friendship while Rev. Mary prepared Salma
for her First Communion. After being sentenced to fifty-five years to
life in prison, Salma gave birth to a son and begged her mother to raise
him, fearful of his being caught in the foster system. She told Rev. Mary
that her limited moments with her baby in the hospital were the most
moving of her life: she had never before known love like the love she felt

1. Cited by Jeanette Rodriguez, *Our Lady of Guadalupe: Faith and Empowerment*
among Mexican-American Women (Austin: University of Texas Press, 2005), 39.
2. This name has been changed to protect the identities of Salma and her
family members.

for her child. Salma had only forty-eight hours with him after his birth and kept him nestled beside her the entire time. Salma's mother is raising the boy, but because Salma is in Chowchilla State Prison in central California, she sees her son only once a year—sometimes less—when *Get on the Bus*, a program of the Center for Restorative Justice Works,[3] has sufficient funding to bus children the five hours to the prison for visitation. Rev. Mary created a portrait for Salma based on a photograph taken of Salma with her baby on one of his visits and sent a copy to her. In the portrait, Salma is with her son within the mantle of the Virgin of Guadalupe: Salma's prisoner number in the painting parallels the "visitor" badge worn by her little boy. At their feet is a banner proclaiming Luke 1:46, "My soul does magnify the Lord."[4]

Salma is one of hundreds of young women who have been touched by the Guadalupe Art Program, founded by Rev. Mary, the first Latina to be ordained to the priesthood in the Episcopal Diocese of San Diego. The program, described by Rev. Mary as a "spiritual empowerment workshop," has been remarkably successful, providing at-risk young women, aged eight through seventeen, from Los Angeles to Tijuana, with an opportunity for self-portraiture and a chance to take a break from their often rigorous lives. In 2003, Rev. Mary was elected to serve on the National Commission on the Status of Women. She eventually became a delegate to the United Nations and displayed artwork from the Guadalupe Art Program in an exhibit at the UN in honor of the thirtieth anniversary of the Year of the Child.

Many participants in the program, living undocumented in North American society, struggle daily with feeling invisible and worthless. They may be forced to go into hiding, living in continual fear of deportation, separated from or made to deny family, even changing their names. Not all who participate, however, are caught in the failure of the United States to provide comprehensive immigration reform. Many are at risk for gang involvement, and many are simply poor and must shoulder responsibilities more affluent young women don't have, such as multiple part-time jobs or primary care for younger siblings when parents are working.

3. For more information, see http://www.getonthebus.us/index.php. For other programs that support incarcerated women, see http://www.womenprisoners.org/, the web site for the California Coalition for Women Prisoners.

4. Salma's story comes from an interview with Moreno-Richardson, August 8, 2009, and has been revised by the author.

When poor and undocumented, young women are vulnerable to danger, threatened by the growing web of human trafficking. As a volunteer chaplain who is regularly called to Juvenile Hall, San Diego, Rev. Mary has met with scores of young women held for prostitution. Although detained for this crime, they are in fact victims of the crime of trafficking; this affects girls and young women from all ethnic and socioeconomic backgrounds. Rev. Mary describes meeting a fourteen-year-old held for prostitution who explained that she had been kidnapped at age nine while walking to school in Oceanside and then trafficked to Las Vegas and Los Angeles. "Our justice system often overlooks the reality of trafficking and criminalizes the victim," Rev. Mary observes. The intention of the Guadalupe Art Program is that these young women be empowered through one of the most significant cultural and religious symbols in the history of the Americas: the Virgin of Guadalupe. For all of these young women, turning eighteen means facing an uncertain future, but while in this program, they have a few moments to dance in *rebozos*, to play, and to create a self-portrait nestled within the sunlit mantle of the Virgin of Guadalupe, to see themselves within the "feminine face of God."

Why is creating a self-portrait such a powerful experience for young females who have probably had only limited exposure to art and the creative process? This essay explores why the process of self-portraiture has not only been a compelling claim for the dignity of female identity in the history of art in the West but also enabled women to locate themselves within the ethical dimension of responsibility to the dignity of the vulnerable self. Rev. Mary's particular addition of the cultural symbol of the Virgin of Guadalupe to this process adds a new facet of meaning and context that enables young women to see beyond their circumstances, to see themselves as bearers of the divine and as worthy of the respect, opportunity, and leisure necessary to creatively engage the self.

What Is a Self-Portrait?

While the answer to this question may seem obvious, there are many dimensions to the meaning of self-portraiture, including the fundamental dimensions of historical, cultural, and social context. These dimensions lead us to ask about the purpose of creating a self-portrait. Is the image idealized or inflated? Expressionistic or realistic? Did the artist include symbolism or allusions, hidden or explicit, with the intention of communicating a particular moment, idea, or cause? The self-portraits of contemporary photographic artist Cindy Sherman (born in Glen Ridge,

New Jersey, 1954) are performative, exaggerated, and full of clues to a particular set of interpretations. The painted self-portraits of Mexican artist Frieda Kahlo (1907–54) are similarly performative, exaggerated, and full of clues, but the differences between what constitutes a series of Sherman self-portraits and Kahlo self-portraits are substantial. Their visual information is based on their contextuality as well as their willingness to convey (or perhaps produce) life experience.

In Kahlo's case, nothing of her actual life experience is withheld: not her physical suffering from polio at thirteen and a horrific bus accident at eighteen in which a handrail pierced her "like a sword," not any aspect of her tumultuous marriage to the muralist Diego Rivera, not even the finely drawn hairs of her famous eyebrows. Kahlo's self-portraits are clearly exercises in both self-exploration and self-explanation. But Kahlo is also interested in representing the conflicting roles ascribed to being female: in *Self-Portrait with Cropped Hair* (1940), painted soon after her divorce from Rivera, she appears in Rivera's suit, having chopped her long hair, now scattered in long shards, like scissor blades, around her on the floor. A verse from a Spanish song is written above her, which translated reads, "You see, if I loved you, it was for your hair. Now that you've cut it off, I don't love you any more."[5] The scissors held between her legs may be a reference to Freud's notion of the female as having to endure the "absence" of her anatomy; her gaze at the viewer seems to inquire, "Do I have to be a man to succeed as an artist?"[6] In her pain over Rivera's betrayal, this self-portrait examines the roles ascribed to her gender, in terms of both personal relationships and profession.

On the other hand, while Sherman features herself in most of her works, primarily in exploration of gender roles, she maintains that they are not self-portraits.[7] Her works do not provide insight into her personal circumstances or biography. She disguises herself: sometimes she is a 1940s film star (*Untitled* #122, 1983), or a teenager sprawled on a linoleum floor in suburban turmoil (*Untitled* #96, 1981, which sold in 2011 for nearly $4 million). Her series *Untitled Film Stills*, 1977 to 1980, explores the clichés of female sex roles through the 1950s and 1960s. They are all images of women alone but as objects of observation, inviting consideration of how women may come to know the self when they are tacitly confronted by sociocultural expectations. Because she both

---

5. Liana DeGirolami Cheney, Alicia Craig Faxon, and Kathleen Russo, *Self-Portraits by Women Painters* (Washington, DC: Ashgate, 2009), 178.

6. Ibid., 179.

7. See the biography on her web site: http://www.cindysherman.com/biography.shtml.

manipulates the camera and occupies the image, Sherman reverses the passive role of women that typically occurs in the scenarios she constructs. If Sherman's works are self-portraits, it is because they manifest an agency that results from intentionality: not only is a woman in control of the portrayal of female sex roles, it is Sherman's own persona that appears in a work created for the public sphere. She is both observed and observer, mediating the distance between what is imposed and what is chosen. Sherman's self-portraits become avenues for the creation of life experience—which arguably enhances self-understanding—rather than ways to deconstruct or analyze personal experience.

The purpose of self-portraiture is thus extraordinarily varied; from commissioned works to private, from psychological to social, self-portraits can be simply manifestations of technique, a way to advertise talent, or a way to wrestle with profound challenges. Self-portraits are essentially the artistic perception of one's existence in a way that requires the distance of separateness and otherness to be able to contemplate and represent the mysterious and ineffable self.

As we will see in more detail in the next section, female artists such as Catharina van Hemessen and Sofonisba Anguissola of the sixteenth century, who are among the first recognized female artists, had also been self-portraitists since their teen years. Such artists rejected any association with the anonymity and invisibility often accorded their gender in society: the self-portrait was their refusal to have their artistic talent possibly mistaken for a man's. No one could view their works and fail to see that the artist is indeed also a woman. Self-portraiture represents the first opportunity for women to proclaim the value of the female self, by itself, without reference to a man and without deference to religion or other authority. Until the advent of women's self-portraiture, the only representations of women in art were goddesses, saints, or the wealthy elite; in the sixteenth century, the female in visual art becomes legitimate as a subject of self-portraiture, through no other avenue but her own talent.

Can the advent of the female self-portrait be traced to the acquisition of female subjectivity in the West? While addressing this question is beyond the scope of this essay, a few things may be said. In the self-portrait, the subject of the work is the artist herself, and the intention to supply the viewer with a visual understanding of the subject, an intention that underlies the lure of visual imagery in the West, is realized. In Existentialist philosophy, the self is defined through the process of involving the self in the world. There is no self without context; furthermore, this relational process of self to itself is defined by agency—I know who I am based on my choice to love someone in particular, to identify with a particular group, to meet a particular goal, to challenge my circumstances.

The self-portrait has thus been liberating for women as the locus of both public proclamation and personal introspection. The distance necessary for the visual representation of introspection was encouraged in the fourteenth century with the manufacture of the glass mirror in Venice.[8] Until that point, only polished metal offered a reflective surface, which provided a distorted or fuzzy image. Simone de Beauvoir writes, "Man, feeling and wishing himself active, subject, does not see himself in his fixed image; it has little attraction for him, since man's body does not seem to him to be the object of desire; while woman, knowing and making herself object, believes she really sees *herself* in the glass."[9] The objectification to which females are accustomed in patriarchal society is part of their visual self-identity; this may indicate a reason self-portraiture becomes a part of the oeuvre of several female artists. Perhaps the rise of humanism and the desire for self-awareness that generates the popularity of the self-portrait in the Renaissance can be traced to the common availability of something as mundane as the handheld mirror.

The History of Women's Self-Portraiture

> *Beatriz*[10] *was seven years old and held as undocumented when Rev. Mary met her through the Guadalupe Art Program in the San Diego detention center. She and her older sister made the journey to the United States with relatives from her native El Salvador but had become separated from them, and now, in a strange country, the sisters were being held indefinitely. Authorities at the center were trying to locate Beatriz's mother, supposedly in New Jersey, but undocumented parents, afraid of deportation, often do not come forward. Rev. Mary put her arm around the child and asked Beatriz to explain her portrait. Tears filled Beatriz's eyes. Her self-portrait features her eyeglasses and unruly hair, and the wide smile she normally wears, as well as*

---

8. See Whitney Chadwick, "How Do I Look?," in *Mirror, Mirror: Self-Portraits by Women Artists*, ed. Liz Rideal (London: Watson-Guptill, 2002), 9.

9. Simone de Beauvoir, *The Second Sex*, trans. H. M. Parshley (New York: Vintage, 1989), 629; cf. Chadwick, "How Do I Look?," 9.

10. This name has been changed to protect her identity. Beatriz's story comes from an interview with Moreno-Richardson, January 30, 2010, and has been revised by the author.

a prominent red heart, drawn with a sword through it. "Why is the sword there?" Rev. Mary asks. "Lo quitaré cuando a mi mama," Beatriz answers ("I'll take it out when I find my mommy"). Rev. Mary never saw her again after that and has no idea what happened to her.

Self-portraits, even in young Beatriz's case, are rarely about depicting merely what the artist looks like. Instead, self-portraits capture a facet of identity at a moment in a lifetime, through a dialectical interpretive stance between the artist as subject and the artist as viewer. While self-portraiture appears as far back as Old Kingdom Egypt and surfaces occasionally as a sort of signature during the Middle Ages, for the most part, the growth of humanism in the late fourteenth and fifteenth centuries coincided with the growth of the recognition of the worth of the individual, which meant a rise in the incidence of self-portraiture among visual artists. By the fifteenth century, when Albrecht Dürer (1471–1528) creates a string of highly confident self-portraits, even placing his twenty-eight-year-old persona in the guise of Christ,[11] self-portraiture begins to become a genre. Some art theorists wonder whether the self-portrait isn't the origin of art itself.[12] This was, after all, the height of the Renaissance, when artists were finally recognized as more than mere artisans or skilled laborers but as interpreters of reality in their own right.

Emerging from the Middle Ages, in which the creators of some of the West's most significant works in everything from manuscript illumination to architecture remain anonymous, the fourteenth century was a time of unprecedented license to give individuality visual expression. It should be noted that self-portraiture among female artists grows simultaneously with that among male artists, even though females until the sixteenth century generally studied art in secret.

According to Frances Borzello, the earliest female self-portraits appear as illustrations to Giovanni Boccaccio's *Concerning Famous Women*, written between 1355 and 1359.[13] In this, Boccaccio relies on Pliny the Elder's report that Iaia of Kyzikos (named "Marcia" by Boccaccio) painted

11. Albrecht Dürer, *Self-Portrait as Savior of the World*, c. 1500–1506, Alte Pinakothek, Munich.

12. Edward Lucie-Smith, *The Self-Portrait: A Modern View* (London: Sarema Press, 1987), 9.

13. Frances Borzello, *Seeing Ourselves: Women's Self-Portraits* (New York: Harry N. Abrams, Inc., 1998), 20.

her portrait "with the aid of a mirror, preserving the colors and features and expression of the face so completely that none of her contemporaries doubted that it was just like her."[14] Even earlier, a manuscript illustrator named Claricia incorporates what appears to be a self-portrait reclining in the tail of the letter Q in a German psalter from Augsburg in the twelfth century.[15] Much of the artistic life of the Middle Ages takes place in the monasteries with the production of illuminated manuscripts; access to the convent, and an education, was often determined by noble birth.[16] While there is evidence of abbesses in double monasteries directing scriptoria from the eighth century onward, it is impossible to determine whether the work produced was executed by a man or a woman.[17]

Female self-portraiture comes into the open in the sixteenth century, when Belgian Catharina van Hemessen (1528–87) paints eight self-portraits from 1548 to 1552 and Italian Lavinia Fontana (1552–1614) paints several self-portraits early in her career. Both were trained by their fathers, as was often the case with female artists. In her 1548 work, van Hemessen is credited with the first self-portrait for either gender showing the artist in the process of painting. While she portrays herself as demure and studious, she also includes signs of obvious technical skill, such as depicting velvet garments and the firm grasp of several brushes. Lavinia Fontana's 1577 self-portrait shows her playing a clavichord, influenced perhaps by Sofonisba Anguissola's (1532–1625) 1555 self-portrait, which is considered the earliest female self-portrait depicting musical skill. Tintoretto's daughter, Marietta Robusti, also trained by her famous father, paints her 1580 portrait before the clavichord as well.

Praised by Giorgio Vasari in his 1568 *Lives of the Artists* as working "with deeper study and greater grace than any woman of our times at problems of design, for not only has she learned to draw, paint, and copy from nature, and reproduce most skillfully works by other artists, but she has on her own painted some most rare and beautiful paintings,"[18]

14. Ibid. See Giovanni Boccaccio, *Concerning Famous Women*, trans. G. A. Guarino, rev. ed. (New York: Italica Press, 2011), 144–45. Borzello notes, "The sin of vanity was always personified as a woman studying herself in the mirror," such as in Ambrogio Lorenzetti's *Vaingloria*, 1338–40; "This may be the reason why, compared with men, so few women artists of the twentieth century incorporated the mirror into their self-portraits" (27).

15. Borzello, *Seeing Ourselves*, 27.

16. See Whitney Chadwick, *Women, Art, and Society* (London: Thames and Hudson, 2007), 44.

17. See ibid., 45.

18. Giorgio Vasari, *Lives of the Artists*, trans. Julia and Peter Bonadella (London: Oxford University Press, 1991), 343.

Anguissola's output of self-portraits rivals that of Rembrandt, who is considered the premier self-portraitist of youth to old age. Anguissola at age thirteen executed a chalk study of herself with an old woman; against convention, she is smiling broadly and raising her hand in a playful gesture. At sixteen, she sketches a more somber countenance, perhaps indicative of her interest to be taken seriously; at age eighteen she paints her mentor Bernardino Campi painting her portrait (c. 1550) in a remarkable and original composition. These self-studies continue into her adulthood, when before her marriage she would sign her portraits "Virgo"; to her marriage portrait, in which she portrays a tender intimacy with her husband; to the several portraits she paints of herself in late life, unabashedly showing every weakness and wrinkle. Anguissola's self-portraits are not studies in vanity, since she often renders herself in black, with little or no jewelry, and hair conservatively pulled back. The works lack the technical details featured in Fontana's work—such as lavish pleated collars—so her portraits might be understood more as attempts at self-exploration. Like van Hemessen, Anguissola paints herself at her easel, but in a more adventurous turn, she paints herself in the manner of St. Luke painting the Virgin Mary (1556). Because of the legend that Luke painted the first portrait of Mary, this motif became common in Christian art in the fifteenth century; in these works, "Luke" is usually a self-portrait of the artist, an early Renaissance allusion that the artist is divinely inspired. For Anguissola to see herself in this tradition is not audacious but testimony to her self-possession. She not only is aware of her talent but soberly conveys that women's creativity is also divinely inspired; an inscription in one of her versions of this motif reads, "I, the maiden Sofonisba, equaled the Muses and Apelles in performing my songs and handling my colors."[19]

The majority of female artists known today from this period were Italian; education of women in Italy proliferates during the Renaissance due to declining male enrollment in universities, a consequence of war and disease.[20] Granted, as Ellen Lubell points out, female artists focused on portraiture (and hence self-portraiture) because they were banned from life-drawing classes, as well as other academic aspects of artistic training.[21] The persistence of female self-portraiture throughout the history of art, however, presents something more significant when the use

19. Borzello, *Seeing Ourselves*, 46.

20. See Cheney, Faxon, and Russo, *Self-Portraits by Women Painters*, 30. Women have studied at the University of Bologna since the thirteenth century.

21. See Ellen Lubell, "Women Artists: Self Image," *Women's Art Journal* 3, no. 1 (Spring–Summer 1982): 12.

of the self-portrait by female artists is for public view. Because artists such as Anguissola and Fontana portray themselves as noblewomen (*gentil* or *nobil donna*), and not as swimming wildly against mainstream current, they could have relied solely on the use of traditional religious subject matter, or even bowls of flowers, to display talent. Instead, they leave a legacy of agency in the effort of women to be considered with respect as equals. Whitney Chadwick writes,

> Every woman who paints a self-portrait . . . challenges in some way the complex relationship that exists between masculine agency and feminine passivity in Western art history. . . . In taking up brush or pen, chisel or camera, women assert a claim of the representation of women (as opposed to Woman) that Western culture long ago ceded to male genius and patriarchal perspectives.[22]

Female agency was typified in motifs such as the biblical story of Judith and Holofernes, which became popular among female artists. Artemisia Gentileschi (1593–1652), trained by her father, paints a particularly striking version of this motif (c. 1620). Gentileschi's troubled life—she was sent to study under her father's friend Agostino Tassi but was raped by him and an associate—spilled into her art, giving her heroines stubborn perseverance. Her most famous Judith (she painted three) slays Holofernes with a searing vigor that has become a symbol of women defeating male dominance. For her self-portrait, Gentileschi paints herself as the "allegory of painting," *La Pittura*, c. 1630 to 1637, in which we can barely see her face, so involved is she in the act of creating. Based on themes and techniques presented in her self-portrait, we see echoes of Artemisia in all her works, rebelling against convention, staking a claim as one of the most important artists of the early Baroque, turning self into art.

Seeing the Self: The Theological Significance of the Self-Portrait

Encouraged by the process of seeing,[23] works of art not only rely on but also engender shared understandings between the artist and

---

22. Chadwick, "How Do I Look?," 9.

23. James Elkins points to the distinction between "vision," which refers to the anatomical activity of the eyes, the light refracting off an object, and "sight" or "seeing," in which the brain must manage the image, locate it within banks of visual memories, and make sense of it. See *The Object Stares Back: On the Nature of Seeing* (San Diego: Harcourt, 1996), 17–22.

the viewer. In the case of the self-portrait, the artist is both subject and viewer; this requires some distance in order to produce an intentioned and recognizable image. In other words, some distance is necessary for any reflection on the nature of the self, visual or not: if I stare at my own face too long in a mirror, I begin to lose sense of what I am seeing, and the reflection becomes distorted. I have to stop and look again later to gain a better perspective. The Jewish philosopher Emmanuel Lévinas (1906–95) might phrase this phenomenon as "consciousness that loses itself in order to find itself."[24] In contrast to the Cartesian ego, in which the self is the centerpiece of reality, for Lévinas, the meaning of subjectivity is to recognize the self as "the one-for-the-other," which requires a displacement of the ego.

Lévinas explains the process of subjectivity as ethical: there is no self, no subject, without encounter with the Other. Paul Ricoeur explains that, for Lévinas, "when the face of the other raises itself before me, above me, it is not an appearance that I can include within the sphere of my own representations."[25] The "face" is the concrete realization, not abstract or conceptual, of the alterity of the Other. I may see the Other as simply an extension of myself, and so only in terms of my needs (which he calls the "Same"), but if the face of the Other pierces the Cartesian ego, pierces the "totality" of everyday, mundane, and even narcissistic existence, I will recognize the Other as the locus of the infinite responsibility the Other requires of me. Lévinas writes,

> The epiphany of the Absolutely Other is a face by which the Other challenges and commands me through his nakedness, through his destitution. He challenges me from his humility and from his height. . . . The putting into question of the Same by the Other is a summons to respond. The I is not simply conscious of this necessity to respond, as if it were a matter of an obligation or a duty. . . . Rather the I is, by its very position, responsibility through and through. And the structure of this responsibility will show how the Other, in the face, challenges us from the greatest depth and the highest height—by opening the very dimension of elevation.[26]

24. See Emmanuel Lévinas, *Basic Philosophical Writings*, ed. A. Peperzak, S. Critchley, and R. Bernasconi (Bloomington: Indiana University Press, 1996), 85.

25. Paul Ricoeur, *Oneself as Another*, trans. Kathleen Blamey (Chicago: University of Chicago Press, 1992), 336.

26. Emmanuel Lévinas, "Transcendence and Height," in *Basic Philosophical Writings*, 17.

To be a subject means that the "Same," the ego, is irrevocably changed when faced with the event or epiphany, the "height" of recognition, of the Absolute Other. Lévinas employs the religious term "epiphany" deliberately, since the recognition of the Other that puts the Same into question is a "trace" of the divine. The trace of the Infinite "disturbs the order of the world,"[27] disturbs the comfortable order of the Same, by presenting the self with the Other.

The infinite horizon of responsibility in being-for-the-other means that the self is known and knows only through heteronomy. It is precisely because I am utterly unable to fulfill the needs of another but that I desire to attempt to fulfill them that we may name God present in the moment between awakening to the Other and living life for the Other. The being of God, then, dwells in the sacred history of human relationship, as the moment "through which God may pass."[28] "A God invisible means not only a God unimaginable, but a God accessible in justice. . . . The Other is the very locus of metaphysical truth, and is indispensable for my relation with God."[29]

How might the moment of Lévinasian subjectivity refer to the theological significance of self-portraiture? Art for the public sphere, art that is not private or withheld from public view, is a creative act of communication, inseparable from the artist's self-awareness. Painting a self-portrait requires a certain amount of self-reflection, such that the self becomes an object for subjective understanding. This is as true for children (as we saw in the story of Beatriz above) as it is for mature artists. The paradox of self-identity and objectification, between self and alterity, is the creative fuel behind the intention of a self-portrait. Creating a self-portrait may mean creating a face that is not necessarily included within my usual sphere of self-understanding, thereby differentiating the self for the purpose of recognizing the self as worthy of respect and recognition.

Hence, the distance necessary for the self to confront the self designates the self as worthy of reflection and visual representation; "being *for* the Other," a relationship of ethical responsibility, requires a response to the needs of the Other. In the distance necessary for self-reflection is an opportunity to see in the self the trace of the Infinite, the divine, the promise of transcendence. In his essay "Beyond Intentionality,"

27. Ibid., 62.

28. Emmanuel Lévinas, in an interview with R. Kearney, in *Face to Face with Lévinas*, ed. Richard Cohen (Albany: SUNY Press, 1986), 18.

29. Emmanuel Lévinas, *Totality and Infinity: An Essay on Exteriority*, trans. Alphonso Lingis (Pittsburgh: Duquesne University Press, 2008), 78.

Lévinas writes, "The face 'signifies' [the] beyond, neither as an index nor as symbol, but precisely and irreducibility as a face that summons me. It signifies to-God (*à Dieu*), not as sign, but as the questioning of myself, as if I were summoned or called, that is to say, awakened or cited as myself."[30] The face of the Other summons the self toward the responsibility necessary for subjectivity: this is where the idea of the Infinite, the intuition of God, is to be found. If the self in reflexive, artistic distance posits the self as Other, perhaps a sense of the same ethical responsibility can be cultivated.

Because in becoming subjects we are oriented to the Other with a desire that cannot be explained as something generated by the self, for Lévinas, ethics precedes ontology, which means that we encounter "God," the Infinite, only through reaching beyond the self toward the Other. "The dimension of the divine opens forth from the human face. . . . It is here that the Transcendent, infinitely other, solicits us and appeals to us. . . . [God's] very epiphany consists in soliciting us by his destitution in the face of the Stranger, the widow, and the orphan."[31] The relation to the face is the relation to the Other as vulnerable, "absolutely exposed," "bare and destitute":[32] the command of the Other that I give all I am is described as the power not of force and might but of vulnerability and weakness. When the self is vulnerable, through poverty, the threat of violence, oppression, and discrimination, self-portraiture opens the possibility for recognition of the self as worthy of respect and care.

This possibility points to the significance of the Guadalupe Art Program, which empowers young women vulnerable in circumstance. The purpose of cultivating reflective distance of the self in self-portraiture is profound not only for those who witness it but for the subject herself: the process of engaging one's self for the purpose of valuing the self. It should be remembered that, for Lévinas, the process of subjectivity is not an individual enterprise initiated by the self's existential inquiry; however, in the particular case of women's self-portraiture in history, and in the case of the young women of the Guadalupe Art Program, recognizing the self as worthy of respect when confronted by an environment that denies the dignity of agency to women and to all persons of color, the self as vulnerable must be self-reflective in order to be able to

30. Emmanuel Lévinas, "Beyond Intentionality," trans. Kathleen McLaughlin, in *Philosophy in France Today*, ed. Alan Montefiore (Cambridge: Cambridge University Press, 1983), 112.

31. Lévinas, *Totality and Infinity*, 78.

32. See Emmanuel Lévinas, *Entre Nous: Thinking-of-the-Other*, trans. Michael B. Smith and Barbara Harshav (New York: Columbia University Press, 1998), 104.

engage in the sort of heteronomy, the transcending of the self, that makes one fully human. The incorporation of the self-portrait into the mantle of the Virgin of Guadalupe lifts the self-reflective exercise into the face of the divine feminine, superimposing the self-at-risk onto centuries-old symbolism of the Mother who identifies with the oppressed.

The Virgin of Guadalupe

Alessandra[33] was fourteen when she made the arduous journey from Guatemala City to Tijuana, hoping to eventually reunite with her sister in south Florida. But sex traffickers separated her from the group she was with and held her hostage in a house surrounded by over thirty vicious dogs. "Don't try to escape," they told her, "you would never make it out alive." The dogs, abused themselves, were frenzied by malnourishment; Alessandra, terrified, listened to their wails through the night and their barking during the day, constant reminders of her impossible situation. The traffickers sent "clients" to the house to rape her and pocketed the money. After months of this, she felt that death would be preferable to the life she was forced to live and decided to attempt escape. One late morning, when her captors were drunk and asleep, she prayed, deep within and over and over, like a mantra: "Dios esté conmigo" ("God be with me"). She neared the door and slowly, soundlessly, turned the knob; the door squeaked on its hinges. She held her breath and moved forward. The bodies of the dogs were splayed on the dusty ground, the shadows of their ribs moving in the sun. But for the first time since she had been held, all were quiet, miraculously subdued. Tenderly, she crept down the path to the fence surrounding the shack of a house, opened and closed the gate, and ran into the desert, the heat of the sun burning the ground beneath her bare feet. Eventually, Alessandra arrived in south Florida, but her sister did not come forward for her, out of fear of her own deportation. Alessandra is today thriving in a foster home, going to school, and visiting her sister when she can.

---

33. This name has been changed to protect her identity. Alessandra's story comes from an interview with Moreno-Richardson, January 30, 2010, and has been revised by the author.

Self-portraits created in the Guadalupe Art Program: the divine in each luminous face. Photos courtesy of Rev. Mary Moreno-Richardson.

Miriam of Nazareth was fourteen and unwed when she became pregnant. Alone, frightened, unsure of her future, she relied on God for the strength to set out on the journey of her life, a journey in which she would find her voice as a prophet, proclaiming, "My soul magnifies the Lord, and my spirit rejoices in God my savior. . . . He has brought down the powerful from their thrones and lifted up the lowly" (Luke 1:47-52; NRSV).

As any feminist in Christian theology knows, the image of Miriam, better known to Christians as the Virgin Mary, has been a source of both empowerment and oppression for women in Christian history. Elizabeth Johnson notes, "While a historical woman obviously dwells at the root of this whole phenomenon, there has been a plasticity to her image that has allowed the Christian imagination to create widely different Marian symbols and theologies in relation to spiritual and social needs."[34]

In the history of art in the West, the depiction of Mary's physical beauty pointedly intends to surpass that of any other woman; Sandro Botticelli's depictions of Mary, for example, are strikingly similar to his depictions of the goddess Venus, indicating the possibility of using the same model for both. That Mary's beauty intentionally rivals the goddess, or at least substitutes for her, is also a theological claim. She is alluringly appealing but, as virgin, is also unobtainable; the goddess Venus is also alluringly appealing and, as a fantasy, is also unobtainable. Is it possible that the fantasy of a stunning young woman who would perpetually remain a virgin, inaccessible to men, motivated the celibate priesthood's increasing devotion to Mary from the Middle Ages to the present day?

For actual women, however, comparison to an unobtainable fantasy is highly problematic. Johnson notes several instances in which women must confront the impact Marian fantasy has upon their notion of self. In one, a South African prayer group decides to omit the Litany of Loreto's praise of "Mother inviolate, Mother undefiled" because such degrades their experiences of intimacy with their husbands and the bearing of their children; in another example, a small Christian community in Oaxaca, Mexico, rejects the notion that Mary accepted that her son must be sacrificed for the forgiveness of sin as "God's will" on the basis that no mother would will her child's death, which also means that no God could will such either.[35] In both instances, critiquing the traditional

---

34. Elizabeth A. Johnson, *Truly Our Sister: A Theology of Mary in the Communion of Saints* (New York: Continuum, 2006), 5.

35. Ibid., 8.

theology of Mary led to a more liberating understanding of both the identity of Mary and the identity of God. Mary's image as passive and unobtainable was challenged by women's belief in the intrinsic value of their maternal and sexual lives. Mary is understood less as a goddess and more as a human woman who shares their lives and experiences and yet plays a pivotal role in the story of divine self-revelation. Mary makes sense to women when women find in her a peer rather than an archetype, someone who inspires perseverance as well as encourages a relationship to the divine.

The conquered indigenous peoples of the "New World" found such a peer in the image of the Virgin of Guadalupe. Although the image contains obvious allusions to goddess imagery, her beauty is contextual, not ethereal or inaccessible, as noted is a trend in some Western portraits of Mary. Virgilio Elizondo puts it best:

> She wore the black band of maternity (*cinta*) around her waist, the sign that she was with child. This child was her offering to the New World. The Lady was greater than the greatest in the native pantheon because she hid the sun but did not extinguish it. Thus she was more powerful than the sun god. . . . The Lady was also greater than their moon god, for she stood upon the moon, yet did not crush it. However, great as this Lady was, she was not a goddess. She wore no mask as the Indian gods did, and her vibrant, compassionate face in itself told anyone who looked upon it that she was the compassionate mother.[36]

Guadalupe's symbolic power is not in the historic Western ideal of femininity as passive or dependent; if it were, the image of Guadalupe would have supported the European hegemony that oppressed the indigenous peoples. But Elizondo notes her compassionate agency here, as though the best of what the Náhuatl[37] understood of themselves was reflected in her.

Elizondo explains that whereas the Spanish worldview is based on linear, rational thinking, individualism, and the salvation of particular souls, the Náhuatl worldview is intuitive and communal, such that the

36. Virgilio Elizondo, "Our Lady of Guadalupe as Cultural Symbol: The Power of the Powerless," in *Beyond Borders: Writings of Virgilio Elizondo and Friends*, ed. Timothy Matovina (Maryknoll, NY: Orbis, 2000), 121.

37. Jeanette Rodriguez uses the terms "Náhuatl" (who had been conquered by the Aztecs before the Spanish conquest of Mexico), "indigenous," and "Indian" interchangeably to refer to the people of central Mexico in the time of Cortes (about 1519). "Aztec" she uses to refer to the dominant group in direct conflict with the Spaniards. See her essay in this volume, as well as *Our Lady of Guadalupe*, 2.

well-being of the cosmic community precedes the salvation of the in-dividual; "For the Europeans, conquest of self—and others—was the measure of the human, while for the Amerindians, harmony within the self and with all creation was the measure of the human."[38] The Náhuatl language reflects this communal thinking in its employment of *disfrasismos*, the complementarity of seeming opposites: for example, "world" is expressed as "heaven-earth," and personality is not located in the mind but in *rostro y corazón* ("face and heart").[39] "Face" was under-stood as the gateway to the person, the "embodiment of self," according to Elizondo.[40] Both Elizondo and Jeanette Rodriguez agree that "for the Náhuatl, knowledge of reality was the result of 'seeing' through intuition, symbols, interrelationships, and movements, best expressed through *disfrasismos*."[41] Hence, when the worldviews of the Spanish and Náhuatl met, the result was catastrophic, because "rather than integrat-ing Indian society, the Spanish destroyed it and attempted to replace it. The result was the *mestizaje*, the Mexican people."[42]

When the *Señora* appeared to Juan Diego in December 1531 near Tenochtitlán (now Mexico City), a decade after the city's brutal fall to the Spanish, on the hill of Tepeyac, site of a sacred temple to the Aztec goddess Tonantzin, the indigenous people had been stripped of history, language, religion, and thousands of lives. The bishop refused to believe such a vision had come to an Indian, but the *Señora* insisted to Juan Diego that it was he to whom she had chosen to deliver her message. Returning to the bishop, Juan Diego unfolded his *tilma* and an image of the *Señora* appeared behind a cascade of Castilian roses. Her skin is olive, her hair black, her eyes gentle, her hands folded "in an Indian manner of offering, indicating something is to come from her."[43]

Since then, Guadalupe has been the "Mother of a new humanity," according to Elizondo: a humanity that persists in the affirmation of its own dignity, despite every external effort to subdue it. The authenticity of the image has been disputed, of course, and some historians have argued that the indigenous connection to the image was more through

38. Virgilio Elizondo, *Guadalupe: Mother of the New Creation* (Maryknoll, NY: Orbis, 1997), xvi.

39. Rodriguez, *Our Lady of Guadalupe*, 8.

40. Virgilio Elizondo, *La Morenita: Evangelizer of the Americas* (San Antonio, TX: Mexican American Cultural Center, 1980), 18.

41. Rodriguez, *Our Lady of Guadalupe*, 8.

42. Ibid., 9.

43. Ibid., 27; cf. Elizondo, *La Morenita*, 1.

the goddess Tonantzin than Mary.[44] Elizondo's theology of Guadalupe is based on the effective power of her symbolism as having surpassed the objective historicity of the event; this means that regardless of whether the apparition is objective "fact," it is the sort of guiding mythology that establishes and preserves a culture, which in turn establishes and preserves a people. She has become patroness of Mexican and Indian peoples, patroness of the Americas, Madonna of the Barrios, *Nuestra Señora de Guadalupe*, "the symbol of the new Indian Catholicism as distinguished from the foreign Catholicism of the conquerors."[45]

Five hundred years later, she is invoked by the sick, the poor, the disenfranchised; she has been carried on banners in marches of oppressed *campesinos* led by César Chàvez and Dolores Huerta in demonstrations from the late 1950s to the 1970s, one of which covered 250 miles, from Delano to Sacramento, California, in 1966. In 1968, on one of several hunger strikes Chàvez would undergo, twenty thousand pilgrims visited him over the twenty-five-day period, bringing him images of Guadalupe while keeping vigil. She is invoked because she represents the divine as power shared rather than subjugating power; this energizes people who seek only the respect of their rights as workers and as human beings, not the sort of power that seeks to conquer, dominate, or destroy.

Conclusion

When Gloria was fifteen years old, she wrote the following prose poem after her experience in the Guadalupe Art Program in San Diego:

> It seemed like a normal day—I come home, eat, do my homework, go to sleep. But at 3:00 a.m., my father cries: "Get up—we're leaving! Grab some clothes and let's go." I don't know where we're going, but he rushes me into a black van, packed with little kids and grandmas. We drive for hours, the van stops, we're rushed out and head up a hill—there's a fence cut open. People slip through, but before I get to the fence, we hear a siren: THIS IS THE UNITED STATES BORDER

44. See Louise M. Burkhart, "The Cult of the Virgin of Guadalupe in Mexico," in *South and Meso-American Native Spirituality: From the Cult of the Feathered Serpent to the Theology of Liberation*, ed. Gary Gossen and Miguel Leon-Portilla (New York: Crossroad, 1993), and Stafford Poole, *Our Lady of Guadalupe: The Origins and Sources of a Mexican National Symbol, 1531–1797* (Tucson: University of Arizona Press, 1995). These writers assert that the image on the *tilma* could not be authentic and that there was no widespread conversion of native peoples during the time that the image appeared.

45. Rodriguez, *Our Lady of Guadalupe*, 45.

PATROL! STOP! I see in my father's face disappointment and rage; I can smell his fear. I grab all my strength, force myself onto my legs and rush everyone through, thinking "I've made it, I'm safe." But they have taken my father, my hero, the one who gave me a chance for a better life. He calls to me, "I'll be right there with you every step of the way, right there in your heart—God will guide you to a new life!" I look inside myself and am comforted by what he said—I love you, Dad, and one day we will be together again.[46]

Gloria has endured deportation from the United States three times since she was two years old. She is currently living with relatives in Rosarito, Mexico, a beachfront town south of Tijuana. Her story, and the other stories told by the Latina youth featured here are unbearable, but, remarkably, each young woman finds hope in an idea of herself as persevering, led by a vision of a future with family, and finding home again. Each of these young women speaks longingly of finding and being reunited with loved ones as the fundamental experience of self-identity—the ancient echoes of a native culture long gone but reverberating in the *mestizaje* symbol of the Virgin of Guadalupe. Finding sanctuary within oneself, she provides a symbol of what Mexicans call *dar a luz*, "giving birth"—literally, to "give light" where there was darkness.

The ethical responsibility we have for one another, that which makes us human, is underscored in every encounter with a face that draws us toward community; this Lévinas calls the "human inversion of the in-itself and the for-itself into an ethical self, into a priority of the for-the-other."[47] These young women learn through the Guadalupe Art Program to turn that longing for the other into a sense of respect and care for the self; through their art, they have taught us about the divine in each incomparable, unique, luminous face.

46. Her name has been changed to protect her identity. This is a shortened version of her work; collection of Moreno-Richardson.
47. Lévinas, *Entre Nous*, 202.

Contributors

Susie Paulik Babka is assistant professor of theology and religious studies at the University of San Diego. She earned a PhD from the University of Notre Dame in systematic theology, specializing in the doctrine of the trinity and Christology. Her research focuses on the relationship between visual art and theology; her publications include work on the *Gnadenstuhl* motif in art and the impact of popular culture on Christology. She is currently working on a book titled *Suffering, Kenosis, Presence: Exploring the Incarnation through Visual Art* (Liturgical Press, forthcoming). Her future projects explore the relationship between maternity and theology and how art and culture may be theological resources for interreligious dialogue.

Colleen Mary Carpenter is associate professor of theology at St. Catherine University in St. Paul, Minnesota, where she teaches systematics. She is author of *Redeeming the Story: Women, Suffering, and Christ* (Continuum, 2004) and numerous articles and book chapters on feminist theology, ecotheology, and the religious imagination. She was awarded the Denny Prize for Distinction in Writing for her article, "Red is the Colour of the Morning: Resurrection in the Writings of Terry Tempest Williams" (*The Way*, April 2009). Carpenter grew up outside of Chicago and spent most of her life in cities before moving to rural western Minnesota in 1999, where she learned about the theological importance of sustainable agriculture and the beauty of the prairie. Before she returned to the Twin Cities, she worked with the School Sisters of Notre Dame at EarthRise Farm, an organic farm and earth spirituality center. Her current book project is titled *Is the Earth Holy?*

Laurie Cassidy is associate professor of religious studies at Marywood University in Scranton, Pennsylvania. She is the coeditor, with Alex Mikulich, of the award-winning book *Interrupting White Privilege: Catholic Theologians Break the Silence* (Orbis, 2007). Her second volume, *Religion, Culture and Economics in Conflict and Conversation* (Orbis, 2011), was coedited with Maureen O'Connell. Her work as a social ethicist is informed by thirty years of giving spiritual direction and retreats around the United States. Her teaching and research explore how Christian mysticism can be a resource for personal and social transformation, particularly in responding to contemporary culture.

M. Shawn Copeland is associate professor of systematic theology at Boston College, where she teaches graduate students preparing for a doctorate in theology and undergraduate students in the PULSE Program and the Interdisciplinary Program in African and African Diaspora Studies (AADS). Copeland has taught at St. Norbert College, Yale Divinity School, and Marquette University and as adjunct faculty member of the Institute for Black Catholic Studies (IBCS) at Xavier University of New Orleans. Copeland lectures frequently on topics related to theological anthropology, political theology, and social suffering. At the same time, she is recognized as one of the most important influences in North America in drawing attention to issues surrounding African American Catholics. She is author of *Enfleshing Freedom: Body, Race and Being* (Fortress Press, 2010) and *The Subversive Power of Love: The Vision of Henriette Delille* (Paulist Press, 2009) and is the principal editor of *Uncommon Faithfulness: The Black Catholic Experience* (Orbis, 2009).

Rebecca Berru Davis recently completed her theological studies in the area of art and religion at the Graduate Theological Union in Berkeley, California. She is interested in the intersection of art, faith, and justice as a way to understand the spiritual and religious expressions of those located on the margins of society. Her research is focused on women, particularly Latin American and Latina women's creative activity evidenced in the home, the church, and the community. With more than twenty years of teaching, museum, and arts advocacy experience, she continues to explore ways in which the arts are illuminative, inspirational, and prophetic. Davis' current research and curatorial project, *Picturing Paradise:* Cuadros *by the Peruvian Women of Pamplona Alta as Visions of Hope*, continues to unfold as it is exhibited in university galleries and museums throughout the country. For more information about the exhibit, see www.convida.org or write to rdavis@ses.gtu.edu.

Michelle A. Gonzalez (Michelle Gonzalez Maldonado) is associate professor of religious studies at the University of Miami. She received her PhD in systematic and philosophical theology at the Graduate Theological Union in Berkeley, California, in 2001. Her research and teaching interests include Latino/a, Latin American, and feminist theologies, as well as interdisciplinary work in Afro-Caribbean Studies. She is the author of *Sor Juana: Beauty and Justice in the Americas* (Orbis, 2003), *Afro-Cuban Theology: Religion, Race, Culture and Identity* (University Press of Florida, 2006), *Created in God's Image: An Introduction to Feminist Theological Anthropology* (Orbis, 2007), *Embracing Latina Spirituality: A Woman's Perspective* (St. Anthony Messenger Press, 2009), *Caribbean Religious History* (coauthored with Ennis Edmonds, NYU Press, 2010), and *Shopping: Christian Explorations of Daily Living* (Fortress Press, 2010).

Jayme M. Hennessy is associate professor of religious and theological studies at Salve Regina University in Newport, Rhode Island. A liturgical musician and theologian, she is interested in the relationship of the arts to Christian spirituality and moral theology. Her research and teaching bring together virtue ethics and religious symbolic images to examine the ways in which images contribute to the cultivation of the emotions and the construction of Christian identity. The study of the *Pietà* image, its history and how women have experienced this image, has been central to her research regarding the contribution of symbolic images to the cultivation of compassion in the Christian life. In addition to the *Pietà*, her research, teaching, and writing have focused on the Christian virtue of mercy and the symbolic images that constitute the art of mercy.

Elizabeth A. Johnson, Distinguished Professor of Theology at Fordham University in New York City, teaches in both undergraduate and graduate programs. A former president of the Catholic Theological Society of America, the oldest and largest society of theologians in the world, and a former president of the American Theological Society, an ecumenical association, she is the author of numerous books, including *She Who Is: The Mystery of God in Feminist Theological Discourse; Women, Earth, and Creator Spirit*; and the notable *Quest for the Living God: Mapping Frontiers in Theology of God*. Translated into more than a dozen European, Latin American, and Asian languages, her work focuses on the mystery of God, dialogue with science, Jesus Christ, the problem of suffering, ecological ethics, and issues related to justice for women.

Maureen H. O'Connell is associate professor of theology at Fordham University where she teaches social ethics, religion and politics, and theological aesthetics. She authored *Compassion: Loving Our Neighbor in an Age of Globalization* (Orbis, 2009) and coedited with Laurie Cassidy the College Theology Society's annual volume, *Religion, Economics, and Culture in Conflict and Conversation* (Orbis, 2011). She has contributed to volumes on religion and politics, religious ethics for millennial students, and contemporary American Catholic studies. She has explored the arts as a source of ethical wisdom and a catalyst for moral action in an image-laden manuscript, *If These Walls Could Talk: Community Muralism and the Beauty of Justice* (Liturgical Press, 2012). She currently serves on the board of the College Theology Society and Society for the Arts in Religious and Theological Studies. She is also the Faculty in Residence at Fordham's Lincoln Center campus.

Jeanette Rodriguez is professor at Seattle University and teaches in the Department of Theology and Religious Studies, Women Studies, and the graduate School of Theology and Ministry. Rodriguez is the author of several books and articles concentrated in the areas of US Hispanic theology, theologies of liberation, peacebuilding, and genocide studies. Her works include *Our Lady of Guadalupe: Faith and Empowerment among Mexican American Women; Stories We Live* (University of Texas Press, 1994), *Cultural Memory: Resistance, Faith and Identity* (with anthropologist Ted Fortier, University of Texas Press, 2007), and *A Reader in Latina Feminist Theology* (with Maria Pilar Aquino and Daisy Machado, University of Texas Press, 2002). She served a term as president of the Academy of Hispanic Theologians in the United States, has served as vice-chair for Pax Christi USA, and is presently a board member of the *National Catholic Reporter*. Rodriguez holds a PhD in religion and the personality sciences from the Graduate Theological Union, Berkeley, California.

Susan A. Ross is professor of theology and a faculty scholar at Loyola University Chicago, where she is the chairperson of the Theology Department. She is the author of *Anthropology: Seeking Light and Beauty* (Liturgical Press, 2012), *For the Beauty of the Earth: Women, Sacramentality and Justice* (Paulist Press, 2006), *Extravagant Affections: A Feminist Sacramental Theology* (Continuum, 1998), and over fifty journal articles and book chapters and is the coeditor of six books and journal issues. She is the recipient of a Louisville Institute Sabbatical Grant, the Book of the Year Award from the College Theology Society in 1999, and the Ann O'Hara Graff Award of the Women's Seminar of the Catholic Theological Society of America in 2001. She is currently president of the Catholic Theological Society of America (2012–13) and also serves as vice president and member of the editorial board of *Concilium: International Theological Journal*.

Kimberly Vrudny is associate professor of systematic theology at the University of St. Thomas in St. Paul, Minnesota, where she also serves as founding project director for HIV/AIDS initiatives through the university's Office for Service Learning. She is the author of *Friars, Scribes, and Corpses: A Marian Confraternal Reading of* The Mirror of Human Salvation (Peeters, 2010). She is also coeditor of two books, the most recent with Robin Jensen, *Visual Theology: Forming and Transforming the Community through the Arts* (Liturgical Press, 2009), which includes her essay, "Deforming and Reforming Beauty: Disappearance and Presence in the Theo-political Imagination of Ricardo Cinalli." The second is with Wilson Yates, *Arts, Theology and the Church: New Intersections* (Pilgrim Press, 2005), which includes another essay she authored, "Spirit Standing Still: Documenting Beauty in Photography." She served on the staff of *ARTS: The Arts in Religious and Theological Studies* for sixteen years (1993–2009).

Mary Ann Zimmer, ND, is assistant professor of religious studies at Marywood University in Scranton, Pennsylvania. She is the author of *Mary 101: Tradition and Influence* (Liguori Publications, 2010). Her work has appeared in *Religion, Economics, and Culture in Conflict and Conversation* (Orbis, 2011), *Women and the Shaping of Catholicism* (Liguori Publications, 2009), the *Proceedings of the Forum on Religion and Public Life* for the Community of Christ, and *In the Embrace of God: A Feminist Reader in Theological Anthropology* (Wipf & Stock Publishers, 2005). Her research interests include church congregations as a resource for constructive theology, feminist approaches to popular religion, and the concrete effects of theological verbal and visual formulations.